Julian

CW00797257

# The Battle of Britain: Victory and Defeat

AIR CHIEF MARSHAL LORD DOWDING, GCB, GCVO, CMG
FIRST BARON DOWDING OF BENTLEY PRIORY
(APRIL 24, 1882 – FEBRUARY 15, 1970)

# THE BATTLE OF BRITAIN:
# Victory & Defeat

*A Full Account of the Removal
of Air Chief Marshal Sir Hugh Dowding
from Fighter Command
Without Reward or Recognition
after he had won the Battle of Britain
A Saga of Heroism and Treachery*

## J.E.G. DIXON

**Woodfield**

First edition, published in 2003 by

WOODFIELD PUBLISHING
Woodfield House, Babsham Lane, Bognor Regis
West Sussex PO21 5EL, England.

ISBN 1-903953-40-5

# CONTENTS

# FOREWORD

by

## Air Chief Marshal Sir Christopher Foxley-Norris
GCB, DSO, MA, RAF (RETD.)
### Chairman, Battle of Britain Fighters Association

Ever since the Royal Air Force was formed in 1918 as an independent fighting arm, its directing strategic thought became centred on the potential of the offensive bomber. It was, in fact, its *raison d'être*. This preoccupation originated with the fear engendered by the virtually unopposed German raids on London, by Zeppelins in 1917 and by Gotha bombers in 1918.

Until 1936 this doctrine of "the only defence is offence" was buttressed by the conviction that "the bomber will always get through."[1] This notion was challenged in the period 1936–37 by a few far-seeing individuals, who conceived of the possibility of creating a true defence; and from then until 1940 a fierce debate between the proponents of offence and those of defence disturbed the complacency of the Air Staff. The dispute was resolved in favour of the 'defenders' — but only just, and only temporarily.

The Royal Air Force was formed by an amalgamation of the Royal Flying Corps and the Royal Naval Air Service. Whereas the latter were flying sailors, the former were soldiers who learnt the basics of flying. The new RAF was dominated by ex-soldiers — and indeed nearly all the officers who rose to the top in the 1920s and 1930s were ex-Army men. Now, the army and the navy are inspired by diametrically opposite, yet perhaps complementary, traditions and purposes. The one is essentially offensive, the other defensive.

The one constant concern and preoccupation of the English throughout their history has been, in the words of Arthur Balfour, "this eternal question of our safety against invasion." That security had been guaranteed by the British Navy. It is not going too far to suggest that the English have always had a love affair with their Navy, and refer with admiration to the creation of the first fleet by King Alfred. The place occupied by the Navy in the minds of the British people is stated by Sir Walter Raleigh at the outset of his history of air warfare in the First World War, *The War in the Air*: "The British navy is

6

a great trust, responsible not so much for the progress of the nation as for its very existence."[2]

When armies engaged in battle in civil wars in England, the engagements were offensive on both sides. When English armies took the field on the continent of Europe, it was to wage offensive wars. The role of the navy was by contrast predominantly the defence of the British Isles and their peoples. The protective ethos is as natural to the navy mind as the offensive ethos is to the army. Little wonder, then, that most of the army men who rose to become the commanders of the RAF thought only of offence. That is certainly the case with Hugh Trenchard.

There is always the exception to the rule. Air Chief Marshal Lord Dowding was also an army man. Whatever the explanation of his mental and moral development, his strategic vision saw things differently from his contemporaries, even from Trenchard himself, and convinced him that no war could be prosecuted successfully without first ensuring the security of the home base. In that his thought is in tune with centuries-old English strategic ideas. Is it overstating the case to suggest that the fighter exploits of the RAF, especially in the Second World War, and more especially from the Battle of Britain on, effected some transfer of the affections of the British people from the navy to the air force, precisely because of the protective shield it became and the glamorous heroes it produced?[3]

The Battle of Britain was, like Waterloo, "a damned close-run thing." In 1951, when I was on the staff of the Royal Air Force Staff College, an exercise about the Battle of Britain called *See Adler* was carried out and I was detached to direct it and to write up the setting and conclusion. After a week I went to see the Assistant Commandant and reported the results along these lines: "I am very sorry, but I have applied all the usual considerations to the exercise — such as factors affecting the attainment of the aim, and the balance of forces — and the Germans must win. What do I do?" He said: "Go and fudge it!"[4] So I did, and it has been fudged ever since.

This book is more directly about the late Air Chief Marshal Lord Dowding than about the Battle of Britain; but in pointing out along the way the worst mistakes made by the Germans and some of the mistakes avoided on the British side — which Dowding was alive to on both counts at the time — it makes a contribution to the necessary and unfinished business of defudging the issues.

# INTRODUCTION

## *"Here I stand"*

Today, over 60 years after the Battle of Britain ended victoriously, any mention of the Battle seems often to be associated in the public mind with the dominating presence of Winston Churchill. His speeches that summer stirred and galvanized the nation; especially in his speech to the House of Commons on June 18th, one ringing sentence has come to sum up and to immortalize the struggle: "Never in the field of human conflict have so many owed so much to so few."[5]

Churchill of course did not win the Battle of Britain. Of few men can it be said that this man alone won the battle. Yet, if the Battle of Britain can be said to have been won by any one man, that man was Air Chief Marshal Sir Hugh (later Lord) Dowding. For true it is that we could have won the Battle of Britain without Churchill; we could not have won it without Dowding.

In March 1941, when the Battle of Britain had been over for four months, the Air Ministry issued a slender pamphlet on the Battle and summed it up in these words: "Such was the Battle of Britain in 1940. Future historians may compare it with Marathon, Trafalgar and the Marne." Yet the Air Ministry summarily removed Dowding from his command without reward or explanation, and even withheld recognition of him in their pamphlet.

Having established the historic and global significance of the Battle as the saving of Britain from probable invasion and defeat, the Air Ministry ignore the rôle and the very existence of the chief architect of the victory. Indeed, for most of those four years they regard him as a thorn in their side rather than, especially in 1939–1940, as Britain's likely only saviour.

The Air Ministry's collective attitude toward Fighter Command was one of endemic superiority, for Fighter Command was but one of many Commands. Moreover it was entirely a local affair, restricted to the British Isles, whereas the Air Ministry was self-consciously aware of its world-wide strategic concerns and responsibilities.

This distinction between the Air Ministry and Fighter Command was stressed as recently as 1990 at a conference at the Royal Air Force Staff

College to mark the occasion of the Battle's 50th anniversary. An Air Ministry historian characterized Dowding's remit as "parochial" in asserting the better informed global vision of the Air Ministry. "Newall . . . [he said] as CAS . . . had to take a wider strategic view than the more parochial concerns of a C-in-C." This judgement was repeated even more recently, in 1995, in the article on Dowding in the *Oxford Companion to World War II*: "His [Dowding's] vision, necessarily, was a narrow one and he was no politician."

Global, strategic, parochial: what do these terms mean? In the context of the times, and still in some writings today, they are used to disparage Dowding and Fighter Command by reducing their rôle to a local theatre of war, and to elevate the vision of the Air Ministry and the War Cabinet to an altogether higher plane of wisdom and importance.

A more accurate distinction would be to say that these terms were used more in a geographical and temporal, than a strictly military, sense. If this distinction is valid, then global and strategic mean nothing more than remote, and hence forgettable or expendable, because beyond help.[6]

In this view parochial becomes the concern with the immediate situation and what is possible in the present. Dowding and the Battle of Britain parochial? We must give fervent and constant thanks that there was a man who saw clearly what had to be done and did it. While the air marshals in Whitehall either did not see what had to be done, or, seeing, did nothing for fear of their political masters or to protect their jobs and promotions, Dowding alone took a stand on an unshakable principle.

In order to do what he did — to create Fighter Command from the ground up, to prepare it for war, and to lead it when war came — he had to tread on many toes and incur unpopularity and even hostility. He fought with the Air Staff; he went over the heads of the Chiefs of Air Staff; and he stood firm against Churchill and the War Cabinet, at a critical moment when no one else did, when vital issues at stake threatened to weaken his forces and imperil the security of the kingdom.

Dowding conceded that it would have been perfectly possible to have good relations with the people on the Air Staff. But in order to realize that end, desirable though it was, Dowding would have had to acquiesce in many recommendations and urgings which he disagreed with for sound reasons. In rejecting or opposing them because their implementation would be wasteful or dangerous, Dowding never lost sight of essential priorities. Always was the security of the base. All his and Fighter Command's strategic and tactical thinking were devoted to that end.

Dowding's gaze was penetrating and whole. He understood what was happening, and acted upon that understanding. He knew the first principle of war: the security of the base. The entire issue at stake in the Battle of Britain was that security. If Britain succumbed everything was lost. He pursued that aim singlemindedly. He let nothing deter or deflect him from that course. If the price of that dedication was to find himself held in disfavour in the Air Council and by the Air Staff, it was a price he was willing to pay. And they certainly made him pay it.

# ENDNOTES:

Many of the passages quoted in this book, being well-known, are not referenced. Regrettably, the references to a number of passages quoted which should be referenced are missing, having been mislaid during two moves.

## NOTES TO FOREWORD AND INTRODUCTION:

1. Stanley Baldwin in the House of Commons, 10 November 1932.
2. For this and the preceding quotation, see Alfred Gollin, *No Longer An Island* (London and Stanford, 1984), p.2.
3. We are convinced that had the Germans attempted a sea-borne invasion in 1940 the Royal Navy would have regained in full measure any admiration and affection lost to the Royal Air Force. But of course the "miracle" of Dunkirk had already restored to the Navy some of its glamour. (Author).
4. See *The Battle Re-Thought*. A Symposium on the Battle of Britain (Airlife Publishing, 1991), p.2.
5. I quote but one source, published in 1959, by someone who should have known better, being intimately involved in Government as he was at the time: "There were . . . people milling around, looking dejected; the country could easily br defeated within a few months. Where should we all be then? So much depended on Churchill." R.F. Harrod, *The Prof* (London, Macmillan, 1959), p.227.
6. That is the story in a nutshell of Singapore and Malaya.In the autumn of 1940 Air Chief Marshal Sir Robert Brooke-Popham, having been recalled from retirement at the age of 61, was appointed Commander-in-Chief Far East of the air and land forces. In one despatch to the Air Ministry he wrote: "Let England have the super-Spitfires . . . Buffaloes are quite good enough for Malaya." The mind reels. But Brooke-Popham was soon to change his mind. No sooner had he suffered his early reverses from the Japanese attacks than he sent an urgent request to London for large air reinforcements, including long-range bombers. "One of the early responses he received from an uncomprehending Whitehall was the priceless advice, 'All war experience shows the uselessness and wastefulness of attempting to gain air superiority by bombing aerodromes at long range.' This was precisely what the Japanese had just tried with exemplary results!" It was also, let it be added, the very core of the Air Ministry's strategic doctrine! And of course within the "wider strategic view" of the Air Ministry were Malaya and Singapore.

# Part 1

# Laying the Groundwork

# CHAPTER 1

# *Dowding and the Air Ministry (I):*

# *Living in the Past*

The official history of the Royal Air Force in the Second World War by Richards and St. George paints a glowing picture of the Royal Air Force and the Air Ministry as they were in 1939:

> The principle of a unified Air Force [we read] . . . had triumphed over all opposition; thanks to that . . . it was possible to fight the air war with efficiency and economy. Up-to-date equipment, sound organization, correct principles — these were all very vital. . . . The Service was well staffed and well led. In the Air Ministry alone there was an enormous array of talent.

The reality was different. We need, for the moment, only draw attention to one over-riding failure. The entire strategic policy of the so-called "unified Air Force", which came to be known as the "Trenchard Doctrine", was anchored on the creation of a bomber force which would strike at the enemy from the moment of the outbreak of war and destroy his war-making capacity and his will to fight. By September 1939 all the Air Force's bombers were hopelessly obsolete; and 80 per cent of the aircrews could not even find a designated 'target' in daylight in friendly skies.[1]

A truthful and objective history of the Air Ministry, with emphasis on the directorates of Planning and Operations during the few years preceding the war, would go some way to undermining the trust and faith that the British people came to place in the integrity and reliability built up over the course of the years in the Royal Air Force since the earliest days of its history.

The public will have difficulty in understanding this statement, for the simple reason that they do not know the structure and workings of the Air Ministry and the Royal Air Force.

We must begin by making a distinction between the Royal Air Force and the Air Ministry. At the very mention of "Royal Air Force", one thinks at once of the exploits of the fighter pilots, the bomber and maritime crews, the special operations forces, the pathfinders, and all their legendary aeroplanes and weapons. The names of Spitfire, Mosquito, Lancaster, Beaufighter, Hurricane, Tempest, Mustang and Sunderland have become by-words in the vocabulary of students of the air war and admirers of the RAF.

What is easy to overlook is the administrative organism and machinery which governs and runs the Air Force: in a word, the Air Ministry.

The Air Ministry is made up of a Minister, the Secretary of State for Air, who is an elected politician appointed to that position by the Prime Minister; his deputy, with the title of Under-Secretary of State, who is also an elected politician; and, under them, the whole panoply of officers from Air Chief Marshal down, NCOs, airmen, and civilians (again, from deputy minister to the humble clerk), who, like a huge department of State, create and implement policies and administer all the affairs of the Air Force.

Making up essential ruling elements of the Air Ministry are the Air Council and the Air Staff. The Air Council is the supreme policy-making body of the Air Ministry. The Council comprises the Minister, who is the President of the Council, and his deputy, plus the air members, senior air officers who are responsible for such essential functions, *inter alia*, as research and development, training, personnel, and supply.

The Air Staff comprises the senior officers responsible for executing the policies of the Air Council; the departments responsible for advising and overseeing the functions of the operational Commands; and perhaps above all the directorates whose staffs draw up plans relating to vital defence needs and equipment, and the advising of their head, the Chief of the Air Staff (CAS), who, in his turn, advises the Minister. An important position on the Air Staff was the Vice-Chief of the Air Staff (V-CAS), who, being responsible for liaison with and the daily operations of the operational commands, was in close and daily contact not only with the CAS, but also with the Minister and the Under Secretary of State.

From May 12, 1940, the Minister was Sir Archibald Sinclair, and his Under-Secretary, who had been in office since 1938, was Harold Balfour. The Chief of the Air Staff was Air Chief Marshal Sir Cyril Newall, until succeeded on October 25 by Air Marshal Sir Charles Portal; and his V-CAS was Air Vice-Marshal William Sholto Douglas.

The Royal Air Force **is,** in its very essence, the squadrons and stations, the aeroplanes and the men and woman who fly and service them, and the Command headquarters which direct their operations.

It is inevitable, it is almost traditional, that there will be misunderstandings and friction between the people 'at the sharp end', who do the dangerous and dirty work, and the people 'at the top', who, too often comfortable and secure in their official positions, issue directions.

The 'operational' men and women would have it no other way. Similarly, many of the 'brass' would pull out all stops to **prevent** their being posted away **from** their cocoons of safety and their desks of authority and **to** a position in the field which offered neither of those commodities. These differences create between them a gap which is difficult of bridging, an alienation difficult to overcome, almost an antipathy. Certainly very different ways of thinking.

To the Air Ministry mind, the commands, stations and squadrons feel that their roles are far more important than all the others and should get priority of treatment in supplies and the best people. To the men and women of the squadrons and stations, on the other hand, the Air Ministry — and even at times their own Command Headquarters — are seen as being divorced from reality, out of touch, and unaware of what is going on. It is fairly certain that important disagreements will lead to recrimination on both sides.

Air Chief Marshal Sir Hugh Dowding, as the first Air Officer Commanding-in-Chief of a vital operational command, made sure that he never fell into the traps of complacency, reaction, or arrogance. But he learnt the hard way.

In the six years before he became the very first head (Air Officer Commanding-in-Chief: AOC-in-C) of the new Fighter Command, he was, successively, the Air Member for Supply and Research, 1930–1935, and Air Member for Research and Development, 1935–1936. It was in the former capacity that he signed the Certificate of Airworthiness of the airship R.101, which crashed in France just two days later with great loss of life. I bring this matter up for an important reason.

Hough and Richards in their history of the Battle of Britain described thus Dowding's dilemma, and his lesson: "Not all Dowding's decisions between 1930 and 1936 turned out well. Within a few weeks of his first appointment, trusting to the experts, he cleared the airship R.101 for her maiden flight to India. The disaster at Beauvais made him very wary in future of trusting to experts without strong proofs of their correctness."

This statement itself lacks 'correctness' and calls for modification. The 'decision', such as it was, was not Dowding's. New as he was to his post, he would not have had the time to study the experts' opinions. For the fact is that the best informed opinion was against the flight of the R.101. Charles G. Gray, the author of *A History of the Air Ministry,* is very specific:

> The [R.101] was foredoomed to failure. Its structure and its design had been severely criticised in this and other countries. Its trials had been unsatisfactory. And the Air Ministry had been warned in print that it would come to grief. Unhappily, for political reasons, the ship was ordered to start for India, and the Air Ministry and the RAF had to obey orders.

The Air Ministry and the RAF "had to obey orders"? Despite the traditions and constitutional requirement subordinating the military to civilian control, the statement cries for examination. First, who had to obey orders? The Air Ministry and the RAF were not abstract organisms trained to obey orders like automata. They were human organizations made up of thinking men and women — especially, at the top, of men who were trained to use their judgment. Who were the men who obeyed orders? If the senior officers in the Air Ministry who received the political orders did not agree with them, they had the option to refuse them, or to resign. Why then did they obey them? Did they fear to confront their political masters? Or did they place their careers ahead of their convictions? These men were the high-ranking officers who formulated the policies and directed the affairs of the Royal Air Force, many of whom were still in positions of authority in the early days of the war.

The order was a political order, and a political blunder. The explanation of the order lies in the fact that the R.101 was a Government-built airship. It was in competition with the R.100, a private venture. The R.100, which was designed by the fertile, imaginative brain of Barnes Wallace, was a magnificent airship. It flew to Montreal and back without incident and in record time. But after the crash of the R.101, the Government ordered the destruction of the R.100; it was dismembered and crushed, and the pieces sold as scrap metal.

It was from this experience that Dowding acquired his distrust of politicians and their ways, and his scepticism toward the senior air marshals of the Air Ministry — a distrust and a scepticism that were to be justified in later years.[2]

Dowding established himself as one of the most forward-thinking officers of the Air Force. As Air Member for Research and Development he pushed for the improvement and production of radar and of the advanced fighters which were to be christened the 'Hurricane' and the 'Spitfire'. He had to fight for these things, and to overcome the opposition of officers living in the past.

One such — and we are speaking of officers of very high rank and many years' experience (or, perhaps, of a few years' experience repeated many times) — resisted the recommendation that the cockpit of a new fighter (it was the Gladiator) be closed. "Gad! [we imagine him saying] I flew in an open cockpit, and what was good for me is good for these young fellers!"

Dowding, when in Fighter Command, was occasionally invited to Air Ministry conferences to decide on the equipment needed for new types of aircraft. "At one of these [Dowding has written] I asked that bullet-proof glass should be provided for the windscreens of the Hurricane and Spitfire. To my astonishment the whole table dissolved into gusts of laughter. . . ." Dowding silenced them with his retort, become celebrated in Air Force circles, "If Chicago gangsters could have bullet-proof glass in their cars I could see no reason why our pilots should not have the same." It is an eternal black mark on the record of the Air Ministry that the windscreens of the Spitfires and Hurricanes were being replaced by bullet-proof glass as late as the summer of 1940.

It took the Air Ministry policy-makers and planners a long time to get over their most basic prejudices and blindness. Shortly after the fighting broke out on the Western Front, Squadron Leader Basil Embry (later Air Chief Marshal) was in the thick of it. When he was shot down, he, like dozens of his fellow-airmen, was totally unequipped and unprepared for imprisonment or for evasion, let alone for escape. Earlier that year, he had actually written to Bomber Command recommending that aircrews be issued with the type of button compass that had been used by pilots and observers in the First World War. It was a regulation button with a difference: the inside of the button was a compass, which was obtained by unscrewing the top of the button. The reply he got was that the Air Ministry banned their use since, if the enemy learnt of it they would cut off all the captured airmen's buttons, and "how *infra dig* and embarrassing that would be."!

One wonders how such men got to the top echelon of the pyramid of authority in the Air Force. Here is one opinion, that of G/C Ira Jones:

> Towards the middle of September, 1919 . . . I saw the first complete list of officers who had been granted permanent and short-service commissions

in the RAF's peacetime establishment. It was a real puzzler. How the Powers that Be had decided on those selected I cannot imagine. . . . One name on the list made me shudder. It was that of one of the greatest cowards I had known.

When it came to war in 1939, some of these people had risen to high rank and now occupied positions of authority in the Air Ministry. The Germans committed the same blunder when they came to create the Luftwaffe. Field Marshal Milch blamed Goering: "Göring has put his old First World War comrades too much to the fore, and these are obviously not equal to the burdens of leadership that war places upon them."[3] Similarly some measure of the blame for the *débâcle* that was to ensue in 1940 must rest on the shoulders of such throwbacks to 1918. Embry also writes:

> [A] counter-attack was made [at Arras on May 21-22, 1940] without air support for the simple reason that no aircraft were available. Lord Dowding has told us since that pre-war planning had made no provision for fighters as part of the Expeditionary Force![4] I do not know the names of the high-ranking strategists of the time, but it is obvious that . . . they had not learned the lessons of World War I. My friends and I had always thought that during the period 1918-39 there were too many high-ranking officers with little practical experience of air warfare at the head of the RAF.

When Dowding went to Fighter Command he was faced with the huge task of creating a new organization from the ground up, to be constructed around the new fighters and the inchoate radar system which he had been instrumental in bringing into being. His task would have been forbidding even if he could count on the complete cooperation of the Air Staff from the beginning. But he knew the Air Staff and its workings. The Air Ministry at times gave the impression that the cooperation it accorded to Fighter Command was against its better judgment.

Every bit of evidence suggests — and both Air Ministry and Dowding supporters agree — that the relations between Dowding and the Air Ministry became strained, if not actually acerbic. Dowding had more direct dealings with the Deputy-Chief of Air Staff than with any other senior officer of the Air Staff. The incumbent throughout 1940 was Air Vice-Marshal William Sholto Douglas. What motive Douglas had many years later to depict their relations as other than they were, while not beyond our ken, tells us much about him. This is what he wrote:

I have never been at all happy about the way in which Basil Collier has spoken in the official history about what he describes as the "important differences of our outlook between Dowding and the Air Staff," any more than I have liked being described by him elsewhere as Dowding's "ex-officio critic." There is in these statements a serious lack of understanding of the relationship with Dowding that I have known and valued over a period of many years, as well as an insufficient appreciation of the way in which Commanders-in-Chief conducted their official relationship with the Air Staff. In these relationships there was a great deal more give-and-take and understanding between us than is implied in the expression "ex-officio critic." As with the controversy over the use of wings, too much has been made of the difference that did admittedly exist at times in our opinions.

If I managed to advance my own opinions in a way which won support that did not mean that I was unduly criticising Dowding, any more than it meant that he was unnecessarily criticising me. We were much too experienced, as professional airmen, for that; and we had too keen and profound an appreciation and respect for each other for such trivial indulgences.[5]

A "serious lack of understanding" on Collier's part? He understood only too well. We do not know where Douglas got the notion that Dowding had respect for him. All the evidence points in the other direction. Dowding's personal assistant, Flight Lieutenant Francis Wilkinson, recounted a telling incident to his successor, Robert Wright:

As the momentum of the enemy attack increased, so did the strain for Dowding. But there was no relaxation of his tight control over what was happening. At times it seemed that only he and a few of his senior officers and those who were doing the actual flying and the controlling of it knew how serious the situation had become. It was not a matter of a straight fight — that would have been all too easy to handle — and never for a moment would Dowding drop his guard. It might have meant running the risk of a possible blow from some quarter or other which could damage his Command.

"I think it was that which led him to have at least some of those awful rows with those people at the Air Ministry," Francis Wilkinson once remarked. "Some of them up there simply didn't seem to know what was happening, or understand what it was all about. One day an Air Commodore from the Air Ministry came to see Dowding. It was right at the time when we were very low on pilots who really knew how to fly. I listened to him in astonishment when he said to Dowding: 'But I don't understand what you're worrying about. . . . You've got plenty of aeroplanes and pilots.' I thought poor old Stuffy would have a fit."

Douglas's motive in falsifying the nature of the relations between himself and Dowding is transparent. Douglas wrote his autobiography in 1956. Dowding's achievements were so great, and their greatness so manifestly clear, that they eclipsed Douglas's and made him appear of little account. Douglas wanted to be seen by posterity as enjoying relations of mutual respect with the saviour of Britain. It would make him look good in the eyes of history. An airman who tries to ingratiate himself with a superior is scorned by his fellow-airmen. They have vulgar, airman-like, expressions for it, better left unsaid here.

It was, and still is to this day, frequently charged also against Dowding that he was an unwilling co-operator. No allegation could bring into sharper focus the fundamental split between Fighter Command and the Air Ministry and their conflicting outlooks, values and, apparently, aims. This criticism of Dowding has been repeated by pro-Air Ministry, anti-Dowding critics since 1940. There is much evidence in the voluminous files of correspondence between Fighter Command and the Air Ministry to support the latter's view that Dowding was not doing what the Air Ministry wanted; and that the Air Ministry was not doing what Fighter Command needed. And the tone of recrimination is very evident.

On the other hand, the Air Ministry would be hard pressed to produce the records in support of its counter-claim of its supposedly matchless cooperation with Fighter Command.

One fact is incontestable: there have been many criticisms of the Air Staff and their blunders both from without and from within the Air Ministry. There has never been a breath of criticism of Dowding from within his own Fighter Command Headquarters.

One must ask: If "the Air Ministry were very supportive of Fighter Command and **everything that it did**", why was Dowding 'at war' with them? What was the nature of his complaints, what the cause of "those awful rows with those people at the Air Ministry"? Surely a strange way to thank those selfless people for their unstinting support? In what way was Dowding "not a good cooperator"? Is it possible that he rejected, or accepted with ill-grace, all that support the Air Ministry gave to Fighter Command and, presumably, its approbation of "everything that it did"? (In chapter 6 we examine fully the implications of Dowding's being in the Air Ministry's eyes "not a good cooperator".)

The rows, disputes and recriminations erupted from the differences of views held by the two sides as to what should be done, by whom and with what, at many crucial moments before the Battle of Britain and, especially, during the Battle itself.

If one surveys the war from the strategic outlook of the War Cabinet and takes stock of the regions where Britain had possessions and interests to protect, the task of assessing their dangers, threats, needs and demands involved the drawing up of a catalogue of priorities.

The Air Ministry's vision, while still global, was less so, for it considered only air force requirements, not navy or army, let alone the political. Indeed, its view was restricted even more, for, being everywhere on the defensive it saw things largely in tactical terms at this stage, not strategic.

From the Air Ministry's perspective, in 1939 and 1940, whilst there were Air Force bases in many parts of the world, there were three immediate competing demands on the resources of the RAF. One was the needs of the Air Component in France, rendered critical after the Germans launched their assault on May 10, 1940. The second was the call from North Africa for Hurricanes to reinforce or replace their Gladiators. And the third was the attempt to thwart the German occupation of Norway.

The first and last of these issues were settled at the same time, at the end of May and the beginning of June, with the Dunkirk evacuation and the failure of Churchill's Norwegian misadventure. As for the second, the demand was actually met by the courageous or rash decision — depending on the outcome — to ship Hurricanes to the Middle East. This was in August and September — a time when, however, the shortage of front-line fighters at home was being remedied.

The Air Ministry had the additional responsibility of overseeing its other operational commands: Bomber and Coastal Commands. These, however, were in relative limbo, since the war was in its infancy and it was too early to implement any policies or directives that may have been laid down with respect to long term strategic goals. But what of Training Command? There was one area of the Air Ministry's responsibilities which called for immediate action, and where action was both urgent and possible. But the need was woefully neglected. Air Vice-Marshal Keith Park reported on what he found on taking over his training group at the end of 1940:

I was worried daily from July to September by a chronic shortage of trained fighter pilots, and it was not until the battle was nearly lost that Air Staff of the Air Ministry assisted by borrowing pilots from Bomber Command and from the Royal Navy. In December 1940 when I was posted to Flying Training Command, I found that the flying schools were working at only two-thirds capacity and were following peace-time routines, being quite unaware of the grave shortage of pilots in Fighter Command.

The Air Member for Training at that time was Air Marshal A.G.R. Garrod. He was appointed to this post only in July of that year; even so it seems clear that in his first six months, when a new broom is traditionally meant to sweep clean, and where a cleaning, or a clean-out, was a matter of national emergency, he did not take the first essential measures which cried out for action.

In 1940 and 1941 Churchill habitually cast a critical and disapproving eye at what he called the "cumbersome machinery" of the Air Ministry. (It can only have been out of personal loyalty to his old friend Archibald Sinclair that he left him there as the Air Minister for the entire war.)

The Air Ministry had once in the 1920s and '30s been a lean and trim organization that got things done with relative efficiency and despatch, even if more through economic necessity than by design. Once the programmes of rearmament, re-equipment and reorganization got under way in 1936, and more especially so in the immediate aftermath of the Munich crisis of 1938, the rapid expansion of the RAF resulted in an excessive growth and staffing of the Air Ministry.

The bureaucracy which grew up, and which rapidly became tumescent, caused the machinery to become cumbersome. The many superadded layers of functionaries only exacerbated the difficulties which Dowding experienced in getting decisions from them. And it was an easy matter for the Air Staff to find reasons to blame Dowding for what went wrong.

## NOTES TO CHAPTER 1:

1. Even the aircrew trade of Navigator was not created until 1939.
2. Can it be doubted that this experience lay at the root of his interventions with the War Cabinet in May and June of 1940 in a desperate effort to resist the Government's intention to send more fighters to France, when there was no opposition to it by the Air Ministry authorities?
3. There is another explanation. In the Royal Air Force men were judged and promoted as being members, or not being members, of the Old School Tie syndrome. That is one reason why Douglas Bader was given a sympathetic hearing in the controversy we examine later.
4. Dowding's words are: "No specific provision for field force fighters had been made, and all fighters had to be provided at the expense of the Home Defence organisation." (*Twelve Legions*, p.34.) This blunder on the part of the Air Ministry is at the root of Dowding's subsequent fight with the War Cabinet to retain as many full, operational, front-line squadrons in the U.K. for the battle that he foresaw would come.
5. Our appreciation of Douglas will be found in chapter 8.

# CHAPTER 2

# *Dowding and the Air Ministry (II):*
# *Questions of Doctrine*

It is doubtless a human failing that makes us see our own sphere of interest and action as of overwhelming importance. Conversely, we observe outside events and people through a distorting or reducing glass which would make them appear lower on the scale of relative value. No doubt the officers of the Air Staff, with their global concerns, looked at Fighter Command and its insistent claims on attention as only one Command among several, and considered Dowding a nuisance for his unceasing demands.

Dowding made himself a nuisance — but only with the Air Ministry, for they made some of the fateful decisions that governed the survival or defeat of their country. Dowding sums up the concern that drove him during the years of preparation, from 1936 to 1940: "The defence of the country had been allowed for too long to exist in a state of grave inefficiency. I was continually having to fight that situation while there was yet time."

The state of inefficiency was brought about by neglect, by inconsiderateness, by ill-advised decisions, by the failure to provide essential equipment, and above all by wrong-headed strategic thinking.

One factor which compounded the inefficiency — and which was certain to exacerbate the relations between the Air Staff and Dowding — was the habit that people in the Air Ministry had: of making decisions which directly affected Fighter Command, without consulting or informing Fighter Command.

The foisting on him of the Boulton Paul Defiant is one example. Another, of far greater importance, relates to certain items concerning his emergency operation rooms which were decided on without his knowledge, to be followed by a refusal to reconsider them.

Another, involving Lieutenant-General Sir Frederick Pile, Commander of the Anti-Aircraft Command, who came under Dowding's direction, is explained thus: "General Pile was also having his difficulties over provision of sufficient equipment for his own Command with which he could support Dowding. Pile was also discovering from Dowding, as he later admitted, more of what it meant to have to face squarely up to the obtuseness of officialdom, and he expressed his own delight in learning a little from Dowding about how to try to deal with that. . . ."

Together Pile and Dowding had this pressing matter of shortages for ever on their minds. . . . Pile recorded that at one time Dowding was informed that a certain important committee having to do with defence, of which both he and Dowding had been members, no longer existed. But they were also told that the work of the committee was being done by other people at the War Office and the Air Ministry with no reference to either of them. And then they were told that Dowding was responsible and should make the decision himself.

One of the most frequent causes of the squabbles Dowding had with the Air Ministry was the shortage of equipment of every kind. Not only the dangerous lack of equipment, but the non-delivery of promised equipment. It included everything: machine-guns and light anti-aircraft guns for aerodrome defence; heavy anti-aircraft artillery for defence of the cities and industrial targets; barrage balloons; searchlights; the manning and training of personnel of all trades, especially for the Operations Rooms. And always the expanding of the radar chain of early warning stations around the east and south coast from Scotland to Cornwall.

Radar was still in the experimental stage, and subject to inaccuracies and failings. An essential reserve system of tracking enemy aircraft was provided by the Observer Corps. So essential was it, indeed, that a radar plot of an enemy raid could not be acted upon unless verified visually by an Observer Corps unit. Yet the Observer Corps had been woefully neglected by the Air Ministry.

The Observer Corps became, under Dowding's integrated defence system, an indispensable component of Fighter Command. He not only had it enlarged and expanded, but he had it put on a war footing. And so effective was it that it earned the epithet of 'Royal', and won an admiration and recognition, admittedly in a more limited and less heroic sphere, not far from that enjoyed by the Royal National Lifeboat Institution.

Mention of the sea naturally raises the question of the rescue of airmen who crashed or parachuted into the sea. The RAF had virtually nothing of its own. The Germans, on the other hand, though they had only about six weeks in which to prepare their assault on England following the capitulation of France, organized an air-sea rescue service, involving both high speed launches and float planes, which saved many of their own airmen from either drowning or capture — and the lives of some of ours as well.

Drowning was the more likely fate. Many of our airmen, some already wounded or burned, died by drowning when they could have been saved. Indeed, many uninjured pilots drowned for the tragic reason that they exhausted themselves merely by trying to keep afloat in the water in their heavy flying clothing.

And yet it was not for want of a proven high speed launch. The RAF had itself developed a marine craft for use as a sea-plane tender as early as 1931. *The History of RAF Marine Craft* recounts the development of the 200 Class Seaplane Tender and "a unique section of the service which pioneered the use of high speed rescue crash boats from which came the Air Sea Rescue Service of World War II."

These boats were subjected to rigorous testing, and the tests were fully reported in three articles in The Times in March and April 1932. The first, of March 28, reported: "They are intended for general duties, which may include rescue work in bad weather. . . . (The) trial boat was run for 400 hours in heavy seas. From that series of experiments it was concluded that no wind to be expected in the Channel up to 35 miles an hour could limit its usefulness." We do not know how many of these high-speed rescue craft were stationed in the Channel in 1940, but certain it is that none of them, although under Air Ministry control, were assigned to the rescue of their own pilots. One historian has spoken to the point on this issue:

> There was no co-ordinated command and control of the Channel rescue service. . . . Any boats that could be got out there were, of course, sent; and slight progress was made when Dowding managed to pinch twelve Lysanders and base them around the coast; at least they could drop dinghies if they could find anybody. . . . It is not normally within the airman's range of experience to think about the sea. And yet from the earliest years of flying, aircraft had been designed to operate on and over the water. Indeed, the Royal Air Force itself was created from an amalgamation of the Royal Flying Corps and the Royal Naval Air Service. It was the Air Ministry's, and only the Air Ministry's, responsibility to think and plan ahead. And in this provision the Air Ministry let the fighting men down badly.

There was no excuse; there was still less excuse in matters related to the Air Force's aerodromes. It is almost a repetition of the battle that Dowding had to fight over bullet-proof windscreens. As late as 1937, not a single aerodrome of Fighter Command had a concrete runway. They had only all-grass airfields. Did it matter? Did it matter! Grass fields are subject to inclement weather. So bad was the winter of 1936, Dowding's first winter with the new Fighter Command, that no flying was possible for three weeks at Kenley, a vital link in the system defending London. Collier concludes his account as follows: "Runways were long opposed by the Air Ministry on the ground that they did not lend themselves to the accepted principles of camouflage." But at last persistence triumphed (over boneheadedness). Dowding got his runways.

He did not get all the runways he needed. It was a blessing that the Battle of Britain was fought in a dry summer. Perhaps soggy airfields would have absorbed better the explosion of bombs and done less damage to the grass runways. Perhaps concrete runways would have sustained worse damage than dry or wet grass. The fact remains, however, that the Air Ministry had made no provision at all for the repair of bombed airfields.

Among the conspicuous examples of aerodromes without all-weather runways was Manston, in the south-east corner of Kent. Churchill visited Manston on August 28th and saw for himself the bomb damage still unrepaired. He wrote critically about it to Sinclair, Portal and Ismay the very next day:

> I was much concerned on visiting Manston Aerodrome yesterday to find that although more than four clear days have passed since it was last raided the greater part of the craters on the landing ground remained unfilled and the aerodrome was barely serviceable. When you remember what the Germans did at Stavanger aerodrome and the enormous rapidity with which craters were filled I must protest emphatically against this feeble method of repairing damage. Altogether there were one hundred and fifty people available, and the whole process appeared disproportionate to the value of maintaining this fighting vantage ground. . . . In what department of the Air Ministry does this process now fall?

Air Vice-Marshal Keith Park, the AOC of 11 Group, Fighter Command, was equally incensed — and was in a position to appreciate the fearful consequences of such damage. He wrote in 1965, in an invited contribution to *ICARE*, a French publication brought out on the twenty-fifth anniversary of the Battle (author's translation):

Finally, when the German Air Force had concentrated on bombing my fighter aerodromes, I could get such little help from Air Ministry to repair the bomb damage that I had to borrow some thousands of troops from the British Army to fill in the bomb craters to keep the aerodromes serviceable. For so doing I was severely criticized by the Air Ministry for accepting Army assistance. Had my fighter aerodromes been put out of action, the German Air Force would have won the Battle by 15 September 1940.

Collier has well summarized the acrimonious relations which existed between Dowding and the Air Ministry, and looked behind the façade to catch a glimpse of the personalities.

> Dowding's knowledge of air defence and his understanding of its problems were unrivalled. A bold fighter in the cause of safety first, he had been proven right by events. It was incontestable that, had he been overruled in May, the country could scarcely have withstood the German onslaught in the summer. At heart he did not dissent from the orthodox view that ultimately only offensive measures could bring success. He held merely that the strategists must be careful not to lose the war before they had a chance of winning it. But he had urged his case so vehemently and pertinaciously that his assent to orthodoxy might well be doubted. Consistent and unyielding where others at times were weak and hesitant, he seemed one who might not easily be persuaded to bow to *ex cathedra* rulings where the balance to be struck between offensive and defensive preoccupations was in question. He had not shown himself particularly amenable to guidance in the past, and he might not prove so in the future. Like all men, he had made mistakes, though fewer, perhaps, than most of his contemporaries. But he had been so often right in his frequent conflicts with the Air Ministry that the few occasions when he was wrong were not likely to be forgotten.

Of all Dowding's battles with the Air Ministry none gave rise to greater resistance on the Air Ministry's part, and hence to greater persistence and dogged insistence on Dowding's part, than to instil into the heads of the Air Staff the fundamental task of Fighter Command. That may seem like showing university graduates the alphabet. Such was Fighter Command's struggle. Dowding conceived his role in this battle as being that of mentor and teacher. If he regarded his 'pupil' as being rather backward in learning the lesson he had to impart, he must appear justified in the eyes of posterity.

The lesson that Dowding had to teach was nothing other than the fundamental differences between strategy and tactics, and the fundamentally different aims of defence and offence.

The strategic thinking of the Air Ministry had been dominated by the doctrine expounded by the Italian Air Force's General Giulio Douhet in a series of articles which were collected in a book entitled *The Command of the Air*. His ideas had been reduced to a few simple formulae outside his immediate circle; and these notions had been espoused by none more enthusiastically than by Trenchard, who exercised almost unchallenged authority in the air councils of Great Britain. Douhet's doctrine, extreme though it appeared, was, simply put, that the bomber had become the supreme strategic weapon of war; and that, if it was not yet capable of winning wars alone, unaided by army and navy, it would soon become so.

This doctrine was enunciated at a time when there was no difference in performance between bomber and fighter. The power of air forces was to be demonstrated convincingly by the Italians against the defenceless, naked people of Abyssinia in 1935, and by the Germans against some towns in the Spanish Civil War. It was to be demonstrated once more against Warsaw in 1939 and against Rotterdam in 1940. An historian of air warfare sums up the situation in this way:

> The irony of the situation was that at the very time that the RAF re-emphasized its commitment in the mid-1930s to a strategic bombing force, other British airmen were at the forefront in the development of a theory of air defence. The bomber theorists of the 1920s had rested much of their case on the belief that there was little effective defence against bombing. Douhet wrote that 'the aeroplane is not adaptable to defence' and that 'nothing man can do on the surface of the earth can interfere with a plane in flight'. By the time Baldwin made his remark that 'the bomber will always get through', the disparity in performance between fighter and bomber aircraft was still so low that the prospect of a successful fighter defence seemed correspondingly unlikely.

This was still the attitude and policy which prevailed in the Air Ministry when Fighter Command was created and when Dowding became its first commander. Nothing seems more likely to refute the notion that Dowding was sent to Fighter Command in the belief that the Air Ministry had finally seen the light, than the struggle that he had to wage, for four long years, from 1936 to 1940, in order to build Fighter Command into a strong defensive force capable of withstanding and repelling any assault against the home base.

The shift towards a mixed air doctrine of defence and offence was met with some reluctance by those in the RAF who favoured the bombing strategy. To admit that there was a defence against the bomber was to question the whole basis upon which an independent air force had been built up.

When historians and others, especially critics of Dowding, describe the relations between Dowding and the Air Ministry, they tend to focus exclusively, and narrowly, on issues of equipment and fighter planes. Vital though they were — and still more crucial were the number and quality of fighter pilots — no question exercised Dowding's mind so completely and permanently as the almost insuperable task of making the highest people on the Air Staff grasp the supreme importance of creating in the Fighter Command an effective fighter force and principal fighting arm capable of ensuring the security of the United Kingdom.

The battle might well be a defensive operation; but all future offensive action depended upon its success. The Air Ministry satraps might regard the battle as a mere holding action and see it solely in tactical terms; but it taught the most vital strategic lessons to those with minds clear enough to learn them.

Does anyone think that 'simple' and 'easy' mean the same thing? Then consider this: Dowding set himself the simple task of converting the Air Ministry, even for a short span, to **fighter** thinking, as against **bomber** thinking; of seeing the fighter as both a tactical and a strategic weapon. Simple indeed! But how difficult! It cannot be charged against him, therefore, that the senior officers on the Air Staff had an excuse or justification for their blindness. They either refused to see the situation as it was in the crucial years 1936–1940; or seeing it, took refuge in their entrenched habits of mind and either dug in their heels or buried their heads in the sand.

If Dowding had been totally alone in his mission to convert Whitehall to thinking fighters, he must have failed. The fact is that in 1936 a new office was created in the Government, that of Coordinator of Defence. The first, and only, incumbent was Sir Thomas Inskip.

The doctrine which bears his name, as enunciated in his Report of 1937, challenged the principles of air strategy which had been the very basis of British air policy since the early 1920s. What it did was to question, undermine, and finally to brush aside the policy of parity with the growing German air force, with its overriding emphasis on the offensive, and the bomber.

The policy of numerical parity is little understood — and its aims were not even fully understood by its champions. Essentially it was conceived as a deterrent to inhibit the further expansion of the Luftwaffe's bomber force.

Latterly, when that failed, it was intended as a deterrent to the use by Germany of its bombers in an attempt to deliver a 'knock-out blow' against Great Britain.

Although the British air authorities did not know that the Luftwaffe never had the capacity for a 'knock-out blow', they knew that they did not come within shouting distance of expanding to the point of building such a force themselves.

The doctrine of parity, founded on the concept of a bomber force as both a defensive and offensive deterrent force, nurtured and promoted by the Air Staff, after the successive shocks administered to it by Hitler's cheap triumphs in 1935, 1936 and 1937, lay in ruins after the Munich appeasement of 1938.

The Inskip Doctrine made a clear separation between offence and defence, and laid the primary emphasis on the defence of the home base. The Cabinet accepted Inskip's recommendations on December 22nd, 1937. "The Air Marshals raged and Trenchard declared in the House of Lords that the decision 'might well lose us the war.'"

Inskip's iconoclastic doctrine was not inspired by strategic insight or vision. It found its origin in a Treasury report. From it Inskip realized that it was beyond Britain's economic capacity in the short term to build both defensive and offensive arms. If there had to be a choice, that choice had to fall first on defence. Britain's strength, and Germany's weakness, lay in a long term conflict. The longer drawn out a war was, the greater the certitude that Britain would outlast Germany. The time to construct a heavy, strategic bomber force would come after the security of the home base had been assured. That security could only be attempted — no talk of assured — by the creation of a fighter force. There is, however, little evidence to suggest that Inskip had any idea what would be required to bring into being a fighter force adequate to parry a determined German aerial onslaught, even without fighter escorts.

Notwithstanding the priority given to the defence of Great Britain as a strategic policy by the Government, especially from 1937, the Air Staff never let up on its insistence on the greater importance of a strong bomber force.

The new CAS in 1937 was Newall. The Director of Plans had been Group Captain Arthur Harris, who was succeeded in May 1937 by Group Captain John Slessor. Both were staunch bomber men. Moreover, the Air Staff were totally unconvinced that Fighter Command could put up an adequate defence against a determined enemy onslaught by, say, 1940, no matter how great the resources devoted to its preparations. As late as 1938, the Air Ministry put forward yet another scheme, this one known as Scheme L, which called for a front line force of 1320 bombers, and making allowance for only 554 fighters. "The views of the Air Staff grew increasingly unrealistic during 1938 and 1939. ... By this stage ... the Air Staff arguments had all the appearance of whistling in the wind. The Munich crisis and its aftermath lent an air of unreality to the last-ditch stand of the Air Staff on the bomber deterrent."

Long before Munich criticism of the Air Ministry had been gathering steam. To cite an extreme example: on April 2nd 1938 the Permanent Under-Secretary of the Treasury (who was also the Head of the Civil Service), Sir Warren Fisher, sent an uncompromising report to the Prime Minister, Neville Chamberlain, scathing in its indictment of the Air Ministry, which, he said, had been dishing up nothing but "soothing syrup and incompetence" for some years. He gave the comparative strengths of the German Air Force and the Royal Air Force and concluded that as a consequence "for the first time in centuries our country is (and must continue to be) at the mercy of a foreign power".

Fisher repeated this condemnation after Munich. But the accusation, though no doubt motivated by deep concern for the safety of his country, harked back to the abandoned policy of parity. There was truth in it, and a woeful unfairness. It was unfair because it was the Government, the politicians, who were entirely responsible for allowing Britain's defences to have evaporated to an ineffective obsolescence. The Air Ministry's culpability lay in its over-riding faith in a bomber force.

It was not until 1939–40 that the total failure of the bomber policy hit home. In late 1939 and the early months of 1940, the failure of Bomber Command to hit its targets, or even to find them, produced the effect of half opening the eyes of the Air Staff. When they were forced at the same time to take into account the undoubted successes of the German fighter defences against the bombers, they finally swung round to give realistic support to the needs of Fighter Command.

It is in the light of the reactionary and mulish persistence that prevailed in the Air Ministry over these vital questions of strategy and tactics that must be seen the cause of the disagreements between the planners and Dowding, the acrimonious disputes that took place over the telephone and in correspondence, and Dowding's long, uphill battle to educate the Air Staff in a strategic thinking anchored on the security of the home base.

In his correspondence with the Air Staff, Dowding showed himself a master of sharp rejoinder which does little to conceal the writer's view of the mental equipment of his adversary. Sure of his ground, convinced that he was right, and confident of a favourable reception before the supreme tribunal of his conscience, he was not an easy man to argue with. An expert in air defence, or fast becoming one, for six years holder of the highest technical posts in the Royal Air Force, he had the advantage of understanding many issues better then anyone outside his own headquarters could hope to understand them. Lifted above compunction by the vision of calamity impending, the iconoclast of Bentley Priory demolished, with what sometimes seemed unholy glee, the edifice of pious evasion with which, at times, the hierophants of Whitehall cloaked official reluctance to surrender to his logic. This view is supported by Dowding's personal assistant, Flight Lieutenant Wilkinson, as reported by Robert Wright:

> In what to Dowding was the Air Staff's grave lack of realism there was one of the main reasons for the differences of opinions . . . between him and the Air Ministry. 'The fundamental stupidity of too many people on the Air Staff was almost unbelievable,' Francis Wilkinson has commented. When he was challenged on the reason for his feeling that way, he snapped: 'I didn't just feel it! I knew it from what Dowding was having to put up with. What used to beat me completely was how those people could sit up there in their ignorance and have the audacity to set themselves up to pass judgment on matters that they simply didn't seem to be able to understand.'
>
> The vehemence of that statement was to find some support in my own experience in serving under Dowding later in the year, and an even stronger support when, over the years since then, a closer examination was made of the treatment that was accorded Dowding.

It is hardly surprising, therefore, that when the fighting actually started, the Air Staff would manifest a woeful incomprehension in another area of Fighter Command's concerns:

> In the fighting that started on May 10, the severe losses of aircraft, including fighters, suffered by the RAF caused an alarm in high quarters that was so sudden that to Dowding it approached imbecility. He was told by a Senior officer on the Air Staff of the Air Ministry, who had come to report to him, about the grave losses of Hurricanes that were being reported from France, as though such losses were a complete surprise. 'What do you expect?' Dowding snapped, finding it hard to contain himself. 'When you get into a war you have to lose things, including precious aircraft. That's exactly what I've been warning you about.'

SIR HENRY TIZARD

PROFESSOR P. M. S. BLACKETT

H. E. WIMPERIS

ROBERT WATSON-WATT

## *The Victors of the Battle of Britain:*
### SOME OF THE SCIENTISTS

One cannot help but feel that what then Air Vice-Marshal Arthur Tedder said of Sir Henry Tizard applies with equal force to Dowding: "He didn't suffer fools gladly, and there were lots of fools around." Hence, it is not at all surprising to see that one of the chapters of Dowding's book *Twelve Legions of Angels* is entitled, "Why are senior officers so stupid?"

If Dowding were the only target or victim of jealousy, intrigue, and sheer incompetence, and of attitudes and ideas which belonged more appropriately in "the dustbin of history" or a museum of the obsolete than in the higher councils of a modern, scientific air force, it would already be damnable. The sorry fact is that such attributes seemed rather regular than exceptional in the halls and offices of the Air Ministry.

Two other victims were no lesser men than the two scientists who did more than anyone outside Fighter Command itself to prepare Fighter Command for the victory it won. They are Robert Watson-Watt and Sir Henry Tizard.

Watson-Watt, as he was known in the 1930s, is universally considered to be "radar's greatest pioneer", and the foremost scientist most directly involved in its application to the detection of airborne aircraft. It was his system of radar chains located on the coast round Britain which permitted the early warning of approaching enemy aircraft. This system, unique in the world at the time — and which came as a very great surprise to the German Air Force when they learnt of it — obviated the need for wasteful standing fighter patrols and made of England 'an island again'.

Sometime in June 1936 Winston Churchill, a member of the powerful, political Air Defence Committee, "expressed anxiety about whether the speed of advance in RDF [as radar was known then] was as great as could be attained", and asked Watson-Watt to give him his opinion on the matter. Watson-Watt gave Churchill his "diagnosis of the prime cause of avoidable delays."

> It was that the Air Ministry was stubbornly adhering to a foredoomed policy. It was attempting to force its normal machinery to revolve at an abnormal rate, instead of setting up abnormal machinery to meet a highly abnormal need. Even after acceleration, the normal machinery was already holding up our rate of advance.

Intimately involved with this lack of progress was the professional position of Watson-Watt as an employee of the Air Ministry. The Air Ministry had procrastinated for weeks in making Watson-Watt an offer of a permanent appointment adequate to his duties and responsibilities, and in accord with a strong recommendation made by the Tizard Committee to the Secretary of State for Air. Watson-Watt comments as follows:

> I resented the passage of fifteen weeks without reasoned discussion; I was astonished by the rejection of advice which had been given by Tizard in person, by the Tizard Committee as a body and by Sir Frank Smith. My fury at this treatment ("cavalier" was far from the *mot juste*) was enhanced by recollection of my promise of complete acquiescence in any proposal on which the Secretary of State, the Secretary of the Air Ministry (Sir Christopher Bullock) and Tizard were in real agreement.

That this was not just a personal matter, but one which vitally affected his duties, he made clear in a letter to Sir Frank Smith written on the day after his meeting with Churchill:

> This apparently personal issue was of public importance in two ways. It indicated again the Air Ministry's unwillingness to take emergency measures, although nothing but the pressure of national emergency led me to give so much as a moment's thought to rejoining the Air Ministry. It also inhibited me from full immediate usefulness, since I could not, in face of the Air Ministry's immutable attitude, bring myself to make large scale recommendations of great urgency so long as they might be interpreted in Air Ministry as manoeuvres to magnify the importance of my prospective post.

The treatment of Sir Henry Tizard by the Air Ministry and others was worse. To begin with, he was not an employee of the Air Ministry; he had no official position, but fulfilled the office of personal adviser to the Chief of the Air Staff on scientific matters. He was the Rector of Imperial College London and a renowned physicist, who gave of his time, learning and advice unstintingly, without remuneration, and with the full consent of his Board of Governors, out of a sense of duty to his country.

The priceless worth of his contribution to the Royal Air Force and his country can best be grasped from this appreciation written by Sir Solly Zuckerman in his Foreword to Clark's biography:

> Tizard's single greatest achievement [he wrote] was the encouragement he gave to the development of the chain of radar stations which assured the RAF's victory in the Battle of Britain. None of the scientific ideas behind radar was his, but without his support, backed by the prestige gained through many years of intimate and successful co-operation with members

of the Air Staff, it is doubtful if our defences would have held in those vital days of 1940. Tizard's own place in history is secure for this contribution alone.

Since the first meeting in January 1935, Tizard had been the energetic and forceful chairman of the Committee for the Scientific Survey of Air Defence — the Tizard Committee, as it became known. This committee, comprising a number of eminent scientists, was founded when the potential of Radio Direction Finding (RDF) was first demonstrated. However, Tizard's report to the Air Ministry that "a practical system for detecting and locating aircraft fifty miles away could be developed" provoked a certain resistance. The reaction of one high officer is typical of many at the time. "'Why', said he, 'if that is possible the whole plan of Air Defence will be revolutionized!'" Tizard's retort was to start revolutionizing it without delay. Such was a taste of the opposition to be put up by dinosaurs "resolutely preparing for the last war."[1]

Two other high officials who got on well with Dowding on the personal level, precisely because they understood his problems and the difficulties he had in getting solutions to them, were Lord Beaverbrook and Lieutenant General Sir Frederick Pile.

Beaverbrook was the Minister for Aircraft Production. Every morning he telephoned Dowding to ask him what he could do for him. Always the same answer came back: More Spitfires! Better performance! More speed! Longer range! Heavier armament!

There is no doubt that Beaverbrook derived a double pleasure from treating Dowding with deference. He too had his difficulties with the Air Ministry and its red tape, and became a second thorn in their side; so his visible favouring of Dowding was an extra poke in their collective eye.

But the professional results of the relationship between the two men is what irked the Air Ministry most keenly, for it removed from their authority an important strategic role which was theirs by right, namely, the decision over the types of aircraft to be built. Beaverbrook, on Dowding's urging, gave overwhelming priority to fighters. We have seen the long battle that Dowding had with the Air Ministry to convert them to thinking fighters. But to have the decision removed from them without so much as a 'By your leave' was not likely to endear him, or Dowding, to the Air Ministry.[2]

General Pile was the commanding general responsible for all anti-aircraft units, guns and personnel. His command, as we have seen, came under

Dowding's control. Every morning at ten o'clock Pile would report to Dowding. They had a free and frank discussion of Dowding's needs, and Pile put himself and his resources entirely at Fighter Command's disposal. Pile's daily visits, when Dowding frequently unburdened himself to him, were savoured by Dowding; and the warmth of their personal relations was a salutary counter-balance to the acrimony which so often embittered the relations between him and the Air Ministry.

One cannot but regret that the Chief of the Air Staff did not have the foresight and the character to telephone Dowding every day, after the Battle of France began, or set up an informal weekly meeting with Dowding, and offer him the same encouragement and support that Pile and Beaverbrook gave him so readily.

By the summer of 1940 it was too late: relations between them had already become too strained for any of the senior officers to rise above the rancour they will have felt and to put their duty first. The Air Ministry never forgave Dowding for the sharpness and bluntness of his expression. They were incapable of appreciating the enormity of the burden he bore in fighting the battle, and were equally insensitive to the added burden that they were gratuitously imposing on him.

No one has ever disputed the contention that Dowding's every act and every word were motivated by the imperious need to strengthen Fighter Command and to protect the sanctity of the home base — to save England from invasion and defeat. No Air Ministry historian or apologist has dared to try to account for Dowding's alleged uncooperativeness and supposed 'cussedness' as being a personality defect. They were the product of his having to fight for everything that Fighter Command needed to win the battle to come, and the battle that came.

If one who, having read at least some of the correspondence which passed between Dowding and the Air Ministry, puts himself in the position of the Air Staff and tries to view Dowding from their perspective, Dowding would appear, it is true, a difficult person to deal with. He was prickly, argumentative, stubborn, strong willed, tenacious, obstinate, unyielding. Even a good friend and close associate said of him: "A difficult man, a self-opinionated man, a most determined man, and a man who knew, more than anybody, about all aspects of aerial warfare." One almost feels a tinge of sympathy for the senior officers who had to deal with him. But all incipient sympathy is immediately dispelled by the recollection of how they treated him at the end; and above all by their formal refusal to acknowledge, from that day to this, the fact that if Dowding had not been such a 'cussed' character, we might all be speaking German today.

## Notes to Chapter 2:

1. Tizard's work brought him and his committee willy-nilly into contact with political forces, which constituted further obstacles. How little did even this farseeing scientist imagine what havoc they could wreak! When his committee was dissolved in the summer of 1940, it was due to intrigue both personal and political. That intrigue was the doing of Churchill and Lindemann (the latter, later Lord Cherwell, was then, and was to be Churchill's personal scientific adviser throughout the war.)

   In the light of Tizard's magnificent record of achievement, the news that "he had been forced out brought despondency to the Air Force and alarm to the scientific establishment." Among the scientists who wrote to Tizard, Egerton was appropriately blunt, and thought that his colleague's resignation made it "quite terrifying to realize, when the country is in such danger, that things like that can be happening owing to personal intrigue."

   Reaction among the enlightened air marshals was of a piece. Trenchard was aghast; Freeman was outraged; Bowhill, at Coastal Command, offered Tizard full access to all his stations to pursue his work in ship detection. As to Dowding, he wrote of his resentment of the treatment Tizard had received, and went on to say: "I feel that we all owe a debt of gratitude to you for the commonsense and logical attitude which you have adopted to scientific problems — in fact I always say of you that no-one would suspect you of being a scientist (and I mean that in a most flattering sense). The present witch doctor is firmly established for the time being but witch doctors lead a precarious existence. . . ."

   [Author's note: The witch doctor in question, Professor Lindemann, was to lead a charmed existence during the war.]

   Tizard's position as scientific adviser to the Chief of the Air Staff, Air Chief Marshal Sir Cyril Newall, was only semi-official. When Newall retired and was replaced by Air Marshal Sir Charles Portal in October 1940, Portal did not see fit "to enquire for Tizard's services."

2. Two observations are called for: (1) John Terraine has shown that the claims of Beaverbrook and his champions that the new Minister of Aircraft Production appointed on May 12, 1940, wrought miracles of increased production of Spitfires and Hurricanes are not borne out by the figures. Our statement explains the origin of the impetus. What Beaverbrook did effectively — albeit to the disapproval of the Air Ministry because of his cavalier contempt for 'channels' — was to repair and rebuild damaged fighters with great promptness and in large numbers. (2) The early raids by the RAF's bombers were carried out in daylight, hence the high losses. Bomber Command subsequently reverted to bombing by night, with poor results for three years.

# CHAPTER 3

## *Dowding at Fighter Command*

## *1936–1940*

Few dates in recent English history, seen in retrospect, can be regarded as quite so fateful as April 1st, 1936. For it was on that date that Fighter Command, Royal Air Force, came into being — in name, at any rate — and Air Marshal Sir Hugh Dowding handed over his responsibility as Air Member for Research and Development to become its first Air Officer Commanding-in-Chief. If Clio was the muse of ancient history, Ironia would appear to be the muse of modern history. Indeed, the march of history is a long course of exemplary lessons which should teach men that events have a way of upsetting, reversing and frustrating human plans and men's ambitions.

The deity we have named Ironia was to intervene a second time, and this time present a diversion of the march of history.

The appointment, because of Dowding's age, would normally have been for three years. He would therefore be due to retire on July 14th, 1939. In 1938 his successor was announced. He was to be Air Marshal Christopher Courtney. In June Courtney was severely injured in a flying accident and he could not take up the appointment.

Already, however, in 1936, when his term as Member of the Air Council for Research and Development was nearing its end, Dowding had been notified by the then Chief of the Air Staff, Air Chief Marshal Sir Edward Ellington, that he, Dowding, was to succeed him as Chief of the Air Staff. This news was repeated to him by the then Air Member for Personnel, ACM Sir Frederick Bowhill. Indeed, he had already been notified of his selection for this top job as the head of the Royal Air Force by none other than a former CAS, Sir John Salmond. Hence, when Dowding went to Fighter Command as its first AOC-in-C, he went in the belief that it would be for about seven months. He was therefore surprised to receive a letter written by Ellington in his own handwriting on February 3, 1937, informing him that the Secretary of State for Air had decided on Newall as the next CAS.

Some historians have pointed out that Dowding had no right to expect to be appointed Chief of the Air Staff, because that office is exclusively in the power of the Secretary of State, who may or may not seek advice from any source, and who may disregard any advice he receives. That is correct. And it had happened while Dowding was himself a member of the Air Council. But that being the case, why should no fewer than three of the most senior officers in the Royal Air Force have told him that he was earmarked for the post unless there were solid grounds for it? He was the most senior officer in the Royal Air Force.

This is quite unsatisfactory. These events cry for answers to questions which have seldom been answered. If Dowding was expecting to be raised to the position of Chief of the Air Staff in 1937, why was he appointed AOC-in-C Fighter Command, in the knowledge that he would have a tenure of less than one year? What could he accomplish in a new position, especially one of such importance, in one year? What had happened, or what turnabout had taken place in the thinking of the Air Council, of such significance as to convince the authorities that Newall was preferable to Dowding? It is a great pity that Wright, Dowding's confidant and friend, did not interview and interrogate the officers and politicians, members of the Air Council, still living in the 1960s, at the time of the preparation of his book, to explain the change of heart. If this remote observer may be permitted to speculate, is it not possible that the Air Council saw in Newall a manageable CAS, but Dowding most certainly not? Finally, is it not equally possible that the Air Council had in fact come to that conclusion before Dowding had left the Air Ministry, despite what some officers had unofficially told Dowding? Deighton has stated that the appointment as Commander-in-Chief of Fighter Command "was not due to any friends that Dowding had in the Air Ministry. On the contrary, plans were afoot to deprive Dowding of the promotion to Chief of the Air Staff which had already been promised to him." Dowding himself has commented: "No reason was given [when he was informed], and to this day [in ca. 1966] I have no idea what lay behind this change of policy."

Later Dowding was to comment to his biographer, Robert Wright: "It came as somewhat of a blow. It is always an attractive prospect to reach the top of the tree. But when I look back on this incident, in the light of later events, I see how fortunate this decision really was." When Dowding came to throw himself "heart and soul" into the work of Fighter Command, he remarked many times "how often he came to be glad that he had not become Chief of the Air Staff." Years later, some people, notably Air Ministry people who cannot be counted among Dowding's admirers, tried to spread the word that this 'set-back' was the source of a sustained rancour on Dowding's part which forever after soured his relations with the Air Ministry and made him both uncooperative and a hostile critic. One may believe Dowding or not, as one pleases, when he replied to Ellington on February 9, 1937: "I have always had a rather contemptuous pity for superseded officers who complain of their treatment..., and I have no intention of joining their ranks." Dowding was to repeat this demurral nearly four years later, in circumstances that were to cause him acute distress. But that Dowding had genuine cause for complaint of his treatment in the years ahead there can be no shadow of doubt.

With a devotion to duty and a will-power which we come to see as two of the great driving characteristics of the man, Dowding set to work on the mammoth task of creating and building up the organization, personnel, training and *matériel* that were going to provide an effective defence of the United Kingdom at a period in European and world history which he foresaw with greater clarity and vision than most others was fraught with a danger that was immediate and probable, not distant and unlikely.

In July 1938 Dowding received a letter from Newall, the new Chief of the Air Staff, informing him that, as previously announced, his services would not be required by the Royal Air Force after June 1939. He expected to hand over his Command to Courtney. And indeed Newall telephoned him on February 24 to tell him that his retirement had been reported in a London newspaper that day, but added that it had been decided that "no change would be made during the present year." Dowding had not received the least intimation before this informal telephone call that he would not now be retiring in June. He had been making plans to leave the RAF in a few months' time.

In March Dowding had a long conference with the new Secretary of State for Air, Kingsley Wood, with Newall present, at which he made clear his dissatisfaction at the discourteous treatment he had received in his dealings with the Air Ministry, and that for that reason he was no longer keen to remain in the RAF beyond June.

Later that month Dowding received a letter, not from the Secretary of State but from Newall. In it Newall stated the decision that Dowding was to "relinquish command of the Fighter Command at the end of June, 1939."

Careless readers and people with no mind for nuances of language will discern no difference between the expressions 'no further employment' and 'relinquish command'. Dowding was not one of them. Dowding's use of language was precise and exact. He expected others, especially those in high office, to be equally scrupulous. To him, the one meant 'retirement'; the other implied at least the possibility of 'a new position'. The second expression seemed to him more in keeping with the policy that had been enunciated to him, namely, that officers of his rank could be expected to be employed until they were 60 years of age. Dowding was now 56. However, Newall's letter repudiated this understanding with this offer and request: "In view of the importance of the efficiency of the Fighter Command and the desire to avoid the coincidence of crises and changes in the higher appointments in operational commands, it has been decided to ask you to defer your retirement until the end of March 1940. I hope this will be agreeable to you."

This was followed by an official letter from the Air Ministry at the end of May, a letter which in its tone and substance is curt and inconsiderate to a degree: "With reference to this department's letter of the 4th. August last, intimating that it would not be possible to employ you in the Royal Air Force after the end of June, 1939, I am commanded by the Air Council to inform you that, after further consideration, they have decided to continue your employment until the end of March, 1940." It was scarcely the manner in which the most senior officer in the Royal Air Force — in fact he was senior even to the CAS — should be addressed. Wright comments: "So, for a second time, Dowding had to readjust all his plans about looking forward to the time when he would be among the unemployed."

War was declared on September 3rd, 1939. Dowding had performed wonders in creating the highly technical defensive apparatus with the thousands of trained personnel that constituted Fighter Command. War does worse than disrupt people's lives. Nevertheless, Dowding, in view of his position, and ill-treated though he had been by the Air Ministry, could not have expected the next letter. We can do no better than to quote the entire page which narrates the episode.

> Despite all that had been happening in the rapid expansion of the Royal Air Force, and the cataclysm that had overtaken the world with its immediate threat to this country, Dowding was still under notice, which he fully understood and accepted, that he was to relinquish his command and retire

from the Royal Air Force on 31 March. He had made his plans with that firmly in mind. But at the very last moment, *only the day before he was due to go* (our italics), he received a long letter from the Chief of the Air Staff that threw everything, yet again, into the melting pot. 'On the 20th March last year I wrote to ask you if you would defer your retirement until the end of March, 1940', Newall wrote. He made no mention of that date being the very next day. 'Even at that time of disturbed and uneasy peace your Command was of the very greatest importance, and since then war has intervened with a consequent increase in your responsibilities. In the circumstances it has been decided to ask you to continue in your present position until July 14th of this year, on which date you will have completed four years as Air Officer Commanding-in-Chief.'

With all that was staring the country in the face, this was a postponement of only three and a half months, and in its own way it illustrated the unreality of the thinking of that time when it came to planning for even the immediate future. Newall continued:

> I shall personally be very glad if you are willing to accept this extension, as I feel it would be undesirable for a change to take place at Fighter Command at this stage when we may be on the verge of intensified air activity. Whether that be so or not, I am well aware how high the efficiency of Fighter Command stands today and I fully realise how much we owe to your personal leadership in preparing the command and bringing it so successfully into action.

Despite the upheaval that this latest notice meant for him at the very last moment, Dowding felt that all that Newall was saying was pleasant enough, and obviously well-intentioned, and that after the objection that he had raised a year ago it would not be advisable to go over all that again. But there was nevertheless something of a sting in the tail of Newall's letter, which read:

> As I mentioned to you previously, I have the uncongenial task of informing the more senior officers in the Service when it becomes necessary to call upon them to make way for others in order to keep up a sufficient flow of promotions. I must now confirm the information that, so far as can at present be seen, it will be necessary for you to retire when you relinquish your Command on July 14th next. An official letter to this effect will be sent to you in due course. I know you will appreciate the difficulties involved in this decision, and believe when I say that the Royal Air Force as a whole will greatly regret the conclusion of your active duties in the Service.

There was no lack of decision in this final notice. Dowding was to relinquish his Command and retire. That was stated categorically, and there was nothing he could do but accept it and make his plans with this new date in mind.

In his reply, the next day, Dowding merely stated: 'I shall be glad to continue in my present Command until July 14th of this year.' He added only one other sentence: 'Can you tell me who my successor will be?'

There was no reply to this request. Nor was there any official letter which Newall had said would 'be sent to you in due course': the customary official letter confirming the extension of Dowding's last few weeks of service in the Royal Air Force until 14 July.

Any man or woman who places uncritical faith in authority and their word is a man or woman destined to be deceived. Yet, surely, in view of the situation in which Britain found herself at this moment in her history, at war and totally unprepared for war, the British people had the right to think that, at the very summit of the organizations responsible for their defence and security, the authorities, Service and political alike, who directed those organizations were cooperating with each other in the highest interest of their country. Alas! How, in a democracy, do the people ensure that their elected and appointed authorities do what is necessary when it is necessary?

Dowding had set his sights, and made his preparations, in view of his impending retirement on July 14. He had heard no further word from Newall or the Air Ministry a week before his planned departure. In the intervening three months, events which shattered Europe and changed the face of the world forever — the German *Blitzkrieg,* the resignation of Chamberlain in favour of Churchill, and above all the evacuation of the British Army at Dunkirk and, finally, the total defeat and collapse of the French Army and of France — seemed to produce little impact on the cocooned enclaves of the Air Ministry, unless it was a confusion bordering on panic. Was Dowding to pack up and leave, with the war about to be launched against the British Isles? Or was he to assume that he was to stay, without instructions or request? He thought it better to inquire, and so settle the matter. He telephoned Newall. In the course of their conversation, Dowding delivered what was tantamount to an ultimatum to Newall, saying: "If you want to get rid of me, then get rid of me, but don't do it in this way." It produced its effect — whether a desired effect it is impossible to say, but an effect of immeasurable benefit to the Royal Air Force, to Great Britain, and to all of mankind. Dowding received a letter from Newall on July 5th. Among other things, he asked Dowding to stay on again. It is to be noted that this letter gave Dowding at least nine days to change his plans this time.

This letter of Newall's also produced from Dowding a reaction such as no Chief of the Air Staff can ever before, or since, have received from an officer of Dowding's position and stature. Newall asked for it and Newall got it. On July 7th. Dowding, understandably insecure and resentful, wrote as follows to Newall:

> I should like you to cast your eye down the following record.
>
> Feb. 8th 1937. Letter from Sir E. Ellington [Chief of the Air Staff]: "It has been established . . . that an Officer of your rank will be employed as far as possible up to age of 60."
>
> Aug. 4th 1938. Letter from Air Council 'unable to offer you any employment in the RAF after the end of June 1939.'
>
> Feb. 23rd 1939. Paragraph in *Evening Standard* announcing my impending retirement and naming my successor.
>
> Feb. 24th 1939. You telephoned and told me that the Air Ministry proposed to reply that 'no change would be made during the present year'.
>
> March 10th 1939. Interview with S of S at which you were present. Said I was not willing to extend service unless I had the confidence and support of the Air Council hitherto denied to me. Verbal assurance.
>
> March 17th 1939. Reminder to S of S that I awaited an answer.
>
> March 20th 1939. Letter from you asking me to defer my retirement till end of March, 1940.
>
> March 30th 1940 [one day before date of retirement]. Request from you to defer retirement till July 14th 1940.
>
> March 31st 1940. My reply accepting and asking who my successor would be. ( No  reply or acknowledgement received.)
>
> July 5th 1940. Letter from you asking me to defer retirement till October 1940.
>
> Apart from the question of discourtesy, which I do not want to stress, I must point out the lack of consideration involved in delaying a proposal of this nature until ten days before the day of my retirement. I have had four retiring dates given to me and  now you are proposing a fifth. Before the war, as I told the S of S, I should have  been glad enough to retire; now I am anxious to stay, because I feel there is no one else who will fight as I do when proposals are made which would reduce the Defence Forces of the Country below the extreme danger point. I would therefore suggest that I should not be called on to retire otherwise than at my own request before the first retiring date given to me, viz April 24th 1942, or the end of the war, whichever is the earlier.

Perhaps his tutelary deity had taken a leave of absence at this juncture, for Dowding did not get his way. It was almost as if he suspected something, for he sent a copy of this letter to the new Secretary of State for Air, Sir Archibald Sinclair.

Sinclair had been appointed to the Air Ministry by his friend Churchill on May 12th, two days after Churchill became Prime Minister. It seems that some member or members of the Air Council or Air Staff were not slow in working on Sinclair, for, despite the visible evidences of Dowding's accomplishments, he or they took little time in convincing Sinclair that Dowding's appointment should be terminated. Martin Gilbert wrote in the sixth volume of his historical biography of Churchill:

> To challenge these new and large-scale air attacks [of July 9 and 10], British fighters moved with skill and daring, and with inevitable loss. But pressure had already mounted against the head of Fighter Command, Sir Hugh Dowding, and only a few days before the increased German air activity had begun, Sir Archibald Sinclair told Churchill that he had been considering removing Dowding from his Command, at the latest after four months. Churchill opposed Sinclair's decision, writing to him on July 10:

>> Personally, I think he is one of the very best men you have got, and I say this after having been in contact with him for about two years. I have greatly admired the whole of his work in the Fighter Command, and especially in resisting the clamour for numerous air raid warnings, and the immense pressure to dissipate the Fighter strength during the great French battle. In fact he has my full confidence. I think it is a pity for an officer so gifted and so trusted to be working on such a short tenure as four months, and I hope you will consider whether it is not in the public interest that his appointment should be indefinitely prolonged while the war lasts. This would not of course exclude his being moved to a higher position, if that were thought necessary.[2]

That did the trick. Sinclair oscillated, this time in the right direction. On that very same day, July 10th, he wrote in reply to Dowding's letter — and what a change in tone and attitude! It was, said Sinclair, "my wish that you should remain in command of our Fighter Squadrons, upon whose success in defeating the German attack upon our munitions factories during the next three months will almost certainly depend the issue of this war."

It is easy to distinguish, in this simple-seeming statement, the influence of Churchill's grasp of events and the contrasting contribution of the Air Minister. That the outcome of the war depended on Fighter Command, and that the issue would be decided in the next three months, had been the theme of one of Churchill's inspiring speeches. But to suggest that Dowding was "in command of our Fighter Squadrons" and that the Germans would attack mainly the munitions factories reveals more than anything else that Sinclair was totally out of touch with the realities of Fighter Command and of probable German aims.

Sinclair concluded his letter thus: "I could give you no higher proof of my confidence in you and, although it seems superfluous, let me add the assurance of my full support." (The change that is to take place in Sinclair's attitude in the next short three months, without a word of explanation, will stagger the mind and justify Dowding's distrust of the politician's word.) Newall wrote too, and apologized to Dowding. But he explained that among the other considerations he had to weigh when making changes in command was the need "to maintain an adequate flow of promotions into the higher positions in the Service." Poor Newall! The very fate of the country is to be decided by an imminent massive aerial onslaught by enemy bombers, and Newall and the Air Staff are wrestling with problems of "an adequate flow of promotions" in the RAF! How deadening to the mind and clear thinking are the transition from peace to war and the routines of a bureaucratic system!

Finally, Dowding also received an official letter from the Air Ministry. And what a change! "I am commanded by the Air Council to refer to personal correspondence between yourself and the Chief of the Air Staff and to enquire whether you would be good enough to accept an extension of your employment with the Royal Air Force until 31st October 1940."

The change in tone must have been gratifying. But the new date showed a certain calculation. For it would seem to have been arrived at from the estimated three months during which the success or otherwise of the German attacks and of Fighter Command's defences would be decided.

Were Sinclair's confidence and expression of support genuine? Was Newall's apology genuine? If they were extending Dowding's 'employment' by only three months, they could afford to be conciliatory and reasonable. On the other hand, Sinclair and Newall were gentlemen of the old school; and after they had reviewed the record of changes in Dowding's retirement date, they must have realized that Dowding had every reason to complain of "cavalier treatment."

Was the Air Ministry's new courtesy genuine? The question is important, for the Air Ministry had the means to make and break officers' careers. Up to now, the relations between Dowding and the Air Ministry had been stormy, and they were at that point deteriorating. Well, they too could afford to be courteous, since Dowding would be out of their hair for good in three months. Finally, one is not to know whether their courtesy was genuine or not, for they were simply following the instructions of Newall and Sinclair.

The picture was to brighten suddenly for Dowding in an unexpected way. Three days later, on July 13th, Dowding was included among the guests who dined at Chequers with the Prime Minister. Churchill and Dowding talked about the forthcoming battle and Fighter Command. Dowding wrote to Sinclair about it the following day. The Prime Minister, he said, "was good enough to tell me that I had secured his confidence, and that he wished me to remain on the Active List for the time being, without any date for my retirement being fixed. He told me that he had written to you on the subject."

Dowding being Dowding, he took pains to ensure that Sinclair knew about his, Dowding's, role in this new development. "In case you should think that his intervention was something more than coincidence, I may tell you that neither he nor any other minister was made aware of my approaching retirement through any action or word of mine."

The Luftwaffe's assault, on shipping in the Channel initially, had already begun on July 9th; and Messerschmitts had already, on the 9th, begun to look, successfully, for prey. With his retirement deferred indefinitely, it appeared, Dowding was able to turn his attentions single-mindedly to the battle. Yet doubts must have nagged at the back of his mind, for a whole month elapsed before Dowding received confirmation.

Finally, on August 12th, with the battle joined in earnest, he received a letter from Newall. "When I wrote to you on July 13th, I could not see any alternative to indicating the end of October as the time for your retirement. [No alternative? Newall is sparing in his explanation. How had things changed?] In the present circumstances, however, I fully realize the disadvantages involved in this decision and I am now glad to be able to say that it has been decided to cancel the time limit to the period of your appointment as C-in-C Fighter Command. I sincerely hope that this information will be agreeable to you."

Dowding still had to wait a further ten days to receive an official letter to confirm that 'information'. He received, on August 22nd, at a stage in the battle when his vital airfields and sector stations were being subjected to damaging and worrying attacks, a letter from the Air Ministry which reverted to their customary clinical formality. "I am commanded by the Air

Council to refer to their letter dated 13th July 1940, reference 809403/38/57c and to inform you that they have decided to cancel the time limit to the period of your appointment as Air Officer Commanding-in-Chief, Fighter Command."

With his eagle eye and his sensitivity to nuances, Dowding noted that Newall's letter referred to both "the period of (his) appointment" and his "retirement". The Air Ministry letter, on the other hand, mentioned only "the period of (his) appointment". He noted also that Newall had made no reference to Churchill's letter to Sinclair and to Churchill's wishes in the matter.

And here, presumably, the matter stood, but leaving Dowding in the dark as to when his appointment would terminate, and whether at the end of it he would be retired or offered a new appointment.

Dowding felt once again free to devote himself to the defence of his country, seemingly secure in his belief that in a fortnight's time he would not be receiving yet another deadline and notice of termination of employment, during that most crucial and precarious time when it seemed that the German concentrated attacks against the sector stations might prevail. But Fighter Command stood firm, Dowding never wavered in his control of his resources, and the Germans made a strategic blunder by switching their attack to London in the belief that what was left of Fighter Command would be forced to defend the capital in maximum strength and so expose itself to destruction by the Luftwaffe's superiority in fighters.

They were grievously mistaken.

But other clouds were gathering on the horizon for Dowding.

## NOTES TO CHAPTER 3:

1. This weird rationale did not prevent the Air Ministry from bringing out of retirement an officer aged 61 and sending him out to Singapore of all places, in 1940 of all times, as Commander-in-Chief of air and land forces.

2. The reader is asked to bear this encomium in mind when it comes time for Churchill to defend Dowding. (See chapter 7.)

D.C.S. EVILL, SASO
FIGHTER COMMAND HQ

KEITH PARK
AOC 11 GROUP

SIR QUINTIN BRAND
AOC 10 GROUP

RICHARD SAUL
AOC 13 GROUP

## *The Victors of the Battle of Britain:*
## THE AIR VICE-MARSHALS

# CHAPTER 4

# *The Tactical Dispute:*
# *11 Group and 12 Group*

The historical record, and the actual results of the protracted air battles over England in August, September and October of 1940, are beyond dispute. Yet the debate, or controversy, about tactics lingers on, like a dead horse whose owner refuses to accept the fact of its demise.

The dispute in question, always lively, sometimes acrimonious, is called the 'big wings' debate.[1] This controversy has, regrettably, become so inescapable a feature of any book that deals with the Battle of Britain, and, even more regrettably, with the fate of the Commander of Fighter Command, that, much as we would prefer to by-pass it, the fact remains that its lingering malodour demands a final treatment of the antisepsis of truth.

The 'wings' dispute refers to the disagreement between two factions within Fighter Command and between Fighter Command and the Air Ministry over the question whether single squadrons or pairs of squadrons acting together, or wings of three or more squadrons under a single commander, were the more effective answer to the German daytime attacks. It is important also because some writers have claimed that the Air Ministry found in Dowding's and Park's refusal to use massed wings of fighters adequate grounds for removing them at the end of 1940. We do not intend to review the whole controversy and its history; instead, we will limit ourselves to an examination of the practical outcome of the 'wings' as they were formed, used, and led. In the event that the reader does not know the main issues, they are easily stated.

For purposes of defence against aerial attack by enemy forces, the Fighter Command divided the United Kingdom into regions on geographical lines. Each region was defended by a Group, with each Group deploying a certain number of fighter squadrons based at certain Air Force stations. The regions closest to the enemy protected the most vital potential targets: airfields, aircraft manufacturing plants, heavy industry, ports, centres of government. The two Groups closest to the enemy were the one defending the south and south-east, including London, and the other defending the east coast and central England, including the industrial Midlands.

When Fighter Command was established in 1936, and during the following three years when Dowding was building its foundations and infrastructure, the only threat to Great Britain came from Germany, whose bombers would have had to fly across the North Sea. At that time, therefore, the brunt of the defence would have been borne by 12 Group, defending the east. For that reason, it was on the east coast that the first radar early warning stations were erected. After the defeat of France in June 1940, however, and the subsequent occupation of French airfields by the Luftwaffe, the main thrust of the aerial assault came from the south; and the tactical centre of gravity shifted menacingly onto 11 Group.

There was an additional factor, one which made all the difference in the world between success and failure. That was that bombers taking off from France would have fighter escorts, an impossibility for bombers starting from Germany because of the range. As the battle evolved, the German tactics, which changed constantly, were devised to entice the British fighters into the air, to be dealt with by the German fighters, while the bombers carried out their work of destruction.

The strategy devised by Dowding, and followed without deviation throughout the Battle, was to take such measures as were required to conserve Fighter Command in being as a fighting force, and thus ensure that there were always squadrons in the south to meet incoming attacks, while other squadrons were held in the north and west to defend their own areas.

No one who studies the Battle of Britain will come close to understanding how it was that the German Air Force, with its numerical superiority and the advantage of the initiative, failed to secure a victory by destroying Fighter Command as a prelude to establishing air supremacy and to invading England, without first appreciating the role of the system of control exercised over the RAF's fighter squadrons **from the ground.**

The chain of radar stations around Britain established through the genius of Watson-Watt and Tizard, received signals indicating enemy aircraft or formations approaching. The information was not always accurate or complete: we are talking about the earliest, pioneering days of radar: but the interpreters did well to form an estimate of numbers, altitude, and bearing.

The masses of information were received at Fighter Command HQ, analysed and 'filtered' there, and passed on to the Groups. The Group Headquarters passed the relevant information to Sectors, who 'scrambled', or despatched, a certain number of fighters, according to Group's instructions. The number of fighters — one or two sections, one squadron, or two squadrons or more — depended on the number available, the estimated number of enemy aircraft, and the distance between enemy and interceptors.

The essence of the defensive system is summed up in the concept and the word: Control. The radar receivers plotted both enemy aircraft and defending fighters. The fighters were 'controlled', that is, they were under strict orders to fly where and when they were so ordered to do in order to effect an interception. For the Group HQ and sectors alone could 'see' both; and the sector controller alone could direct his fighters to a position from which to intercept the enemy most advantageously to the defenders. It was only when the fighter leader actually sighted the enemy aircraft that he was released from control, and only then did he deploy his fighters and give instructions for engaging the enemy.

Air Vice-Marshal Keith Park, the AOC of 11 Group, whose squadrons were based relatively close to France, hence to the attackers, never had sufficient time in which to send off more then two squadrons together to meet any one raid; and, because of the sheer limitations of his airfields, he did not have the resources to send more than two; most often it was a single squadron, or even half a squadron. For it was essential to keep other squadrons in readiness in anticipation of other raiders coming in. As it was, Park's resources were such that it was not unknown for some squadrons to be 'scrambled' three, four, or even five times in a single day.

To the north of 11 Group, in 12 Group, as the battle wore on, some people, nobly motivated, seeing the 11 Group squadrons constantly outnumbered, believed that, because of their greater distance from the action, they had the time to assemble three, four, or even five squadrons in a wing, and thus meet the enemy on more even numerical terms and inflict heavier casualties on them. This idea of wings took such a hold on the minds of some pilots that, feeling justifiably frustrated by being left out of the action, they began muttering criticisms of Park, and even of Dowding, for not trying out a few wings of several squadrons.

Now, few men knew more about air fighting and fighter tactics than Park. Numerical superiority is a principle of war as old as the hills; no commander would have seized the opportunity more keenly and promptly than Park, had he been able.

In 12 Group, one pilot in particular was noted for his enthusiastic and vocal championing of the 'wings' idea. He was Squadron Leader Douglas Bader. Bader was the commanding officer of 242 (Canadian) Squadron. He had been appointed to his command — his first squadron command — by the AOC of 12 Group, Air Vice-Marshal Trafford Leigh-Mallory.

He liked Bader's aggressive spirit; he seized on Bader's ideas, and gave him full authorization to put them into effect, and appointed him wing leader.

The first wing, comprising three squadrons, was first formed in early September. Bader led it on its first operational patrol on September 7th. This wing was further engaged against the enemy on September 9th. On the 11th, a wing of four squadrons, but without Bader and 242 Squadron, made a successful interception. And on the 15th, Bader led for the first time a 'big wing' of five squadrons. (In Appendix "A" will be found a comprehensive analysis of the claims made, and the actual results achieved, by the wing, by 242 Squadron, and by Fighter Command as a whole.)

Two sets of reports have been consulted in the preparation of the claims of enemy aircraft destroyed and/or damaged by Bader's wing. They are:

(1) Reports of Wing Patrols and Fighter Tactics submitted to Fighter Command Headquarters by Leigh-Mallory on September 17th.

(2) "The All-Canadian Squadron", a narrative of 242 Squadron's and Bader's wing actions written by Wing Commander F.H. Hitchins of the Royal Canadian Air Force.

Readers, especially readers of a later time, have been, and may continue to be, surprised by the extraordinary discrepancies between the claims of enemy aircraft destroyed put out by the Air Ministry, and the actual numbers destroyed.

The figures believed by historians today to be reliable are those released after the war as a result of researches made into the records maintained by the Quartermaster General of the Luftwaffe. An indispensable record of these events is to be found in the magnificent compilation published under the title of *The Battle of Britain: Then and Now*, edited by W.G. Ramsey, which gives precise details of each aircraft destroyed and damaged during the Battle.

If the results submitted to the Air Ministry by Fighter Command[2] as a whole are seen to be off the mark, sometimes widely, the summing-up by Wing Commander Hitchins in his narrative borders on the fantastic. He wrote: "During 1940 No. 242 Squadron had fought three campaigns — The Battle of Dunkirk, the Battle of France and the Battle of Britain. It had lost 17 pilots, killed or missing, in the course of the year's operations, eleven during the French Campaigns and six in the later actions over Britain. All but three of these pilots were Canadians. Against these losses it boasted a record of at least 87(?) enemy aircraft destroyed (the incomplete state of records leaves some doubt as to the precise number); 62 of these had been destroyed during the Battle of Britain when the squadron led the Duxford Wing. The five squadrons forming that wing had amassed a total of 158 enemy aircraft confirmed for a loss of only nine pilots and 15 aircraft." (Read that last sentence again!)

Equally remarkable are the comparative figures put forward by Leigh-Mallory in the concluding "Summary" of his report:

| ENEMY CASUALTIES | | OUR CASUALTIES | |
|---|---|---|---|
| enemy a/c destroyed . . . . . | 105 | pilots killed or missing . . . . | 6 |
| e/a 'probables' . . . . . . . . . . | 40 | pilots wounded . . . . . . . . . | 5 |
| | | aircraft destroyed . . . . . . . | 14 |
| | | aircraft damaged . . . . . . . | 18 |

These results have, of course, been contested. They seem all the more difficult to understand when considered in the light of the narrative account of each patrol in Leigh-Mallory's own report. In what follows, we either quote directly or summarize.

First Wing Patrol. "The three Squadrons were at a disadvantage through the loss of any element of surprise and also through the necessity of having to climb up to the enemy. There was the added disadvantage in that when attacking the bombers, the German fighters were coming down on them [our fighters] from the sun.

Second Wing Patrol. "The Spitfire Squadron (19) climbed to 23,000 feet to attack the fighters whilst the Hurricanes climbed to attack the bombers. The number of escorting fighters was large enough to enable some of them to dive on our fighters as they attacked the bombers . . . ."

Third Wing Patrol. "As 74 Squadron went into the formation of Ju.88's they were attacked by enemy fighters (He. 113's) diving on them, but continued their attack on the main formation. AA fire which had drawn our fighters' attention to the enemy was troublesome during the engagement, and hampered the plan of attack."

Fourth Wing Patrol. "The leader saw Spitfires and Hurricanes, belonging to No.11 Group, engage the enemy and waited to avoid any risk of collision. As the Hurricane Squadrons went in to attack the bombers, Me.109's dived towards them out of the sun, but, as the Spitfires turned to attack them, the enemy fighters broke away . . . In the meantime the Hurricanes were able to destroy all the Dorniers that they could see and one of the Squadrons saw a further small formation of Dorniers . . . and promptly destroyed the lot."

Fifth Wing Patrol. The leader of the Wing found that he was at a tactical disadvantage as he had not had time to reach his patrol height, with the result that this formation was attacked by Me.109's, as they were trying to get into position. Because of this, the leader of the Wing told the Spitfires to attack the bombers, and the Hurricanes to...engage the fighters. "The results of the engagement were satisfactory so far as it went, but . . . it was impossible to break up the bomber formation and so achieve the same tactical superiority as in the Fourth patrol."[3]

We have presented the claims made by 12 Group for the success of its wing operations for what they are worth. It is no part of our intent to discuss how the pilots, the squadrons or the Group arrived at these figures. We know today that all the claims made by Fighter Command were considerably greater than the actual results. Our main purpose in presenting the foregoing figures and those to be quoted shortly is to discover to what degree the wing operations, looked at as a whole, were successful. (In chapter 6 we consider what bearing these wing operations had on Dowding's removal from his Command.)

The reader has seen from the tables in Appendix "A" that the numbers of enemy aircraft which Bader's wing claimed to have destroyed turned out to be wildly erratic. That is not the point. The point is that the pilots and squadrons believed them. We feel that that belief was sincerely arrived at. Whether or not Leigh-Mallory himself believed them we do not know. Dowding had something to say about it, as we shall see. Let us look at the total picture of the wing operations.

During the period covered by the 12 Group report, the 'missing' dates — September 8, 10, 12 and 13 — saw no wing operations because of bad weather.

After September 15th, however, the only days on which the Duxford wing was not 'scrambled' were the 19th, 25th, 26th, 29th and 30th. The 30th was the last great daylight battle. The German Air Force lost 47 aircraft against 20 RAF fighters and eight pilots killed or wounded — this without the help of 12 Group and the Duxford wing.

On every other day except September 27th, Bader's wing, of three or five squadrons, was 'scrambled' eleven times on seven days and failed on every occasion to intercept plotted enemy formations. Leigh-Mallory and Bader, in particular, blamed their failures on 11 Group for calling on them too late. On many of these occasions there was in fact no request from 11 Group. The major reason for the failures is that the Duxford controller, Wing Commander A.B. Woodhall, whatever his merits as a controller, never controlled Bader; he merely 'requested' or 'suggested' where Bader might look. On some days he permitted Bader to take his wing up on a free-lance, and fruitless, hunt.

We said that Bader's wing carried out a successful interception on September 27th. On that day the enemy raids were numerous and heavy. The Duxford wing was 'scrambled' three times. On its second patrol Bader, contrary to Woodhall's suggested vector, led his wing on a random search. He was lucky: he found 'bandits'. One writer has described the scene thus:

> It was almost exactly noon. The Wing was up-sun and higher. He [Bader] observed the Bf109s. There were about a hundred. They had no formation. They had no bombers to escort. They seemed to have no purpose. There was no logical pressure point to attack, no focus. A co-ordinated attack was pointless. He instructed the squadron leaders: 'Break up and attack.' Now, each section aimed for a point in the milling mass of fighters. It was a classic 'bounce': up sun and above the enemy.

The wing claimed thirteen enemy aircraft 'destroyed', five 'probables', and three 'damaged', for the loss of five fighters and two pilots killed. In point of fact — following Ramsey's Battle of Britain — the Germans lost to Bader's fighters only four or five of the seventeen Me109s destroyed over England that day.

We now come to the wing's record in October. From the last days of September the Germans changed their tactics yet again. Being unable to sustain the losses inflicted on their bombers throughout August and September, the Luftwaffe resorted almost exclusively to incursions by bomb-carrying Me109 and Me110 fighters flying at altitudes of 20,000 feet, 25,000 feet, and even 30,000 feet. Wood and Dempster put the new situation succinctly:

> These tactics were difficult to counter because of the height at which the
> German fighters flew. Above 25,000 feet the Me109 with a two-stage super-
> charger had a better performance than even the Mark II Hurricanes and
> Spitfires then coming into service. Moreover, raids approaching at 20,000
> feet or more had a good chance of minimizing the effect of radar observa-
> tion and were difficult for the Observer Corps to track, especially when there
> ere clouds about. Secondly, the speed at which the formations, unencum-
> bered by long-range bombers, flew was so great that at best the radar chain
> could not give much more than twenty minutes' warning before they
> released their bombs. Thirdly, Park had no way of telling which of the sev-
> eral approaching formations contained bomb-carrying aircraft and should
> therefore be given preference.

Despite these difficulties, 12 Group persisted in sending up wings of
three, four, or five squadrons under Bader on days when the weather was suitable. Those days were: October 1, 2, 5, 7, 8, 10, 11, 13, 15, 17, 19, 25 and 29. Bader
and his wing failed to make a single interception on any of those patrols.

Let us now summarize the results of all Bader's wing operations from
September 7th to October 29th:

| | | | |
|---|---|---|---|
| operations . . . . . . . . . . . . . | 37 | enemy aircraft destroyed  . . | (?)[4] |
| interceptions  . . . . . . . . . . | 7 | fighters/pilots lost  . . . . . . . | 7/9 |

One of the most persistent critics of the big wings was the late Group
Captain Tom Gleave, who was the official historian of the Battle of
Britain Fighters Association. Gleave is quoted by Norman Gelb in his book,
*Scramble,* as dismissing the results of the wings:

> 12 Group was supposed to cover Biggin Hill, Kenley, Northolt and the
> other 11 Group airfields while 11 Group squadrons were off the ground
> meeting the Hun coming in. It failed to do this. I know of at least one oc-
> casion when Keith Park rang up 12 Group and said, "You're supposed to be
> looking after my airfields."

> He got no change out of that. Of thirty-two Big Wings sent off by 12
> Group, only seven met the enemy and only once did the Big Wing get there
> first, before the bombs were dropped.

On June 25th, 1990, a conference was held at the RAF Staff College,
Bracknell, to mark the fiftieth anniversary of the Battle of Britain. (The proceedings were published by the RAF Historical Society under the title: *The*

*Battle Re-Thought)*. Gleave repeated there this figure; and he was challenged by (the now late) Air Marshal Sir Denis Crowley-Milling to state his sources: "I do not know where Tom Gleave got his figures from . . . ." Gleave informed this writer later, in reply to his query, that he did not have his papers with him and could not satisfy Crowley-Milling with any assurance.

Crowley-Milling was one of the most stalwart champions of the wings. He was a junior pilot in Bader's 242 Squadron. His case leans heavily on the 12 Group report. It was this writer who gave a copy of the report to the Air Marshal in 1989, and Crowley-Milling never ceased to wave it about thereafter in vindication.

When Leigh-Mallory's report was received at Fighter Command Headquarters, it was forwarded to the Air Ministry a few days later with a brief covering letter from Dowding. The key paragraphs read:

> The figures of enemy losses claimed in the table attached to the report can, in my opinion, be regarded only as approximate. It will be seen from these figures that the losses inflicted on the enemy were not increased in relation to the number of our fighters engaged on the later patrol when a large number of Squadrons took part. Nevertheless, the losses incurred by the Wing were reduced and I am, in any case, of the opinion that the AOC No. 12 Group is working on the right lines in organising his operations in strength.

Air Marshal Crowley-Milling also quoted this document at the Staff College conference, emphasizing the last sentence. However, it is important not to rest on one's laurels. One wonders whether the air marshal ever asked himself why Leigh-Mallory never issued subsequent reports on the wings' failed operations.

On September 25th, 1940, Dowding, doubtless after having studied the report and the accompanying table more attentively, expressed his scepticism about them to Leigh-Mallory without beating about the bush: "I read a great many combat reports, and I think I am beginning to pick out those which can be relied on and those which throw in claims at the end for good measure."

This is a most serious suspicion and charge: it comes as close to an accusation of 'cooking the books' as it can without saying it in so many words.

On October 15th, Air Vice-Marshal Park had issued new tactical instructions. He concluded by saying: "Bitter experience has proved time and again that it is better to intercept the enemy with one squadron above him than by a whole wing crawling up below, probably after the enemy has dropped his bombs."

The 'experience' of which Park speaks is not an oblique criticism of the 12 Group wings. Far from it: Park had deployed wings of two and three squadrons since Dunkirk. His 'bitter experience' had been learnt from the lessons of his own wings in September and October.

In response to the increased enemy activity from September 7 on, Park countered with wing formations. Accordingly, a wing was formed at Debden on September 11 and its two component squadrons, nos. 17 and 73, led respectively by Squadron Leader A.G. Miller and Squadron Leader M.S.W. Robinson, had a successful interception. Further wing operations were carried out with the addition of 257 Squadron, commanded by Squadron Leader R.R.S. Tuck, on four occasions. Of the eleven wing operations, only one, the first of two on September 27, was successful.

After September, 257 Squadron ceased to operate with the wing. The other two squadrons continued to operate as a wing until October 20, but had no contact with the enemy and seldom saw any enemy aircraft.

A feature of the Duxford wing on its third patrol has gone little remarked and less commented. On this occasion, on September 11th, Bader was at 12 Group Headquarters, and 242 Squadron did not take part in the wing patrol.

This September 11 patrol comprised four squadrons. One of the squadrons was taking part in its first action in the wing operations. It was 74 Squadron. This famous squadron had had an exceptionally busy time in 11 Group. From July 7th until the end of August, it had been stationed at Hornchurch, and often deployed to Manston; and like all 11 Group squadrons, it had been in the thick of the fighting for many weeks, until being withdrawn to another group for a comparative rest. It was during 74 Squadron's fighting in the south that its commander had established himself as a fighter leader *sans pareil*. He was Squadron Leader A.G. 'Sailor' Malan. Malan was the greatest fighter pilot and leader in the Battle of Britain — of the whole war, in our view. His fame was renowned when he went to 12 Group.

Malan and his squadron moved to 12 Group on September 4th. Two days later, accompanied by Flight Lieutenant H.M. Stephen, one of his flight commanders, Malan had an interview with Leigh-Mallory, who wanted to discuss with the two pilots their views of wing formations. "Malan was happy enough to be part of the Big Wing idea (according to Stephen's recollection), if only as a way to get back into action. The only thing he insisted upon was that he and his Tigers should be on top in the air, above everyone else."

It is significant that in this participation in a wing operation, each squadron acted under the independent orders of its own commander; and that this action was 74 Squadron's only participation in a wing operation.

In most of September and half of October, when Bader was putting his wings into the air, his and Malan's squadrons were the only two squadrons stationed at Coltishaw. Malan and 74 Squadron took no part in Bader's wings.

In one biography of Malan, a slim volume inadequate to its subject, the author makes no mention of it. We turn to Bader's biographer, Laddie Lucas, and surprisingly he does not mention this joint occupation of the same base either.

On October 15th, Malan and 74 Squadron moved back to 11 Group, returning to Biggin Hill. He, and they, must have rested up long enough. It is not difficult to envisage Malan trying to persuade Bader to move down with them. But Bader and 242 Squadron stayed put.

It is probable that Malan must by then have wearied of the inaction, for the Squadron Record Book noted on the day of its return to Biggin Hill: "Should now get back into our stride again." And get back into their stride again they did. If we accept the account given by Group Captain Ira Jones in his history of 74 Squadron, they were successfully directed by Sector Control and intercepted numerous high-flying Me109 and 110 raiders, on some occasions even with the advantage of sun and height.

Other squadrons had their successes as well. In the month of October, 379 enemy aircraft were destroyed. Of this number no fewer than 241 were fighters. On the last day of major engagements, October 29th, 33 German fighters were destroyed for the loss of 12 RAF fighters.[5]

Having established, as we believe, the failure of the Duxford wings, we feel obliged to attempt to explain the failure. We are fortunate to have a detailed account in Bader's own words of how he operated his wings. Bader was interviewed by the historian Alfred Price in connection with his research, and the following account is based on them.[6]

> The five squadrons were deployed at two airfields: Duxford with three Hurricane squadrons, and Fowlmere with two Spitfire squadrons. The Hurricane squadrons took off in flights of three in formation abreast; when the lead flight was "getting towards the far hedge the next three would

be taxiing into position"; and so on until all squadrons were airborne. Bader led and climbed on the directed course at 140 m.p.h. until all flights had caught up.

The Spitfire squadrons, flying much faster aircraft, had to throttle back in order to stay with the Hurricanes. They acted as escorts to the Hurricanes, for they flew 5000 feet above the Hurricanes, and were under instructions to tackle the enemy fighters while the Hurricanes attacked the German bombers.

The five squadrons and the ground controller did not have the same radio frequency and could not therefore keep in touch. The controller would give the wing leader instructions, and he in turn "would have to keep changing frequency from squadron to squadron."

When it came to engaging the enemy Bader would not "personally . . . control the Wing". His objective was "to get the Wing into the right position". From that point "my section of three would go down, followed by everyone else. As soon as we had made one pass, the formation was broken up."

It is perfectly clear from this outline of how the Duxford wing was worked that it contains the seeds of its own failure. The wing could not climb as fast as a squadron and much crucial time was lost in the take-off and climb. In fighter interception operations during the Battle of Britain time was of the essence. Even a few minutes lost in reaching the advantageous altitude was often enough to make the difference between a successful and a failed interception. (Bader constantly blamed 11 Group for calling on them too late.)

Bader did not direct the wing in the fighting: after the initial 'pass' it was broken up and each pilot was on his own. He did not even direct or control the Spitfire squadrons since he could not see them, and in any event they knew what they had to do, for the squadron commanders directed their own squadrons. So one wonders again: what was the purpose of the wings? The wing leader had only two decisions to make in the entire operation: to manoeuvre the cumbersome mass of 40 to 56 aircraft into position, and to give the order to attack. The 'wing' would have been infinitely more effective if each flight of three had taken off as an independent unit and climbed at full throttle under the direction of the sector controller.

We have laid stress on the time factor. Bader's preoccupation was with the delay in being sent off. Why? Because he did not have the time to reach an advantageous position relative to the enemy. What was that position? Always above him: never climbing to meet him.

Bader's idea of actual air fighting is of a piece with his fascination for big wings. He constantly preached three over-riding principles:

> He who has the height controls the battle.
>
> He who has the sun achieves surprise.
>
> He who sees them first shoots them down.

These principles trip off the tongue like lines learnt by rote. Moreover they seek an ideal situation. The test of the fighter pilot is his performance in a situation not of his making. The above maxims may be the lessons of hard won experience, but of experience hard won by others — in the First World War at that. Furthermore, most successful fighter pilots considered that superior height was only a marked advantage in action against other fighters, and not an essential condition against bombers.[7] The ideal position against individual bombers was behind and slightly beneath.

When Jeffery Quill, Supermarine's chief Spitfire development test pilot, arranged a posting to 65 Squadron in order to get some battle experience, he made a point of talking to the pilots, who had "begun to develop definite ideas about air fighting and tactics as the result of hard experience." Among the pilots was the New Zealander Al Deere. "I learned much," wrote Quill, "which I have no doubt contributed to my own subsequent survival. From this and other sources I acquired . . . many nuggets of sound advice such as 'Get in as close as you can; you're usually further away than you think'; "You get shot down yourself by the man you don't see'; 'If you hit a 109 don't follow him down to see him crash — another will get you . . . ;' 'You need eyes in the back of your head'; 'Scan the sky constantly — it's essential to see them before they see you'; 'Never get separated if you can help it — and don't hang about on your own.'"[8]

The failure of the big wings, and persistence in their use in the teeth of their failure, calls precisely into question the leadership of Bader, and of Leigh-Mallory who never ceased to encourage and support him.

Let us first address the question of Bader's experience of air fighting and leadership. He was appointed the officer commanding 242 Squadron on June 24th by Leigh-Mallory, shortly after the squadron's return from France. Previously, the squadron had had more than their baptism of fire in France, and had returned to England exhausted, 'browned off', in disarray, and with little equipment. Bader set about working the squadron up to full strength, putting it through a strenuous training programme, and by these and other useful measures restoring to it its fighting spirit and *esprit de corps*. The single most salutary factor in this restoration was the example of spirit, skills and energy set by Bader.

SQ. LDR.
ROBERT WRIGHT

On July 9, 10 and 11, the squadron carried out convoy protection patrols and encountered a small number of enemy aircraft. "The remainder of the month passed with an uneventful routine of convoy patrols, base patrols and 'scrambles', but without success. "Convoy and interception patrols followed uneventfully day after day" until August 18th.

This day presented a matchless opportunity for 12 Group. Over a hundred Ju88s flew across the North Sea, unescorted by fighters, to bomb airfields in Yorkshire. This raid was entirely in 12 Group territory. Only six enemy bombers were shot down. On the next day Coltishall itself was attacked, but 242 Squadron Hurricanes were 'scrambled' too late to intercept. This blunder was, of course, a failure of commanders and controllers, not of the squadrons. The daily routine of uneventful 'scrambles' and patrols went on until the end of August.

On August 30th, 242 Squadron suddenly found itself engaged in the type of action they craved. With Bader leading the squadron of fourteen Hurricanes on a patrol over North Weald, in 11 Group, they were vectored on to an enemy raid comprising "a vast number" of Me 110s and He 111s. On this occasion the results claimed and the actual enemy losses tally very closely. The squadron claimed to have destroyed five Me 110s and seven He 111s for the loss of none of their own.

Alister Raby, writing in *The Battle of Britain: Then and Now* about this engagement, states: "As No.12 Group to the north of the main fighting was comparatively rested and out of things, at the end of August Air Vice-Marshal Leigh-Mallory decided to bring down the Hurricanes of 242 Squadron . . . from Coltishall to Duxford to join Nos. 19 and 310 Squadrons on

Gp. Capt.
A.G. 'Sailor' Malan

Wg. Cmdr.
Alan Deere

Gp. Capt.
Peter Townsend

Sq. Ldr.
J.M. 'Ginger' Lacey

## The Victors of the Battle of Britain:
### Some of "The Few"

daily standby. Flying as a squadron under Wing Commander Woodhall's guidance, Bader's men claimed twelve enemy aircraft for the loss of none of their own in the defence of North Weald on August 30."

The following seven days in the history of 242 Squadron are recorded differently by two writers. Hitchins states: "From August 31st to September 6th the squadron continued its patrols over Duxford, Northfields (sic), North Weald and Hornchurch without making contact with the enemy." Raby, on the other hand, continuing his narrative quoted above, says: "Leigh-Mallory was impressed [by Bader's results] and authorised Bader to lead the other two Duxford squadrons as a wing and several days were spent practising three-squadron formation take-offs."

The success of August 30th by 242 squadron, we must note, was achieved by a squadron of fourteen fighters, and was the first success the squadron had had in six weeks of patrols. Next we note (if we follow Raby's account) that the wing of three squadrons had been formed for only a few days before its first operational patrol, and that those few days it had "spent practising three-squadron formation take-offs."

What is clear from the foregoing is that Bader himself had had little experience of aerial combat before leading the wing, and that the training of the wing in air fighting itself had been minimal or non-existent.

Indeed, the other two squadrons, nos. 19 and 310, had had no more battle experience. The Order of Battle of this period shows that no. 19 Squadron spent the entire three months of July, August and September at Duxford and appears to have as little action as 242 Squadron. No. 310 Squadron, whereas formed in July, only became operational in early September, so that the first wing engagement of September 7th was its initiation in battle.

The squadrons added later to the wing had an equivalent experience. No. 611 Squadron was based at Digby, in 12 Group, in August and September; and 302 Squadron was based at Church Fenton and also saw **its very first action** in the wing operation of September 15th.

If we are to sum up, we come to the inescapable conclusion that the pilots of the four squadrons discussed above had little fighting experience and less wing experience, under a leader who himself had had no experience in wing tactics and fighting. And we come to the equally inescapable conclusion that one squadron of battle-hardened veterans of air fighting under determined leadership, as 242 Squadron was, accomplishes wonders, on condition that the leader obey the controller, not just follow his 'guidance'.

Bader's record in the Battle of Britain can be shown by pointing out that the sum of his experience of air fighting was acquired in only eight actions in the month of September, yet this limited experience was the basis of very decided views on how to win the battle. The concept of wings as preached by Bader was entirely theoretical, and not borne out by experience. A more intelligent wing leader, J.E. 'Johnnie' Johnson, came to the conclusion later that the optimum wing formation for air fighting was two squadrons: "My own later experience on both offensive and defensive operations confirmed that two squadrons of fighters was the ideal number to lead in the air."

Bader's courage, will-power, fortitude, and skills as a pilot are justly renowned. He had other qualities. He was a dynamic and tireless leader who was 'keen as mustard' and desperately anxious to prove himself — that is, perhaps, one key to his character: his relentless drive to excel others — but also to shoot down the enemy and — why not say it? — earn himself glory. That he was an inspiring leader of men who encouraged them and helped them to rise above their fear is attested to by all who served with him. But Bader was also — self-confident is too mild a word: cocksure, convinced of his own rightness, with a touch of arrogance, in both his ideas and his own powers.[8] He 'knew' with complete assurance that the 'big wing' was the answer. He did not have that tincture of humility, that golden gift of detachment, which might have made him pause and stand back and seek the reasons for the repeated failure of his wings. Instead, he blamed others.

A fellow-pilot has explained this obsession with wings on his part:

> Douglas Bader was completely wrong on tactics at the time. He was very brave. But he'd been out of the air force for ten years. He lagged completely behind in modern concepts. All he could think of, as far as I could see, was the old First World War flying circuses, which had nothing to do with what we were up against in the Battle of Britain.[9]

Bader would seem hitherto to have been almost exempted from criticism and questioning by his heroic personal qualities. On the other hand, Dowding's heroic qualities — and we mean, 'heroic' qualities, but of a different order — did not protect him from criticism and examination. Nor should they. Heroic qualities are no guarantee of right thinking and right ideas.

Bader chafed under direction which he disagreed with, he did not take orders easily, he resisted control. This impatience with being 'controlled' by a man sitting at a desk on the ground led him to challenge the very heart of the defensive system of Fighter Command which had been built up over four years: the control of the squadrons by Sector Stations up to the very moment of sighting the enemy formation they were being vectored to intercept. Bader believed that the Sector Controller should only guide and advise where the enemy might be found, and that the squadron or wing leader was the only person capable of deciding when, where and how — and indeed whether — to meet the enemy. The narrative accounts of his patrols in 12 Group's Report, together with the Price interview, make it clear that that is how he led his wings. If he saw fit, he went charging off in any direction in pursuit of the enemy — even on occasions when he was under orders to patrol and protect 11 Group's airfields. Nothing could better illustrate this union within him of cocksureness and thirst for action. He occupied only a very small part of the sky and saw only a very small portion of the total tactical picture. Yet he knew best what to do.[10]

Another leader, if a less flamboyant and self-publicizing character, has pinpointed this failing of Bader's. He is Squadron Leader (later Air Chief Marshal) Harry Broadhurst. He it was who was leading wings of two and more squadrons from Wittering, also in 12 Group, as early as June. He told 'Johnnie' Johnson: "Sometimes in 1940 our control and reporting system was unreliable so that plotting enemy raids on the ops [operations] tables at Fighter Command and 11 Group was not always accurate. I remember at least one occasion when there were no hostile plots on the table and yet some of our chaps were shot down. It was, therefore, very important for a fighter leader to obey the controller's instructions so that, down in the hole, he would know exactly where the leader was. If, like Douglas [Bader], you went darting about all over the place, it upset the whole plotting table. So, when I led the Wittering wing, I obeyed instructions and did what I was told to do."

Another fellow-pilot has corroborated this view, and has supported his opinion with evidence which should put an end to this 'wings' dispute once and for all:

> From a fighter pilot's point of view, I hold that Bader's wing concept was wrong, and I consider that the German fighter tactics against the American daylight bombers prove my point. The Germans faced the same problem in 1943 as did Fighter Command in 1940, but with vastly more experience behind them. . . . Having tried the mass formation technique, they resorted to small mobile formations of fighters concentrated in time and space, but operating independently. They found that too many fighters tied to a single leader sterilised flexibility of action and thought on the part of individual pilots.

In the story of the Bader wing operations, the lack of success in intercepting the enemy must be attributed in equal measure to Woodhall, who despite his virtues as a calm and steadying controller, failed to control and direct Bader, instead of allowing him to charge off where and as the whim took him. The ultimate blame must be laid at the door of Leigh-Mallory, who, as Air Officer Commanding, not only permitted but encouraged Bader to persist with the wing patrols, and failed to instruct Woodhall to carry out his duties properly.

It would not be surprising if we learned that Bader also had an idea about the larger conduct of the Battle. We are indebted again to Price for it. Bader believed that "the Battle should have been controlled from Fighter Command HQ, where they had a map of the whole country and knew the state of each squadron . . . ."

The author of *Big Wing* accepts Bader's view uncritically and elaborates:

> Instead of assuming control and direction of the air defence of Britain, which was the C-in-C's job, Dowding left the conduct of the battle to a subordinate commander, A V M Park of 11 Group. A map of the whole of England lay on the plotters' table at Fighter Command. It showed every Fighter airfield, with the location and state of readiness of every squadron on the board above it. The difference was paramount. A controller at the Fighter Command operations room would have seen the enemy position as it was plotted. With the whole picture spread out in front of him, he would instantly have realised the need to scramble squadrons from the further away airfields first against the enemy.

A more complete and comprehensive ignorance of the Fighter Command system cannot be conceived. It would be equally unsurprising if Bader's opinion was not shared by the real authorities. Group Captain Townsend records these opinions:

> Douglas Bader . . . wanted control by Fighter command, by Dowding himself in the last resort. But as Commander-in-Chief, Dowding was far too preoccupied with strategic problems to follow the battle blow by blow. He left that to his Group Commanders.

'Bader's suggestion beats the band,' was Park's comment. 'It would have been impossible for one controller to handle fifty squadrons.'[11]

As many writers and commentators on the Battle of Britain have demonstrated a failure to understand the distinctions between the tactics of air battle and the techniques of air fighting, so also many have failed to understand the differences, admittedly delicate at times, between tactics and strategy. That Bader should have so signally failed to study and understand the principles underlying the entire defensive system of Fighter Command, and the specific respective roles of the Commander-in-Chief, and the Group Commanders within that system, is reprehensible to an unheard-of degree. But that Bader, a mere squadron commander — moreover, a squadron commander only newly appointed in June 1940, after having been out of touch with military flying since December 1931 — should presume to know better than the two men most responsible for having created Fighter Command and themselves masters, respectively, of strategic and tactical matters, is a manifestation of arrogance which boggles the mind.[12]

An explanation of Bader's single-minded stubbornness may be found in the very chain of early-warning stations which made possible a successful defence by Fighter Command. It is too little realised that the RDF system of the day was a closely guarded secret. Even so, it is difficult to believe that any squadron commanders were not *au fait* with radar; it would have been the duty of the AOC and Group controller to ensure that they were informed, and hence aware of the crucial importance of obeying instructions. As we have seen, Woodhall never 'controlled' Bader. But Bader was on intimate terms with Woodhall, and had close relations with Leigh-Mallory; so it is inconceivable that Bader was not fully informed about RDF and the system of operation. If such was in fact the case, his contumacy becomes all the more unforgivable.

Another explanation, one which goes part way to attenuating the criticisms levelled against Bader, lies in the nature of the fighter pilot. The fighter pilot is, of necessity, an individualist. He may not be an extrovert, but in temperament and philosophy he is a man who acts better alone, who is hampered by the close presence of others, a crew, for whom he, and he alone, is responsible. He may like, even love, the company of his peers; he may even be a good team man on the ground; in the air he must be a considerate team player with an eye to the well- being of his comrades. But when all that is taken into account, the fighter pilot is one who revels in the man-to-man combat, like a boxer, or a knight of old. He loves to win; and keenly accepts the challenge of measuring himself and his personal skills and courage against a worthy opponent.

It follows that the fighter pilot is a lover of freedom, of the limitless air and the sky. He feels the rhapsody of the clouds and the stars, and a kinship with the eagle. The free chase is in his blood: anything less is servitude, imprisonment.

It is to the credit of Sir Henry Tizard, a fighter pilot of the First World War himself, that when the radar detecting stations were being erected round the British Isles, he was the first to appreciate the restrictive effect that the system of control that he was creating would have on the fighter pilot. "The fact that radio direction-finding could pin-point a plane's position more accurately than any system of dead reckoning was, perhaps a little grudgingly in some cases, now being accepted. But the new system being evolved . . . did something considerably more drastic since it meant that the fighter pilot, the ultimate personification of Yeats's airman with his 'lonely impulse of delight', was now to be ordered about the sky in a way totally new to him. Tizard, with his instinctive understanding of how flying men thought . . . did more than any other man to make the new system acceptable."[13]

This is not quite the end of the story of air tactics and fighting. The practice of flying a squadron in three or four vics of three aircraft was being found impractical early in the battle. Some squadrons lost a number of aircraft and their pilots without ever seeing the enemy. The pilots were so intent on keeping station in the formation that they had no time or occasion to look around them. Yet here was Bader insisting on formation take-offs and landings, and on keeping his massed squadrons in formation in the air.

'Sailor' Malan was an early critic of and rebel against "rigid 'book' tactics". "To Malan a fighter aircraft was simply a 'flying gun'. . . ." In this he was following the example of his predecessor of 74 Squadron, the illustrious 'Mick' Mannock, who taught that "Good flying never killed a Hun."[14]

Malan was not alone. The Polish pilots scoffed at such "pretty flying", good only for air shows, and both ridiculous and dangerous in battle. And many of the Polish pilots had had not only more flying experience than the British, but considerably more battle experience against the Germans. One Polish pilot, Karol Pniak, of 32 Squadron, "was appalled at the British flying formation." Adam Zamoyski describes an incident: "On his first sortie Pniak, who was flying in the last threesome, dropped back to cover the weaver, and was severely reprimanded by the squadron commander after landing." Pniak based his action on his ten years' experience and thirty wartime operational sorties. "That is why (he explained) I could in no way accept the commander's opinion, and I struggled in my poor English to explain that their way of flying was useless and dangerous."

The Polish fighters had, paradoxically, a further advantage. They had not had the advantage of radar and radio-telephones, and hence relied on keeping a sharp look-out. They consistently saw enemy aircraft long before their Royal Air Force comrades.

Similarly, their experience had taught them to act cooperatively, to fight together as a team. Bader's formations inhibited this necessary practice; as did his corollary method of fighting. His flights of three attacked together, after which each pilot was on his own. The Poles fought together, and looked after each other, and were not often surprised.

SQ. LDR.
DOUGLAS R. S. BADER

They were the bravest of the brave; their reputations spread, and every RAF squadron wanted some Poles with them. No. 303 Squadron became legendary, and was the highest scoring of all squadrons engaged in the Battle.

Initially, Dowding had his concerns about how the Poles would fit in. He modified his views about them very quickly. So much so, indeed, that he paid them this ultimate tribute: "Had it not been for the magnificent material contributed by the Polish squadrons and their unsurpassed gallantry, I hesitate to say that the outcome of the battle would have been the same."[15]

In concluding this section, we have to record that no other squadron commander or wing commander thought as Bader did. They understood the system and obeyed orders. Subsequent champions of Bader and defenders of his ideas stand on shifting sands. Their championship may indeed be an act of loyalty or nostalgia. But it may also be something else.

Leigh-Mallory's role was quite different. In the early stages of the Battle he followed Dowding's directives and re-strained Bader. But Bader pressed and persuaded, until Leigh-Mallory saw the tactical merits of his ideas. He saw more: he saw in Bader's tactics a potential challenge to Dowding's and Park's leadership. He had the well-placed connivance of Sholto Douglas at the Air Ministry. And the two ambitious men exploited the challenge to the full, as we shall see when we come to examine the Air Ministry conference of October 17 in chapter 6.

## NOTES TO CHAPTER 4:

1. A book published in 1997 deals in greater detail with the 'wings' dispute than any previous study. It is *Bader's Duxford Fighters: The Big Wing Controversy* by Dilip Sarkar. There are important differences between us. To take one example: Mr Sarkar, although also finding the wings as led by Bader to have been useless, refuses to criticize the man who became a hero to him.

2. Results that were accepted by the Air Ministry without attempts to verify by field researchers.

3. It is important to stress that the reader should study the comparison of the tabulated results and these narratives. It will show a marked discrepancy between them. Above all, one will be struck by the remarkable results claimed, while always complaining of being at a tactical disadvantage.

4. It will never be possible to calculate, from the figures and information available, how many enemy aircraft were destroyed and damaged by pilots of Bader's wings during their operations. The fact 1) that their claims of the first five patrols have been shown to be totally unreliable, and 2) that **they only managed to make two more interceptions in the next 32 patrols** demonstrates as forcefully as anything can how ineffective they were.

5. We have said that Air-Vice Marshal Park operated small wings of fighters in 11 Group whenever the situation was favourable. He wrote a large number of reports on the air fighting, and they frequently included an account of his use of wings. In Appendix "B" we reproduce his entire report on "Wing Formations" of October 1st 1940, and the sections on "Wing Formations" of his report of November 7th 1940. We consider these statements authoritative.

6. The taped interview is reproduced by Dilip Sarkar in his book, cited in note 1 above. The first observation made by Bader was this: "You are the first author who has ever come to see me about it. Despite everything published about my Wing, you are the only one. . . ."

   That statement itself is incomplete. Many Battle pilots have written a about the Battle, critically of Bader, and they knew what was going on. And Bader himself became fully aware of the dispute between 11 and 12 Groups when it broke out into the open in his presence at the Air Ministry meeting of October 17.

   This author met Bader on three occasions between 1976 and 1984, twice in Winnipeg and once in London, and, although I did not interrogate him, it was clear from our discussions that he was unrepentant in his views, and he went to his grave convinced that he was right.

7. 'Sailor' Malan developed his ideas of air fighting from his own experiences and drew up *My Ten Rules of Air Fighting* while at Duxford. They were subsequently pinned up in many a pilot's room. He would not have approved of one of Bader's pilots, Sergeant R.V.H. Lonsdale, who is recorded in *The Bader Wing* on at least two occasions as expending all his ammunition in prolonged bursts of 10 seconds and 15 seconds against an enemy aircraft.

   Malan recommended one- or two-second bursts, on the grounds that it was difficult to hold an enemy steadily and accurately in one's sights for longer, and that you left yourself vulnerable to attack by another enemy whom you would not see.

   We can add two comments: 1) Did Bader not *teach* his pilots about air fighting? 2) Prolonged firing over-heated the barrel and rendered it useless if it did not actually destroy it. Not something to endear oneself with the armourers on whom your life depended.

8. Arrogance is, regrettably, the word. In the Price interview we have quoted Bader also says: "The Battle of Britain was not won by Malan, Stanford-Tuck and myself, who got all the accolades, it was won by kids of 19 or 20, who maybe shot down nothing or just one before being killed themselves." He repeats it: "So don't think that it was Bader and Tuck who won the Battle of Britain".

Price's next question was: "If they shot down nothing, how did they contribute?" Bader answers: "Well, by being determined, by going off to fight and being prepared to die if necessary, that's the point." One is not enlightened. No one ever made the mistake of thinking that Bader won the battle. One admires Bader's generosity, but is flabbergasted by his notion of who won the Battle. Battles and wars are won by killing the enemy, not by being killed oneself.

9. Bader himself confirms this critical view in his Foreword to 'Johnnie' Johnson's book, *Wing Leader*: "Never let it be forgotten that our generation of fighter pilots learned the basic rules of air fighting from them (our famous predecessors of World War I). When I was a cadet at Cranwell I used to read their books time and time again and I never forgot them."

10. In the Price interview he states, after being asked whether any day in the battle was a special day, or a turning point in the battle: "Nothing like that ever occurred to us, we were only thinking in terms of our own engagement, not the overall scenario. . . . My only vision was confined to my Wing getting at the enemy, not what the rest of Fighter Command was doing."

A portrait of Douglas Bader at his most dogmatic, reactionary and aggressive is presented by Larry Forrester in his biography of Robert Stanford Tuck, in a dispute between Bader, Tuck and Malan over the respective merits of the .303" Browning machine-gun and the 20mm cannon. The interested reader is referred to *Fly For Your Life*, pp. 192-195.

11. If that was indeed Bader's idea, he would not have liked the result, for Dowding would not have let him wander all over the sky at his own behest.

12. In the Price interview, as we have seen, Bader disclaimed any knowledge of Fighter Command as a whole. One wonders when Bader conceived the idea that the Battle should have been conducted from Fighter Command HQ.

13. The poem by W.B. Yeats in which this imaginatively expressive line occurs is entitled *An Irish Airman foresees his Death*.

14. Bowyer, p. 35.

15. Zamoyski, p. 97. See pp. 71–74 and 91–94 for their experience, skills and tactics.

# Part ll

# Victory and Defeat

# CHAPTER 5

## *Machinations in High Places*

We have demonstrated the poor relations that existed between the Air Ministry and Dowding, and the criticisms of Dowding which were circulating in the offices and corridors of Whitehall. When some of those same criticisms and calumnies begin to be circulated in Westminster as well, one is left speculating whether they are having the effect desired and whether an assault on the centres of power would be needed to produce results.

What is remarkable in the enigma surrounding Dowding's removal from his command, after a victory, recognized at the time to be on a scale comparable to Drake's and Nelson's, is that a number of people were acting behind the scenes to undermine Dowding's authority and to effect his removal.

Was there complicity between them? All that can be said, after a careful study of the relevant documents, is that, whereas there is hard evidence to show connivance between certain individuals, there is nothing to show collusion between all of them.

The actors in the drama, in their order of appearance, are these:

    1   Irene Ward, MP, and others unknown
    2   Lord Trenchard and Sir John Salmond
    3   Flt. Lt. Peter Macdonald, MP
    4   Reginald Clarry, MP, and the 1922 Committee.

## 1. Irene Ward, MP

Irene Ward was the Conservative Member of Parliament for Newcastle upon Tyne. Until 1940 she had been little remarked. Then suddenly she burst upon the public scene. On August 17th — this date we will show later to be of some significance — she wrote the following letter to the Prime Minister:

Dear Mr. Churchill,

    I know it is nothing to do with me but I always believe in handing on information as I am sure you'll agree that there are things which shouldn't be withheld.

I'm one of the members who have been kept informed about the views of many people in the Air Force who want a change in the Air Chief Marshall (sic) and have seen the confidential memorandum.[1]

I am told a change may take place and I write to say that on all sides there appears to be among the service people an overwhelming desire that the Commander-in-Chief Bomber Command Air Marshal Portal should be appointed to succeed.

My information is that the RAF would consider it a disaster if the Commander in Chief of Fighter Command were given the supreme office.

I know you'll agree with me that one of our most attractive qualities is loyalty and that the fierce views held by many men in the RAF which they express fully realising the implications must betoken a genuine concern at the present direction.

You've always been a straight speaker yourself so I know you'll forgive me. I thought with no axe to grind I perhaps was in a position to express an opinion.

Yours sincerely,
(Signed) IRENE WARD

Churchill received a typed copy with the original handwritten letter, and this he forwarded to Sinclair with the note: "Archie. Let me have this back. WSC. 21.viii."

This letter calls for certain comments and questions. To that end we feel that a detailed analysis of it would be instructive. We will quote passages from the letter, and add our commentary in the right column.

| | |
|---|---|
| **I know it is noth-ing to do with me** | She involves herself in it nevertheless, even though she also knows nothing about the issue. |
| **I always believe in handing on information** | Without any scrutiny of its merits: in this case, not information but a speculative and defamatory document. |
| **I'm one of the members who have been kept informed** | Members of Parliament? Or of the 1922 Committee? We wonder how many; and who the others were who acted on the 'information'. |
| **who want a change in the Air Chief Marshall** | (she means 'Marshal' — no, she means CAS) The Air Chief Marshal in question is the CAS, Sir Cyril Newall. |

| | |
|---|---|
| **have seen the confidential memorandum** | So the memorandum has been circulated widely. And many senior offices want to see Newall replaced. But what is the connection between the many who want to see Newall replaced and the many who have seen the document? |
| **I am told** | This is the key to the enigma. Who told her? Did the same person also tell all "the members who have been informed"? |
| **Portal . . . should succeed** | No reasons are adduced except the "overwhelming desire among the service people". It is not quite a case of 'anyone but Dowding'. |
| **my information is** | The information was clearly conveyed orally by a person or persons known to and presumably trusted by Miss Ward. Hence the lack of documentary evidence. The people involved were careful not to leave tracks. |
| **a disaster** | It is the general opinion, still today, that Dowding would not have made a good CAS. On the other hand, Portal has been held to be, with certain qualifications, an outstanding CAS.[2] |
| **a genuine concern to express an opinion** | Miss Ward has already conceded that this matter is none of her business, and that she has only been kept informed. She has no information of her own, so she is merely peddling another's opinion.[3] |

The "confidential memorandum" in question accompanying Miss Ward's letter is a three-and-a-half page, single-spaced typed document entitled: "A Weak Link in the Nation's Defences." It comprises three parts: 1) an analysis of the perceived defects and shortcomings of the Chief of the Air Staff, Air Chief Marshal Sir Cyril Newall; 2) Reluctance to Remove Incompetent Officers; and 3) Summary.[4]

The features of this document that strike the reader are: the intimate knowledge that the writer conspicuously has of the Air Force, the Air Ministry, and his intended victim; and the well structured form of its composition. We say 'the writer', for everything about the document — style, unity, and inside knowledge — point to its composition by a single person, and one who has, moreover, a long practice in report writing. This last attribute is demonstrated by the fact that the document incorporates a single thesis whose parts are intimately related. That thesis is that Newall must be removed, both for his own deficiencies of leadership, and because he does not have the strength of character to get rid of other officers whom he, the writer, deems incompetent.

The first part of the paper, detailing Newall's shortcomings — which, taken with the consequences flowing from them, is the 'weak link in the nation's defences' — needs detain us only long enough to note the following allegations:

1)  he has not flown an aeroplane since probably 1915;[5]

2)  he took the decision in July to send 12 Blenheims and 12 Hurricanes to Malta, which needed to refuel in France, after France's capitulation;

3)  until March 1940 he was deceiving the Cabinet as to the strength of the R.A.F. in aircraft;

4)  he was reluctant to remove incompetent officers.

It is irrelevant to our purpose to examine the second and third of these allegations, serious, and damaging though they are. But the fourth item demands comment. The "incompetent officers" are identified, named and criticized. They are: the Director of Intelligence (Air Commodore Boyle); the Air Member for Supply and Organisation (Air Marshal Welsh); the C-in-C Bomber Command (Air Chief Marshal Ludlow-Hewitt); the AOC Training Command (Air Marshal Pattinson); the AOC RAF Forces Ulster (Air Commodore Carr); and the Air Member for Personnel (Air Marshal Gossage). Of these officers, the specific criticisms levelled against four of them should be noted.

**WELSH.** He was appointed Air Member for Supply and Organisation on September 1st, 1937. He was replaced on January 15th, 1940. However, Welsh did not take up his new appointment until May 27th, 1940 — as AOC Technical Training Command — and, on July 7th, 1941, he was appointed AOC Flying Training Command, an extremely important post which he held for somewhat over a year, until being appointed AOC Eastern Air Command Africa, an operational command, in November 1942. (These two latter appointments were, of course, made by Portal.) What is of especial interest is that, according to the writer, "**outside pressure** (our emphasis) had to be brought to bear (on Newall) to remove Air Marshal Welsh from his post (as Air Member S & O).

**LUDLOW-HEWITT.** This officer was AOC-in-C Bomber Command from September 12th, 1937 to April 3rd, 1940, when he was replaced by Portal. The writer again declares that "outside pressure had to be brought to bear (on Newall) to make the change, which was long overdue"; and that Portal was an "outstanding improvement". We shall have occasion, in chapter 7, to review a very different appreciation of Ludlow-Hewitt; and a serious related criticism of Portal.

PATTINSON, we learn, is not fitted to hold "his present appointment as C-in-C Training Command". Training Command then embraced all training functions. On May 27th, 1940 the Command was reorganized into Flying Training and Technical Training Commands. Pattinson was AOC Training Command when the reorganization took place, when he was appointed to head Flying Training Command, a post he held for 14 months. And who was appointed in his place but our friend Welsh!

GOSSAGE is a "typical example" of Newall's deficiencies — in this case, that of not appointing the best officers for the commands and staffs of the RAF. The author makes a specific criticism of Gossage as AMP, in alleging that of "some 40 Wing Commanders promoted to Group Captain, all were taken in strict order of seniority", and "a number of them (were) quite unworthy" of their appointments. We note that Gossage only took up his appointment on April 3rd, and could not have had more than a few weeks at most in which to decide on the promotions. What most probably happened is that Gossage, in view of his newness to the job and not having the time to review the candidates, simply promoted them in order of seniority; or he merely approved the promotions earmarked by his predecessor — who was, of course, Portal. In any event, Gossage was replaced in December 1940, and took over Balloon Command, which he commanded ably for the rest of the war.[6]

What we note first in the foregoing criticism is the sweeping nature of the deficiencies of the officers singled out for attack: there is, except in the one minor case noted, nothing concrete, nothing specific. The judgments are notable for their subjective character. Secondly, the subjectiveness of the criticisms becomes more evident when one considers the number of times the author accuses his victims, including Newall, of lacking character and mental ability — attributes which disqualify the officers in question from holding their appointments. Finally, the judgments and criticisms are made from the perspective of the Air Ministry. Not only that: the author is seen as placing himself in an all-dominant position from which to judge; and in so doing not only loses sight of some of the realities of operational commands, but also shows himself out of touch with events and ignorant of some of the officers he casts judgment on.

Before proceeding, it is pertinent to note here again, as we noted in chapter 1, what the official history of the Royal Air Force 1939-1945 says about "an enormous array of talent" in the Air Ministry and at the Commands and Groups at the outbreak of the war: namely, that among this talent one finds the names of Newall, Welsh, Ludlow-Hewitt and Gossage.

The most detailed analysis of an allegedly 'incompetent' officer, after Newall, is found in a section of four paragraphs of the memorandum subheaded "Fighter Command." We reproduce it here.

> Two of the three duty Senior Air Staff Officers at HQ Fighter Command, and who are liable at any time to be called upon to direct the operations of the whole of the Fighter Command in the absence of their Commander-in-Chief, are Air Commodore Webb Bowen and Air Commodore Bonham Carter. Both these officers retired from the RAF many years ago, and neither have (sic) any knowledge of modern fighters and modern air fighting.
>
> Air Vice-Marshal Nicholl has long passed his prime and is incompetent to hold his present appointment as Senior Administrative Officer at HQ Fighter Command. Indeed, HQ Fighter Command is substantially a one man show and is ruled by Air Chief Marshal Dowding who has definite personality, but unfortunately he has inadequate mental ability and a very slow brain. He is also a classic example of a complete non-co-operator either with the Air Ministry or any other authority. His treatment of his staff is deplorable and he tolerates only 'yes' men. Air Chief Marshal Newall has not the strength of character to deal with Air Chief Marshal Dowding or to insist on having a strong and balanced staff at HQ Fighter Command.

We do not comment on the charge of incompetence levelled against Webb-Bowen and Nicholl, or on their retention in the Air Force. We need only add that, in one respect, the writer was in error, for in the absence or incapacitation of Dowding, neither Webb-Bowen nor Bonham Carter would have been "called upon to direct the operations of the whole of the Fighter Command": that task would have fallen to Air Vice-Marshal D.C.S. Evill, a brilliant, experienced, and highly capable officer, who had been described as 'a tower of strength' during the final operations of the Air Force in France before the collapse.

In point of fact, in this criticism the author demonstrates his ignorance of the operational functions of Fighter Command Headquarters: even the

AOC-in-C of Fighter Command did not "direct the operations of the whole of Fighter Command". If by "operations" we mean the air fighting and their direction, that work was the task of the squadrons, stations, sectors and groups. Fighter Command Headquarters played no role in them.

What appears to be the key paragraph, with its denigration of Dowding, makes him out to be some kind of monster.

If this thumb-nail sketch represents the true view of Dowding as he was perceived by the Air Ministry, it explains, in part, the wretched relations which existed between them. In fact, of course, it is a malicious slander and calumny. What of his "inadequate mental ability" and his "very slow brain"? It is enough to point to the whole structure and operation of the Fighter Command, with its unique radar control system, which was in a very real sense the creation of Dowding, to realize how ludicrous the statement is. Dowding may have appeared a slow thinker, but only because he was method-ical and painstaking.

There was a profound reason for his deliberate and analytical method. By 1940 he had become cautious, and, except in cases of emergency or of over-riding importance, he weighed all factors before making decisions that were bound to have serious consequences, for good or ill.

We wish that its author had given a few examples of Dowding's "deplor-able treatment of his staff." It is a serious charge to make against any com-mander. However, neither of his two Personal Assistants, Francis Wilkinson and Robert Wright, has ever breathed a word of recrimination; on the con-trary, both have praised his qualities and leadership in a manner which few high operational commanders have elicited from their personal assistants. To that we must add his unfailing considerateness and courtesy to the young WAAF plotters at the headquarters filter room, in whose skills he frequently expressed his confidence. Dowding was one of those very rare men who was a terror to those set in authority above him if they exhibited incompetence, stupidity or duplicity, and who became a father figure to his junior staff.

Dowding enjoyed the support, confidence and selfless efforts of many fine and capable men and women. To say that he was "substantially a one-man show" and tolerated "only 'yes' men" is not only a despicable and mendacious calumny; it is also, and especially, a wicked slur on the integrity and courage of his headquarters staff. To say that men of the calibre of Park (who was Dowding's Senior Air Staff Officer before going to 11 Group), McEvoy, Evill, Hamilton, Gleave, and many other fine officers were yes-men deserves nothing but scorn for the writer's judgment.

This further observation is called for. If the author is sufficiently familiar with the personnel of Fighter Command Headquarters to know of these officers' incompetence, it cannot have escaped Dowding's attention either. Did the writer seriously mean to imply that Dowding retained them precisely because they were incompetent, and hence, presumably yes-men? And he would do such a thing in the certitude that, in the event that he, Dowding, were incapacitated, either of them would step into his shoes and, by their very incompetence, contribute by default to the success of the Luftwaffe's attacks and hence to the defeat of Great Britain? The date of composition of this memorandum is of considerable interest, both in itself and in relation to the date of Miss Ward's letter. As it carries no name so it carries no date; but there is internal evidence which enables us to date it with fair precision.

On page 2 the author bases his opinion of Newall's bad judgment on "his personal order to despatch (some aircraft) to Malta and the Middle East on 18/6/40 after France had laid down her arms." Here we have a precise date. The memorandum opens with an allusion to forthcoming events which admit of no two interpretations: "Upon the achievements of the Royal Air Force in the coming weeks, and its development in the coming year will, more than upon any other factor, depend the final outcome of the present war with Germany." This can refer only to the Battle of Britain.

These references therefore date the memorandum towards the end of June. It will be recalled that Churchill made his famous speech about the survival of Christian civilization on June 18th.

It is important to note what the memorandum says and what it does not say. It says that, in view of the coming anticipated Battle, and the outcome of the war, the best man available should be chosen as Chief of the Air Staff, and that Newall was not the best man. The author does not suggest who the best man might be, however. There is nothing in the 'confidential memorandum' to suggest or imply that, if its author's intentions were realized and Newall were removed before his due retirement date, Portal would be his successor. On the contrary, the complaisant wording of his appointment as AOC Bomber Command intimates that he was there for the long haul. And Portal's own submission of May 8th to the Air Ministry, expressing in strong terms his objections to and criticisms of the French Army's ideas about tactical strikes by his bombers against a German offensive, corroborates this conclusion.[7]

Nor is there any suggestion that Dowding should be replaced. What the author wishes to see is a new CAS who will be firm enough "to insist on having a strong and balanced staff at HQ Fighter Command."

Between the composition of the memorandum and the date on which Miss Ward sent it to Churchill, how much had changed! In a period of six to seven weeks, Miss Ward, in her covering letter, says there is to be a change of CAS, almost insists that Portal should succeed Newall, and states the view that "the RAF would consider it a disaster if the Commander in Chief of Fighter Command were given the supreme office."

The questions pile up, important questions to which one cannot hazard even the most tentative or speculative of answers.

What happened in that brief period of July and August to make Portal so favoured? Where did Miss Ward get all her information? Who kept her personally informed? Why was Miss Ward selected for this role in the first place? Who selected her? Was there a third party who recommended her to her informant and mentor?

We come now to the final question: What was done about this document? As we have seen, Churchill minuted it to Sinclair on August 21st. Sinclair locked it away and forgot about it. It surfaced again three weeks later. The following is a letter written by Irene Ward to Brendan Bracken, the Minister of Information.

PERSONAL AND CONFIDENTIAL

7th Sept. 1940
Dear Mr. Bracken,

Referring to our conversation in the Lobby on Thursday I enclose herewith copy of the Memorandum to which I referred.

As from our conversation it seems unlikely that Mr. Churchill will have got my letter may I briefly recapitulate what I said. In the first place that I have no personal interest in the matter at all as I do not know any of the personalities concerned but that from a great many quarters I have been told that the Air Force would welcome the appointment as CAS of Air Marshal Portal and that his appointment would give very much greater confidence to those in the Service than the appointment of C-in-C, Fighter Command.

The Prime Minister has always been outspoken himself so I hope he will forgive me if I adopt the same procedure. I always believe in handing on information which I have been given in good faith. I have tried to check up on the Memorandum and am told by those who have an intimate knowledge of the working of the Air Ministry that the Memorandum is 99 per cent true.

Yours sincerely,
(Signed) IRENE WARD

Bracken forwarded the memorandum to the Prime Minister with the minute: "This stuff is being widely circulated. I think you should see it. Miss Ward, MP, is a rather ferocious female." On September 18th, Churchill minuted it to Sinclair: "To see and return." A full month later, Sinclair wrote to Bracken about it, and her.

PERSONAL AND SECRET

WHITEHALL, SW 1
20TH OCTOBER, 1940.


My dear Brendan,

    I saw and heard your virago and then, because the stuff you sent me was so secret, I locked it away and it has only just emerged from its box when I was looking for something else. I observe that Winston asked for it to be returned so here it is.

    Miss Ward was fairly apologetic. She talked to me and admitted she knew nothing of the subject. On the other hand, she made it clear that she felt she ought to have had an answer and that she was not to be trifled with. I explained to her that it was my fault and that I had tried, unsuccessfully, to see her before the House rose and had then forgotten about it.

    At the same time, I recited to her a prose poem about the officer whom she does not like and told her that he enjoyed my complete confidence and that of the Prime Minister. No doubt, however, she is now telling herself and her friends that events speak louder than words and that, not for the first time, a goose has saved the Capitol.

    An exact duplicate of her precious memorandum reached me from another source and also two other memoranda have also come to me which, although not in precisely the same terms, have obviously been penned by the same hand.

Yours ever,

(Signed) ARCHIE S.

That Sinclair regarded the contents of the memorandum as inflammatory is clear since he locked it up in a box. But that he then forgot about it stretches credulity. If, as he states, Dowding "enjoyed (his) complete confidence," it is reprehensible that he took no action to suppress the calumnies against his two most senior Air Chief Marshals by instituting an inquiry into the sources of Miss Ward's information and the purveyor of the infamous document.

# 2. Trenchard and Salmond

There is pleasure in seeing knaves fall out and go for each other's throats. There is none in seeing good men at odds. Among the greatest figures in the history of the Royal Air Force, outside the ranks of the men who earned renown in air warfare, are Trenchard and Dowding.

Marshal of the Royal Air Force Sir John Salmond is also a greatly respected name. Trenchard and Salmond were deeply involved in attempts, carried on behind the scenes by Trenchard and overtly by Salmond, to have Dowding removed from his command. However, because of the relations which existed between Trenchard and Dowding, we will treat him separately, and first.

## TRENCHARD

Trenchard's and Dowding's careers, like those of most of the officers who rose to high rank or who became known in the Second World War, intersected in France in the First World War and ran along similar lines until converging again in the years 1929-40.

Trenchard and Dowding crossed swords three times in France, in 1916 and 1917.

The first occasion of dispute was over the supply and fitting of the wrong propellers to the aeroplanes of Dowding's squadron, No. 16 Squadron, when Trenchard commanded the Wing. When the propellers arrived Dowding saw at once that they were meant for a different engine from the one installed in his aeroplanes. He telephoned Trenchard and told him so. Trenchard ordered him to fit them anyway.

Dowding had one modified, with great difficulty, and, because of the risks involved, test-flew the aeroplane himself. On landing he found that the hub of the propeller had cracked. He refused to fit the others and telephoned Trenchard to protest. Trenchard then had the correct propellers delivered.

What incensed Dowding was that Trenchard would accept the word of the supplier in Paris, who was no more than a garage mechanic, over the expert advice of the man at the fighting end who had to use the equipment. Dowding was not going to send his men up against the enemy with questionable equipment or needlessly risk their lives. Dowding was not the first, and he would be far from the last, who felt strongly that the 'superior' officers at headquarters who sent down unconsidered commands abused their authority, and that the men at the operational level were in the best position to know their essential needs and whose advice should be sought and heeded by the 'authorities' ensconced in their offices far from the enemy.

The second brush was provoked when Trenchard, keen on establishing air superiority over the Western Front, was urging 'maximum effort' on his squadron commanders. Many squadrons suffered heavy casualties, Dowding's among them. When he judged the losses justified his action, Dowding asked Trenchard to rest and relieve his squadron. Trenchard scorned Dowding as a 'dismal Jimmie', feeling that the request was an implied criticism of his policy. Were Trenchard's scorn, and his policy, justified? Here is a sympathetic historian writing of Trenchard's command in France:

> In the five months of the Somme campaign Trenchard lost five hundred aircrew casualties — well over 100 per cent of his starting figure — and this was a heavy mortgage on the Corps' future. . . . Even when, as Trenchard had feared, the German air force came back on the offensive, he went on throwing his squadrons forward against the superior new Albatros and Halberstadt fighters — if they could get across into enemy territory before being 'jumped'. The climax came in 'Bloody April' of 1917, over Arras and Vimy Ridge. The Red Baron, von Richthofen, averaged a victory a day throughout the month, and in all the Corps lost 316 aircrew, or a third of its strength — and for very little result.

In 1917, Dowding was sent home to take charge of the Southern Training Brigade. He was dismayed by what he found. In order to make up for the heavy losses suffered during the Somme fighting during the second half of 1916, and to pursue the policy of achieving air superiority, the training establishments had been bled not only of their output of pilots, inadequately trained as they were, but also of many of their instructors. Dowding saw at once the grave consequences of pursuing such a policy. He made representations to the War Office. In order to buttress his case, he also wrote to Trenchard's senior staff officer, explaining the situation. This officer showed the letter to Trenchard. Trenchard regarded it as an uncalled-for meddling in his policies, which were approved by the War Office; and it had the effect of exacerbating their relations, which remained strained for several years.

In 1927 Dowding was posted to the Air Ministry where he came under the direct orders of Trenchard. Fraught though their close relations were for potential conflict, it may be that both, aware as they were of the risk, were 'on their best behaviour'. They established an unruffled working relationship which one writer has called "almost cordial." There can be no question but that Dowding had come to know the moral integrity, high ideals, and lofty standards that were hallmarks of both the personal and the professional figure of Trenchard. Can it be doubted that Trenchard for his part recognized the same qualities in Dowding? It was certainly not their sharing the name of 'Hugh' that brought Trenchard to confess one day to his Director of Training: "Dowding, I don't often make mistakes about people, but I made one about you."

One wonders what happened between this event and the summer of 1940, or earlier, to again cause Trenchard to change his mind and his views. One may search the published sources, such as Boyle's honest biography of Trenchard, as well as the unpublished records, and end up with nothing. In the light of these blanks, we are left to speculate on the cause or causes of disagreement or friction between them.

Our knowledge of the integrity of these two men leads us to the only reasonable conclusion, namely, that they locked horns over questions of doctrine. If we accept that premise, all is clear. For Trenchard was, as we have seen, not only a bomber man — "The bomber will always get through" — but an uncompromising, even a dogmatic, bomber man.

Dowding's career, as we have also seen, took him through research and development, the new fighters and radar, and the creation of Fighter Command. Dowding became the expert in defence, the champion of the security of the home base. Thus there arose a basic conflict over two opposing strategic views of the best use of the air arm.

Dowding's was the view of immediate strategic necessity. Trenchard's was the long-term strategic goal. Trenchard's goal could not have been achieved without first ensuring the security of the home base. On the other hand, Trenchard's strategic goal could not have been realised without the fighter. And that was a prospect which never crossed Trenchard's mental horizon. Group Captain Peter Townsend makes the case forcefully:

> Dowding was not a man for half measures. He was resolved to get what he needed to make the 'base' — Britain — safe and secure. On one occasion a senior officer propounded to him at length, as if they were sacred words of truth, the Trenchard doctrine, 'attack is better than defence'. Stuffy disagreed vigorously:
>
> 'It's a shibboleth, a play on words with just enough truth, but not

enough to make it a clear case. Why must it be accepted without question? Only because you think that you are going to do so much damage that the enemy will be smashed right at the outset. And how are you going to do that?' Fiercely he insisted that, 'the one thing vital before going over to the offensive is security of the base. That overrides all considerations.' His unshakeable belief in the principle and his obstinate insistence that all his demands should be met did not endear him to all his brother officers.[8]

Trenchard retired in 1930. But, as a former Chief of the Air Staff and, especially, as a Marshal of the Royal Air Force, he remained closely in touch with all Air Force matters, as he did also with many of the most senior officers in the Air Force, especially at the Air Ministry, and gave freely of his advice to the Air Council. His successor as Chief of the Air Staff was Sir John Salmond. Salmond also retired as Marshal of the Royal Air Force; and in 1940 was working with Beaverbrook in the Ministry of Aircraft Production.

That same year Trenchard and Salmond, as patriotic Englishmen concerned with the fate of their country and the conduct of the war, turned their gaze onto Dowding and the leadership of Fighter Command. They exchanged views at their meetings and in correspondence, and came to a common ground in their dislike of what they saw. Whatever the origin of Trenchard's renewed antipathy toward Dowding, in his letters to Salmond he was doing no less than pushing Salmond to use his influence with the Air Council to bring about Dowding's removal. Salmond for his part was urging Trenchard to involve himself more directly in their campaign. Trenchard's letter of October 4th is revealing in this twofold respect.

Dear Salmond,

Yours of the 3rd September. I have done all I can in the last two or three days of rubbing in about Dowding, and I am going to rub in again to-day. At least I know some of my remarks have got to the right quarters.

I fancy it is too much to ask for any conditions to be made by Portal and I feel it would be difficult for him after what has happened to sack Dowding unless we can get sufficient pressure to bear to bring it about. I fully realise with you, that my activities are so much more outside than inside, but I will see what more I can do. I feel your pressure has done as much good as anything I know from what I have heard from other sources, but I never mention that you and I are working in agreement on this matter as I feel it is more use our apparently being independent but working for the same cause.

This letter is also a deeply disturbing document. It is disturbing on a number of counts. There was connivance between Trenchard and Salmond over two or three months, from September to November, to effect Dowding's removal. Trenchard is using his prestige and influence, by taking advantage of his ready access to all and everyone on the Air Council and in the Air Ministry, to undermine confidence in Dowding. In this he is having some success. Yet Trenchard is keen to preserve his reputation as a straight dealer by making it appear that he was acting, and agitating, as a lone, concerned observer rather than in cahoots with Salmond.

The second paragraph is enigmatic. We will propose an explanation along these lines. Portal's appointment as the next Chief of the Air Staff to succeed Newall, on October 23rd, just nineteen days after this letter, was obviously known to Trenchard. Trenchard could not expect Portal to sack Dowding on becoming CAS "after what has happened".

What is Trenchard referring to here? He cannot mean anything other, or anything less, than Dowding's handling of the daylight battle, which at this date, October 4th, was seen to have more than the edge.

What are the "conditions" referred to? Since this sentence runs into the next and constitutes a single line of thought, he can only have in mind the possibility — instantly to be dismissed — of asking Portal to impose conditions upon Dowding if he is to remain at Fighter Command. (He cannot conceivably mean Portal laying down conditions before accepting his appointment.) The crux of the matter lies, however, in getting "sufficient pressure to bear to bring it about."

## SALMOND

It was Salmond who was to be the bludgeon that would exert the pressure. He it was who was working on the inside — on the inside of the Air Ministry, the Air Council, the Government. He it was also who had the tenacity. His biographer has described him in these terms: "a perfect gentleman who knew how to be ruthless" and as one who was "capable of considered ruthlessness".

One must ask in what way were Dowding's shortcomings, in Trenchard's and Salmond's eyes, so grave as to warrant, and incite, their direct and prolonged interference in Air Force matters? For they were both retired officers, even though former Chiefs of the Air Staff; and Dowding was seen to be conducting a successful defence of the United Kingdom and thereby preventing invasion.

If this interpretation of Trenchard's letter is correct, the perceived short-coming must have lain elsewhere.

Already, on September 12th, Salmond had written to Trenchard to voice his concerns about the night defences. Those concerns sharpened to the point of spurring him to strong and direct action. In a long letter to Trenchard dated September 25th, Salmond apprises Trenchard of his actions, his aims, and his views of both Dowding and Newall. The letter, dated September 25th, is worth reproducing in its entirety. (This is taken from a copy, without signature.)

Dear Trenchard,

This is in answer to your letter received today, and the following is the position. You will remember the copy of a note I sent you, the original of which went to Beaverbrook on the subject of the failure to cope with night bombing. From this it arose that I was told to enquire into the whole situation and I completed a report two days afterwards. On it I put a private note to Beaverbrook to say that I considered Dowding should go. Beaverbrook told me that he had been working so closely with Dowding that he could not take any part in it. Dowding has been seeing a great deal of Beaverbrook and Beaverbrook has formed a very high opinion of him, and had informed the Prime Minister who also, apparently, had the same opinion. I think that Beaverbrook is now a bit shaken on it. I then went to see Sinclair and told him I considered that Dowding should go. I could see that he was frightened of putting it forward, although he is aware that the CAS and the whole of the Air Staff, I believe, almost without exception, are in agreement with me. When I left him I felt he was not going to move in the matter.

Yesterday I was invited to the Air Council to discuss the report [on night bombing]. I told Newell (sic) previously that I was quite prepared to raise the matter of Dowding at the end of the discussion, when any civil member would have left. He seemed a bit rattled at the prospect and said he would think about it during the course of the meeting. Towards the end of the meeting he passed me a note asking me not to raise it. Consequently a major opportunity of getting the opinions of the Service members of the Air Council on the matter has passed by. It is really incomprehensible on the part of Newall as he had told me some days ago how extremely keen he was that Dowding should go and what enormous difficulties he and the Air Staff had had in getting him to accept new ideas regarding fighting at night.

I frankly do not feel that, if he remains in his post, we shall get any move on in the matter, until things have become very much worse. Apart from this, as you and I know, he has not got the qualifications of a Commander in the Field, as he lacks humanity and imagination. He is now living on the reputation he has gained through the successes of the pilots in day fighting, a great deal of which, of course, must be due to his account.

When I saw Beaverbrook he said to me, "If Dowding is to go, why not Newall, as Newall must be responsible too". Personally, of course, I have no objection to coupling them as I think Newall's strategic judgment is completely at fault. As you remember, he backed the Norwegian adventure when local air superiority was an impossibility; the RAF in France and Belgium had, I understand, only three Fighter Squadrons and was refused any more; he will not assist the Navy by reinforcing Malta with fighters, which would enable them to refuel there and consequently stop reinforcements travelling from Italy to Libya, and at this moment is so impressed with the possibility of invasion that he will not even tell off a couple of day fighting squadrons to be trained for the night, even though they could be at once used for day work if invasion took place.

If you see Beaverbrook I would very much like you to bring up the matter of Dowding, and also Newall, because I believe that with these two in the saddle, we are not getting the best we should expect.

It is difficult to conceive of a more damming indictment of Dowding, especially coming, as it does, from a former Chief of Air Staff and addressed to another former Chief of Air Staff. But the letter is an equally damning indictment of the writer.

The letter is firstly remarkable for its vagueness. The conspicuous absence of detail to reinforce the allegations against Dowding serves to suggest two things: first, that Trenchard knew what Salmond was talking about; second, that they had talked, and continued to meet.

The descriptions of Beaverbrook, Sinclair and Newall as being, respectively, "shaken", "frightened", and "rattled" — while subjective judgments of states of mind, and hence notoriously subject to error — offer, if remotely accurate observations, revealing insights into Salmond's toughness — ruthlessness? — and the relations of these three men with Dowding. It was well known that Beaverbrook was one of Dowding's staunchest champions. But his aircraft factories were being bombed!

Sinclair had recently written to Dowding assuring him of his unswerving confidence. Newall was, it is true, apt to dither, and was fearful of the prospect of a showdown with that formidable character, Dowding. In the background, present but unnamed, was Churchill.

Churchill was Dowding's most admiring and unflinching supporter. Beaverbrook and Sinclair knew this. If, therefore, they, the schemers, were to get rid of Dowding, they were going to have to convince Churchill. The prospect was not an enjoyable one.

Salmond was not daunted. He saw Churchill and put his case against Dowding to him. At the top of the letter quoted above, he had written in his own hand (with an arrow pointing downwards towards the text of the letter): "My views, which I eventually explained to the P.M. He practically blew me out of the room."

The fifth paragraph is interesting for the light that it shines on conflicting views held by various authorities of larger strategic issues.

> 1) On Norway: Newall "backed the Norwegian adventure" — because Churchill **ordered** it, and Newall was dominated by Churchill. (Salmond would have opposed it. So would Dowding — on the ground that air supremacy was out of the question.)

> 2) On the sending of fighters to France: The opposition put up by Dowding is one of his most courageous actions. Newall only supported him after Dowding had taken his historic stand against Churchill. Apparently Salmond would have sent more. Trenchard urged the sending to France of every squadron that Fighter Command possessed.

> 3) On Malta: Salmond would also have stripped Fighter Command by "reinforcing Malta with fighters". (Strangely, Irene Ward's anonymous paper says that Newall gave "his personal order to despatch 12 Hurricanes and 12 Blenheims to Malta.")

> 4) On invasion and night fighters: The immediate threat at this time was in fact invasion. This threat required the maximum strength in day fighters. The real danger was posed by the critical shortage of fighter pilots. (These inter-related issues are examined thoroughly in chapter 7.)

Salmond's judgment is quite clearly wrong in three out of four of these crucial strategic issues. In those three he demonstrates, not a global vision, but ignorance of the first essential of war, namely, the security of the base — that is, the defence of the United Kingdom. One wonders how he came to arrive at those judgments. What is clear is that, despite his differences with Newall, Salmond's ideas were also those of the Air Staff's.

Finally, Salmond's specific indictments of Dowding deserve comment:

1) Newall and the Air Staff had "enormous difficulties . . . in getting him to accept new ideas regarding fighting at night." (This criticism will be addressed also in chapter 7.)

2) Dowding "has not got the qualifications of a Commander in the Field". As usual, Salmond is vague and subjective in his allegation, and fails to support it with facts. However, we note Dowding's success for "by the end of the month, it became apparent that the Germans could no longer face the bomber wastage which they had sustained" — in other words, the daylight battle was essentially won. And have we not already seen that when Salmond saw Churchill on or about October 6th, i.e. a couple of weeks after this letter, "he practically blew me out of the room." We shall also see in chapter 7 what Churchill thought of Dowding's "ideas regarding fighting at night."

3) Dowding "lacks humanity and imagination." (i) On imagination: It might be an asset; it might on the other hand be an obstacle to lucid thinking and vigorous logic. If, however, imagination is the gift which enables its possessor to anticipate present dangers and to foresee future developments, the reader is invited to judge for himself whether Dowding was possessed of imagination by studying chapter 10. (ii) On humanity: no greater error, no more scurrilous accusation, could be made. Where could Salmond have got such a notion? Dowding was renowned, above all, for his concern for the men under his command — and under his care. He had demonstrated it — to Trenchard of all people, who could have set Salmond right — in the First World War. Between the wars, when Dowding was the Chief Staff Officer, HQ Iraq Command, a post he held from September 1924 to May 1926, he was under orders to carry out the policy of bombing unruly Arab tribesmen. Dowding argued that warning leaflets should be dropped first, a measure that was accepted and spared many lives. Finally, in 1939-40, his pilots, who never saw him, by some subtle and mysterious process of communication, were keenly aware of his profound solicitude. Dowding himself wrote: "In the early stages of the fight Mr. Winston Churchill spoke with affectionate raillery of me and my "chicks". He could have said nothing to make me more proud; every chick was needed before the end."[9]

Salmond reiterated his denigration of Dowding's leadership and command by adding: "He is now living on the reputation he has gained through the successes of his pilots in day fighting". If he had said such a thing to the pilots themselves at the time, he would have felt a stronger blast than the one, relatively mild, "which practically blew (him) out of the room." Salmond's resort to vituperation can have been the result not of a considered professional judgment but only of a deep personal antipathy; and the

(Successes)

accolade, appended as an afterthought — "a great deal of which (reputation)
. . . must be due to his account" — is too grudging to conceal the bias or to
attenuate the slur.

There is a profoundly disturbing feature about Salmond's intervention in
Air Force matters to effect important changes. It is that a retired officer, even
though a former CAS, should involve himself so directly and persistently as
Salmond did, an involvement made doubly disturbing by his flawed judgment
and knowledge of people and events.

In 1936, we recall, Salmond was one of the three most senior officers in
the Royal Air Force who informed Dowding that he would be succeeding
Ellington as Chief of the Air Staff in 1937. One wonders, as in the *volte-face*
made by Trenchard, what brought about this 180° reversal of attitude. We
cannot but conclude that Salmond's about-face was motivated by personal
antipathy.

Salmond wrote of bringing pressure to bear to effect the changes which
he deemed necessary. Miss Ward's anonymous memorandum also mentioned
"outside pressure" which had to be brought to bear to remove Welsh and
Ludlow-Hewitt from their appointments. Who was it who had brought
this pressure to bear on Newall? Now we are witnessing Salmond himself
exerting his considerable influence and strong 'outside pressure' — on
Trenchard, Beaverbrook, Newall and Churchill — to get rid of Dowding.
One wonders whether poor Newall suspected that while Salmond was urging
Newall to remove Dowding, he was simultaneously scheming to remove
Newall himself.[10]

## 3. Macdonald

In the summer of 1940 Peter Macdonald occupied two offices: he was, as
Flight Lieutenant Peter Macdonald, a reserve officer in the RAF; and as Sir
Peter Macdonald he was the MP for the Isle of Wight.

As an RAF officer he was the adjutant of the 242 (Canadian) Squadron,
whose commanding officer was Squadron Leader Douglas Bader. As we have
seen, Bader was the chief proponent of the "big wing" tactics; in Macdonald
he had a sympathetic lieutenant and a faithful servant.

His squadron was normally stationed at Coltishall, a few miles north of
Norwich. Throughout September and October, however, when Bader formed
his wings, 242 Squadron moved to Duxford, a few miles south of Cambridge.
This location permitted ready travel to London, a situation which Macdonald
availed himself of freely.

Macdonald's doings in the cause of Bader's ideas and discontent, and in furthering Leigh-Mallory's ambitions, are dealt with fully in the next chapter, because his intervention led to an immediate reaction and unpleasant repercussions. He is introduced here in order to underscore his twofold responsibilities. As an MP he will have known Irene Ward. A measure of cooperation and an exchange of views are almost certain to have taken place. Macdonald may well have been one of the informants who "kept (Miss Ward) informed" about some Air Force matters. Macdonald and Miss Ward were also, of course, members of the 1922 Committee.[11]

## 4. Sir Reginald Clarry and the 1922 Committee

In early November, when the daylight Battle was manifestly won — and when the night battle was beginning to get ominous — another salvo, another surreptitious broadside, was fired against Dowding. This one emanated from the 1922 Committee.

The 1922 Committee, or, to give it its full name, the 1922 Conservative Private Members Committee, is composed of all Conservative Members of Parliament who are not Ministers of the Crown and who are in receipt of the Party Whip. Its function is to keep an eye on the policies of the Government and the administration of the Government departments by the Ministers.

Its powers are nil, but its influence considerable. It would be a brave, and perhaps foolhardy, Minister who declined an invitation to give an exposition of his policies or practices to the Committee.

In November 1940, the Vice-Chairman of the 1922 Committee was one Sir Reginald Clarry. On November 6th, he wrote the following letter, in longhand, to Mr. Churchill:

My Dear Prime Minister,

In the chair of the 1922 Conservative Private Members Committee held today, the Executive Committee were requested to meet and hear certain criticisms of the Fighter Command (RAF) brought forward by several members.

This meeting was held and I was requested to represent to you the lack of confidence in which Sir Hugh Dowding is held in certain quarters of the personell (sic) of the Force, and the grave concern felt by my Executive. It will be my duty to report to the full Committee at their next meeting, and any reply you care to give me to this representation will be greatly appreciated.

I am, my dear Prime Minister,
Yours very sincerely
REGINALD CLARRY

The records of the 1922 Committee meetings are held in the Bodleian
Library, Oxford. These records do not constitute minutes: they note solely the
subject-matters discussed, one line per subject, in the tersest fashion. The
record of the meeting of November 6th does not even mention this concern
"brought forward by several members." There is no record of any reply from
the Executive Committee. There is no record of any reply from the Prime
Minister, directly or by deputation. Furthermore, the records do not note any
reference to the matter at the next meeting of the full Committee. This letter
appears to constitute the full representation made to the Prime Minister.
There is no suggestion of a meeting having taken place between Clarry and
the Prime Minister.

Churchill did reply to Clarry, however. A copy is held in the same file
as Clarry's letter. It gave Clarry a merited brush-off, advising him not to
allow the 1922 Committee to degenerate into "a kind of collecting house
for complaints."

One would like to know the nature of the criticisms made of Fighter
Command and of Sir Hugh Dowding in the 1922 Committee. One would
like even more to know the identity of the "several members" who brought
forward the criticisms.

The conspicuous features of this letter are, first, its vagueness, and, second
— although there is no disclaimer — the fact that the 1922 Committee had
no business sticking its nose into the affairs of Fighter Command, and that
the Committee — like Miss Ward — had no knowledge of Fighter
Command and its Commander. It is defamation by innuendo. This, as the
Vikings would have said, is 'nerding's werk'.

* * *

The assaults on Air Chief Marshal Sir Hugh Dowding cited and discussed in these pages show some remarkable common features, and some
equally remarkable timing.

The first thing to note is that every criticism, explicit and implied, was
addressed to Mr. Churchill. The questions impose themselves insistently:

Why did they involve themselves? Why did they go direct to the Prime Minister instead of through the normal channels?

The second thing is that Miss Ward and the 1922 Committee had little or no knowledge of the matters they were meddling in. They therefore received their information from another or from others. Macdonald, on the other hand, had direct access to sources of information.

Information is perhaps too mild and vague a word. It is necessary to visualize not just the casual passing of information, but the deliberate briefing of these people, their convincing, and the assurance that they would actually do something about it.

In the case of Irene Ward, she was given a document, with the agreement on her part to send it on to Churchill. The passing of the document to her can only have been in person, from someone she knew. Similarly, this same person must have convinced her, in confidential personal discussion, that the information in the document was reliable. (As we have seen, Sinclair, on receiving it from Churchill, locked it up in a box and later claimed to have forgotten about it. This action cannot have been taken to protect Dowding, for Sinclair knew that other copies were being circulated. In other words, he intended to do nothing about it, for the simple reason that he hoped something would come of it, without action on his part.)

It is equally obvious that the "several members" of the 1922 Committee who had voiced "certain criticisms of the Fighter Command" and who had convinced the Committee of "the lack of confidence in which Sir Hugh Dowding is held in certain quarters of the . . . (Air) Force" must themselves have been briefed on the issues.

One certain conclusion we can reach is that Miss Ward and the 1922 Committee did not act on their own initiative. They were therefore 'put up to it'. We believe, on the other hand, that Macdonald, despite his Air Force position, could have taken the action that he did on his own unprompted initiative. But we also believe that Macdonald could as easily have been persuaded by Leigh-Mallory to tackle Churchill. What most probably happened is that Miss Ward and Macdonald, having themselves been successfully 'enlisted', were the members, or the "several members", who raised the matter in the 1922 Committee.

We have finally to look at the timing of the representations made to Churchill, the specific purpose of each one, their success or otherwise, and the connection between them and the stages of Dowding's tenure and appointment.

The first document, the anonymous one that Irene Ward was circulating, was forwarded to Churchill with a covering letter dated August 17th. Her letter put forward the view that it would be a disaster if Dowding succeeded Newall as Chief of the Air Staff, and that Portal was by far the best choice.

Before this letter was written, Dowding's term of office, as Newall's letter to him of July 10th specified, was due to terminate on October 31st. However, on August 12th Newall wrote again to Dowding telling him that now there was to be **no limit** placed on his appointment as Commander-in-Chief of Fighter Command. The anonymous diatribe against Newall and Dowding had, as we have seen, been composed some weeks before; but its distribution, if any, must have been restricted to insiders or intimates of the author. Now, suddenly, it began to be circulated to a larger audience. It was circulated widely, from August 17th on; that is to say, its larger, outward circulation began exactly five days after the indefinite extension of Dowding's tenure of office. Not only that; its circulation extended throughout September and into October.

Whether or not this document, allied with who knows what other manoeuvres, achieved all its desired effects, the fact remains that some time in October the appointment of Portal to succeed Newall as CAS was made and became known.

Miss Ward's letter did not specify the shortcomings of Dowding which were serious enough to disqualify him as a candidate for the highest RAF office. That was not the case with Salmond's letter to the Prime Minister, and his meeting with Churchill shortly after. Salmond's case was specific: Dowding had failed to meet the night attacks and prepare adequate counter-measures, and for that failure he must be removed.

The Trenchard-Salmond correspondence and campaign against Dowding — according to the documentation that is publicly available — were carried out in September and October. They seemed to bear no fruit, or no immediate fruit.

It was on October 24th that Macdonald had his meeting with Churchill. Macdonald's position as adjutant of 242 Squadron suggests that he wanted to see Churchill to apprise him of Dowding's failure to settle the discord between 12 Group and 11 Group of Fighter Command.

There was something more, something that now needs emphasizing: there was a progressive 'raising of the stakes' against Dowding:

1) in June, the call was to find a Chief of the Air Staff who could deal with Dowding;

2) in August, it was deemed necessary to block his elevation to Chief of the Air Staff;

3) in September-October, it became urgent to remove him from Fighter Command; and

4) in November, the Air Staff wanted nothing less than his definitive retirement.

It seems unlikely that the increasing severity of measures to be taken against Dowding was mere coincidence. It raises the possibility of design, intent, on the part of some person or persons unknown, almost certainly within the Air Ministry, who knew of the criticisms being circulated against Dowding and of the agitations for his removal, and who attempted to further the cause by pulling a string here or dropping a word there.

The final question — and this we can answer with confidence — is: Why Churchill? Churchill was, and was known to be, Dowding's strongest supporter. In order to get rid of Dowding, Churchill had to be persuaded that Dowding was no longer up to it. Churchill was so persuaded. The stream of criticisms and calumnies undoubtedly took their toll. But something more was needed to push him far enough over the line as to convince him of Dowding's inability to deal with the immediate or future operational demands to be required of Fighter Command.

## NOTES TO CHAPTER 5:

1. This memorandum is discussed below.

2. It appears that none of Dowding's most fervent admirers have contested that judgment. It is a judgment that is, nevertheless, open to question. (See chapters 9 and 10.)

3. Miss Ward's 'concern' serves to corroborate the suspicion that the degree of enthusiasm for a cause is in direct ratio to one's ignorance of the facts.

4. Following is the text of the Summary:

> The above mentioned weaknesses in the character of Air Chief Marshal Newall have their reactions on the Air Ministry and on the whole Royal Air Force. It is, therefore, not surprising that many informed officers of medium seniority in the RAF are in despair at the day to day drift, the counter orders which follow orders, the muddles, the waste of effort and the consequent unnecessary loss of life

and aircraft which result from weak higher direction within the Air Ministry. Even more serious is the loss of grip which has seemed to permeate the Air Ministry during almost every crisis which has arisen since the war began.

From the foregoing criticisms it will be obvious that there is the most urgent need to replace Air Chief Marshal Newall as Chief of the Air Staff by the best officer who can be found for the appointment. The change is necessary in justice to the magnificent personnel of the Royal Air Force units and also to the whole nation.

(If these criticisms of Newall are compared with the attacks against Dowding; and if the relative achievements of Newall and Dowding are compared; a comparison of their respective 'fates' is illuminating. Newall, when he was retired in October, was promoted to Marshal of the Royal Air Force and appointed Governor-General of New Zealand.)

This memorandum, it has recently been disclosed, was written by (then) Wing Commander Edgar James Kingston-McCloughry, at the time working in the Directorate of War Organization of the Air Ministry. (See the article, "A Political Intrigue Against the Chief of the Air Staff: The Downfall of Air Chief Marshal Sir Cyril Newall", by Sebastian Ritchie, in *War and Society*, vol.16, no.1 (May 1998) published by the University of New South Wales.)

In my correspondence with Denis Richards, Mr. Richards put forward the idea in his letter to me of April 2nd, 1996 that Kingston-McCloughry was the leading candidate as the author. "I've always understood (he wrote) there were things linking him with the document". Kingston-McCloughry's judgment was warped, it seems, by his failure to be promoted. How little human nature changes! How little men are able to rise above their petty self-interest! We will have much more to say on this theme.

5. This deficiency was undoubtedly true of the great majority of senior officers at the Air Ministry.

6. Likely memorandum author Kingston-McCloughry was, of course, one of the Wing Commanders who was passed over for promotion in this list.

7. This submission is of particular interest in the light of what Sidney Cotton had to say on the self-same issue one day later, on May 9th, 1940, that is, one day before the German *Blitzkrieg* against France. (See Appendix "D".)

8. On the other hand, it is certain that Dowding would have concurred with this judgment by 'Johnnie' Johnson: "The bomber is the true instrument of air power, and the fighter, when used offensively to assist the bomber, is merely a means to an end." If Johnnie were still alive I would write and ask him if he would be willing to amend the phrase 'merely a means' to 'an indispensable means'.

9. In a larger sense, few men can have had a greater concern for humanity and been more horrified by the destructiveness of war. How many other men of Dowding's elevated rank have written a treatise against war?

10. Salmond's hostility towards Dowding may have had a doctrinal origin, for he, like Trenchard, was a committed bomber and 'offensive' man. Yet in 1940 it had clearly become poisoned by a deeply personal animus. (Its origin is probably unknowable, but may lie in Salmond's access to Dowding's correspondence with the Air Staff in 1939–1940 and in his siding with the Air Staff in their dealings with Dowding.)

Salmond's biographer and Henry Probert have nothing to say on the matter.

11. Inquiries and searches have failed to unearth any personal or official papers that would throw any light on the activities of these MPs.

# CHAPTER 6

# The Campaign Prevails:
# End of the Line

The daylight attacks were contained and turned back in September. In October, as we have seen, the Luftwaffe resorted mostly to hit-and-run tactics with bomb-carrying Messerschmitt 109s and 110s. At 12 Group Bader was still massing his fighters in big wings, and still not having any success, against an enemy which was now a far swifter and more elusive prey than the bombers had been.

At the same time Leigh-Mallory's voice was being heeded in the Air Ministry, where the Under-Secretary of State for Air, Harold Balfour, and the Vice-Chief of the Air Staff, Sholto Douglas, were championing the idea of superiority in numbers as promised, on paper at least, by the big wings.

In this chapter we will narrate the events which followed one upon the other in remorseless sequence and which were to culminate, almost as if planned or pre-ordained, in the removal, first, of Dowding, then of Park. The events, presided over now jointly by Ironia and, in the eyes of their admirers, by Tragedy herself, are these:

October 17 . . . . . . . . . . . . . . . . . . Conference at the Air Ministry
October 24 . . . . . . . . . . . . . . . . . . . . . Macdonald sees Churchill
October 27 . . . . . . . . . . . . . . . . . . . . . . Sinclair visits Duxford
November 2/6 . . . . . . . . . . . . . . . . . . . . Balfour visits Duxford:
the 'Duxford Memorandum'
November 13/14 . . . . . . . . Dowding sees Sinclair — and Churchill
November 15 . . . . . . . . . . . . . . . . . . . . Sinclair's telephone call
November 18 . . . . . . . . . . . . . . . . . . . Portal writes to Dowding
November 25 . . . . . . . . . . . . . . . . . . . . . . The End of the line.

## 1. The Conference

This conference, which has achieved notoriety in the Air Force and among historians and taken on certain mythical features, was convened by the

Deputy Chief of the Air Staff, Sholto Douglas, "to discuss major day tactics in the Fighter Force."

This stated purpose is itself misleading and will be examined shortly. Writers who have discussed this conference have themselves been misled by this statement and have gone off on a wild goose chase. The chase has led them to discuss the pros and cons of squadrons and big wings; the tactical ideas put into practice by 11 Group and by 12 Group; whether 12 Group's ideas could work in 11 Group; the mutually hostile exchanges between Park and Leigh-Mallory; the contribution to the discussions, if any, made by Dowding; and, after the draft minutes were sent to the AOC-in-C and to Group Commanders, the misrepresentation of Park's views and the refusal by Douglas to add a correcting statement of Park's to the final minutes.

All that is interesting enough, and important. But the most heat has been generated among historians and others over the presence there of Squadron Leader Douglas Bader. We analysed some of Bader's ideas in chapter 4, and have shown that his contribution to the debate, whereas, ironically, insignificant tactically, became of some importance historically. What the commentators have failed to see is the underlying significance, the portent, of Bader's presence. A superficial explanation is that Leigh-Mallory was himself out of his depth in debating tactics with Dowding, Park and Brand, and leant heavily on Bader to speak for him. The real explanation is to be found in the true purpose of Douglas in calling the conference, and in his conniving with Leigh-Mallory to 'invite' Bader.

The invitation, or summons, was sent on the 14th. Dowding and the Group Commanders were therefore given all of two days' notice of the conference. The notice was accompanied by an Introduction drafted by Douglas; a paper called 'Air Staff Notes on the Operation of Fighter Wings'; and a copy of Leigh-Mallory's 'Report on Wing Patrols Sent up by No.12 Group' of the previous month.

Douglas did not explain why he thought it necessary to discuss tactics **at this particular time,** since the Battle of Britain was essentially over. This belief is stated in the Introduction: "At present it seems that our fighter defence has defeated the GAF [German Air Force] in their attempt this year to gain day air superiority over this country." Note: 'this year'. And 'it seems'. There was no 'seems' about it. The note of belittlement is struck.

Douglas makes it perfectly clear, however, why he wanted the conference: "we must have regard to the possibility that more determined, better organised and heavier attacks may be made in the Spring of 1941, if not before. In consequence it is necessary that the lessons we have learnt should be applied generally to enable the fighter defence to operate at maximum efficiency."

This statement is revealing. The application **in the future** of "the lessons that we have learnt" implies that those lessons have not been applied hitherto. What lessons? The statement also implies, derogatorily, that "maximum efficiency" had not been achieved.

The papers mentioned above are equally revealing: they **all** deal with massed wings of fighters and praise Leigh-Mallory's (and Bader's) use of wings. The Agenda contained nine items for discussion on day tactics, **every one** of which directed the discussion toward approval of 'big' wings.

The minutes of the conference presented three propositions which "he [Douglas] would like the meeting to consider: —"

(1) We wish to outnumber the enemy formations when we meet them.
(2) We want our superior numbers to go into the attack with a co-ordinated plan of action.
(3) If possible we want the top layer of our fighter formation to have theadvantage of height over the top layer of the enemy formation.

It is impossible not to see, it is so conspicuously one-sided, that the discussions, conclusions and recommendations were a foregone conclusion: all was concocted in advance; and Douglas, the Air Staff and Leigh-Mallory had connived to bring about that sole result.

The inclusion among the discussion papers of Leigh-Mallory's report on wing operations was a revealing impertinence. It was impertinent because the figures of enemy losses claimed were wildly exaggerated; it was revealing because the report was a month old. Why was an up-to-date report not included? For the simple reason that Leigh-Mallory had not submitted any further reports — because Bader's wing had had no further successes.

The writing was on the wall, writ large and bold. When and if mass formations of German aircraft again attacked this country, they would be met by even larger mass formations of our fighters. Ah! but under whose direction? Dowding and Park were too much the loyal and dedicated Air Force officers, and hence too far removed from all notions of duplicity, to suspect the existence of the wall, let alone to see the writing. But Park, surely, had received a warning several months before, from Leigh-Mallory himself.

What the writing on the wall said, loud and clear, was that Douglas and Leigh-Mallory were of one mind in the 'wings' dispute and ranged against Dowding and Park, **even though evidence provided by Douglas and Leigh-Mallory was demonstrably untenable.** The conference, Leigh-Mallory's report, and Bader's presence proclaimed their insincerity and fraudulence. How was 11 Group going to muster wings of fighters in the spring of 1941 when 12 Group did not have the time to do it? Such a consideration was irrelevant! It must already have been decided — no doubt between Douglas and Sinclair, with Portal's acquiescence — that Douglas and Leigh-Mallory would replace Dowding and Park.

The purpose of the conference was to undermine Dowding's authority by showing him — or showing him up — as not making the best uses of his limited resources, and by showing him as reluctant or unable to settle the dispute between his two chief group commanders.

Is this speculation? Or is it established fact? It was in the first place a reasonable conclusion deduced from the known facts — until corroborated by an eyewitness:

> In light of what happened later, Douglas succeeding Dowding and Leigh-Mallory succeeding Park, coupled with all I had heard in the various telephone conversations [between Leigh-Mallory and Douglas], I believe this meeting was just part of a move to discredit the two principal figures fighting the battle with a view to the takeover later. . . . (It) was altogether a disgraceful episode and highly discreditable to Douglas and Leigh-Mallory. Bader of course was just a pawn in the game.[1]

## 2. Macdonald and Churchill

One day in October Flight Lieutenant Sir Peter Macdonald went to see Harold Balfour, the Under-Secretary of State for Air, and asked him to set up a meeting for him with Churchill. Balfour, according to Balfour's own account, refused to arrange a meeting with Churchill, contenting himself with reminding Macdonald of his right as an MP to ask to see the Prime Minister. Balfour described Macdonald's request thus:

> Peter returned periodically to the House of Commons in the uniform of a Flight Lieutenant. The position of a serving MP is always a delicate one in relation to his service life. Peter wished to retail to me what was happening between the Groups and the failure of the C-in-C Fighter Command to rectify the position. I asked Peter not to talk to me about RAF affairs, feeling

that it would be wrong for me to listen to a junior officer, even though a Member of Parliament. He then asked if I could arrange for him to see Churchill. I replied that I could do no such thing, but that as an MP he had a right to ask to see the Prime Minister. He saw Churchill and hence down the pipeline came the Churchill enquiries.

Macdonald had his meeting on October 24th and was closeted with Churchill for over an hour.

We must ask by what right an MP who was also a serving RAF officer might take it upon himself to seek a meeting with the Prime Minister in order to apprise him of Air Force matters? And by what means did Macdonald presume to know that Churchill was not already 'in the know' when an officer as lowly as a squadron adjutant seemed to 'know it all'?

The propriety of this action by Macdonald has not been subjected to a critical examination. The few writers who have discussed it have approved Macdonald's initiative, on the ground that it was the business of the Prime Minister, who was also Minister of Defence, to know what was going on. This is to put oneself in the shoes of the Prime Minister, and not in Macdonald's place.

Macdonald, having failed to enlist the direct help of Balfour, who saw its irregularity — but still encouraged him — should have requested a meeting with Sinclair, the minister responsible for air matters. If Sinclair refused to see him, his next step was to write and put his case.

But one cannot fail to ask why Macdonald did not go through the regular Air Force channels. Did he write to Leigh-Mallory or telephone him, as he could well have done, without telling Bader of his action, to suggest a meeting between Leigh-Mallory and Dowding? There is no evidence that he took any such action. (On the other hand, many officers have left behind no evidence of their actions and of many events no record.) But it must be asked: Why did Macdonald do no such thing? For the reason that he would be stepping out of line and risking reprimand.

There is a more profound reason why Macdonald took the course that he did — a course of action, let us not forget, which can only be characterized as highly irregular. That reason — the need for secrecy — has nothing, and everything, to do with keeping Bader in the dark. He could not let Bader know what he intended to do, for the reason that Bader would have vetoed it. And he could not let Bader know because his interview with Churchill was all of a piece with his other activities, as we shall show.

What Macdonald did was to use his position as an MP to influence Air Force policy. Nothing could be more reprehensible. As an MP, his proper activities had to be restricted to the interest and well-being of his constituents and his constituency of the Isle of Wight. As a serving officer of the R.A.F., his activities were necessarily bound to Air Force matters.

Macdonald wore two hats. They were different hats. And they were not interchangeable. Did Macdonald go to the Isle of Wight and inform his constituents of Air Force matters? Of course not. In point of fact, Balfour was culpable by the very fact of advising Macdonald that it was his right — and these are Balfour's own words — "his right as an MP to ask to see the Prime Minister." Precisely: "his right as an MP" — that is, as a Member of Parliament. Macdonald was the Member of Parliament for the Isle of Wight. He was not the Member of Parliament for RAF Station Duxford or for 242 Squadron. But Balfour incriminates himself; for did he not also tell Macdonald: "I asked Peter not to talk to me about RAF affairs, feeling that it would be wrong for me to listen to a junior officer, even though an MP"?

If a writer, especially a writer on historical matters, is justified in assuming the role of Arbiter and Judge, this writer's judgment of Macdonald is harsh indeed. His action smacks of nothing so much as of duplicity.

His deed was an act of treachery against his Commander-in-Chief, in going behind his back to report to the highest authority in the land on issues of which the Commander-in-Chief was fully aware, and **about which he had already formed a reasoned opinion.**

There is worse. Let us read again what Balfour had said about Macdonald's visit and request. If we are to believe the accuracy of Balfour's recollection, "Peter wished to retail . . . the failure of the C-in-C Fighter Command to rectify the position [between 11 and 12 Groups]." What position? Why, the antagonism between Park and Leigh-Mallory over their differing tactical ideas. And how, in Macdonald's view, was this position to be 'rectified', that is, 'put right'? How else than in favour of Leigh-Mallory and 12 Group? — that is, in favour of his squadron and its commander, his CO, Douglas Bader? Does it not stick out a mile that if Macdonald had meant find in favour of Park, and hence of Dowding, he would not have used the word 'rectify' and he would not have needed to see Balfour? He went to see Balfour precisely because he knew that Balfour, like Douglas, was on the side of Leigh-Mallory and not a Dowding supporter.

It is equally impossible to condone Macdonald's action on the pretext that he was intervening in the interest of England's defence, an issue paramount to all others. The fact is that, by the time he saw Churchill, in late October, the daylight aerial operations known as the Battle of Britain were essentially over, and Bader's Duxford wing had had no successes for over three weeks.

What are we to say of Churchill, in agreeing to hear Macdonald? In his place, it is tempting to imagine oneself refusing, and telling Macdonald either to go through the usual channels, or to see the Minister in the first instance. Yet, knowing Churchill as we think we do, and his unquenchable thirst for information, his imperious desire to know what was going on everywhere, his life-long custom of finding out and seeing for himself — and let us not dismiss his propensity for a tincture of intrigue — it is easier to excuse Churchill than it is to condone Macdonald. The temptation we shall resist is to claim that this act of Macdonald's, and the consequences which flowed from it and from Churchill's next move, were to result, **in themselves,** in Dowding's removal. As we shall see, the top brass in the Air Ministry were resolved in their determination to get rid of Dowding anyway, come what may.

But Macdonald's session with Churchill did have immediate repercussions nonetheless. And those repercussions were so baleful that one cannot help wondering whether some sinister agent behind the scenes had not been putting a flea in Macdonald's ear.

The first consequence of Macdonald's action was that Churchill telephoned Sinclair wanting to know what was going on in Fighter Command.

A few days later Sinclair went to Duxford and asked a few questions. Suitably impressed and influenced, he then sent Balfour to Duxford to carry out a fuller inquiry and to report.

## 3. Balfour at Duxford

Balfour spent the day of November 2nd at Duxford, and, ostensibly, spoke at length to and listened to the squadron and flight commanders and to the pilots of the squadrons stationed there. And especially he listened to Bader, and to Stan Turner, one of Bader's flight commanders.

Back in London that evening, Balfour wrote his report. A copy lay on Douglas's desk the next morning, awaiting his arrival. It must have been a heaven-sent answer to his prayers. Or other activities.

An informed and objective critical faculty is one of the most vital functions of intelligence. On the other hand, an over-ready acceptance of what one hears or reads is an indication of prejudice. When such acceptance is provoked by the weight of 'authority', such as a known name, it may be understandable, but no less inexcusable.

A case in point is the exchange of views between Balfour and Douglas, on the one hand, and, on the other, between Balfour and Dowding — the latter fully supported, let it never be forgotten, by his Air Staff at Bentley Priory.

The opinions of Balfour and Douglas, at or near the pinnacle of authority within the Air Ministry, were those of authorities not to be taken lightly. The critical intelligence of Dowding, on the other hand, was a force not to be hoodwinked or trifled with. The 'authorities' might be in 'the driver's seat', in a manner of speaking — they **did** exercise the ultimate authority in questions of careers, or in the 'fate' of all personnel of the Royal Air Force. But the Air Officer Commanding-in-Chief of Fighter Command was the ultimate authority in matters affecting operational control within his Command. Dowding never for one moment lost sight of this, his ultimate responsibility.

We have to analyse three documents. They were written, respectively, by the Hon. Harold Balfour, Under-Secretary of State for Air, by Sholto Douglas, and by Dowding.

## THE 'DUXFORD' MEMORANDUM

Balfour's report, in particular, gives rise to difficulties of interpretation and acceptance, precisely because of his career and authority. Balfour had served with distinction as a pilot in the Royal Flying Corps in France in World War I. He was one of the few pilots of the day who continued to fly in the post-war world, and who not only owned his own aeroplane, but maintained his licence by flying all the latest types. As Under-Secretary of State for Air, he flew the second prototype Spitfire to be built; and he also piloted the Westland Whirlwind, an advanced twin-engined fighter which came close to rivalling the Mosquito. He was a distinguished gentleman, and undoubtedly, as MP for the Isle of Thanet, an adornment of the Conservative Party of the 1930s and early 1940s.

Yet, one must not be influenced by the reputation of the writer: one cannot but examine his words and deeds.

The text of Balfour's report of his visit to Duxford on November 2nd reveals exactly what the objective researcher condemns in the reporting of one's inquiries; namely, an uncritical acceptance of what one hears.

We said above that an uncritical acceptance of what one hears is attributable to immaturity or unintelligence. Neither defect can be said to be Balfour's. To those two we must add a third defect, the commonest of all: in a word, a willingness to hear only what one wants to hear.

Balfour visited only Duxford, and only for a few hours. Duxford was then the home of 19 and 310 (Czech) squadrons. Bader had also flown down with his 242 Squadron for the day, as was their custom. The fact that Balfour listened predominantly to Bader, and that he visited no other squadrons in 12 Group, and none at all in 11 Group, colours his report to the extent that it stands out as one of the most one-sided, and treacherous, documents written within the Air Ministry at this time.

The allegations that he relays in his report to the Secretary of State and the Deputy CAS (Sholto Douglas) the next day are unsubstantiated opinions voiced by Bader. Among them are the following:

> Some pilots of 12 Group's "Balbo Wing Formation" are resentful against 11 Group and its AOC for letting things develop as they have. 11 Group [AOC or pilots?] are accused of jealousy of 12 Group's capacity to shoot down more Germans than they can. 11 Group pilots, in failing to repel the enemy with the forces at hand, are "shaken in their morale".

These allegations are pure Bader and Company — and impure calumny. We need only make these observations: 1) Bader's insistence on his so-called "Balbo Wing Formation" is tantamount to their, and 12 Group's, telling 11 Group how to fight their battle in the south. 2) The admission that they, 12 Group, had "not had contest with the enemy since the end of September" [and here we are in November] despite their having flown "at least one sortie per day" in favourable weather, would have made any intelligent leader look to factors other than being called too late by 11 Group, and make him wonder whether single squadrons could operate in weather not deemed to be favourable for five squadrons operating together. 3) Throughout October enemy action comprised mostly raids carried out by high-flying, bomb-carrying Me109s and 110s, and hence much too elusive for the slow-forming and unwieldy wings. 4) For nearly five weeks, from September 10, 74 Squadron, under the leadership of the supreme exponent of air fighting and leadership in the Battle of Britain, Squadron Leader 'Sailor' Malan, was rested from 11

Group and stationed at Coltishall, where coincidentally 242 Squadron was based. It is significant that Malan's squadron took no part in any of Bader's wings.

### THE DOWDING/DOUGLAS CORRESPONDENCE: NOVEMBER 3 - 6

A point-by-point refutation of the allegations and criticisms contained in Balfour's report is the substance of Dowding's response three days later. (We reproduce it in full in Appendix "C").

The covering letter from Sholto Douglas is another matter, and commands comment. After placing himself, again, squarely in Leigh-Mallory's camp, he reverts to the Air Ministry conference of October 17th — as Balfour had done in fact, gratuitously — to buttress this support, and quotes the three principal recommendations imposed by the 'balbo' champions. In so doing, Balfour and Douglas seem to turn a blind eye to the changed conditions of the battle, of the enemy's changed tactics; and above all they are blithely side-stepping the pointed application of the recommendations in question. Those recommendations, favouring big wing formations, were, as we have already discussed, **not intended** to be put into effect **at that time**: they were pointers to the future. The introductory paper prepared for the conference, let us recall, conceded the success of Dowding's and Park's tactics and handling of the battle; went on to look ahead to a renewal of heavy daytime raids; and asserted the necessity that the lessons learnt should be applied generally "to enable the fighter defence to operate at maximum efficiency."

No one could object to that realistic, and responsible, aim, even if honest tacticians might disagree over the lessons; indeed, it can only be applauded. But one must speculate why the matter is raised again, by Balfour and Douglas, at this juncture, when the attacks are far from "heavier" but conspicuously lighter.

A second issue raised by Douglas's letter is of great interest. He writes: "(the) difference of opinion [between Park and Leigh-Mallory] should be resolved as quickly as possible, . . . and I think that it is for you to put the matter right by an authoritative statement of your views. This would be far more satisfactory than for the Air Ministry to try and act as referee." This strong invitation "to give the Groups an authoritative statement of your views" is repeated in the final paragraph.

It is of great importance to note that here Douglas refers only to the "difference of opinion" between Park and Leigh-Mallory, i.e. to a professional difference over tactics and cooperation between the Groups. But what could Douglas have had in mind when suggesting — not quite 'directing' — that Dowding give the Groups an authoritative statement of his views?

We suggest he had two motives: the one overt, the other covert. The overt intent was that Dowding should issue a directive to Groups; the covert was to use it against him, because Douglas knew what Dowding's views were.[2]

Dowding's statement would have reiterated the view that only the Groups were in a position to assess the immediacy and the level of the danger presented by an incoming raid; and that only the sectors could decide which squadrons to 'scramble' to meet the raiders in their region. He could also have insisted that the Groups re-examine the use of wings in their areas of responsibility while recommending that wings of more than two squadrons should not be assembled.

Douglas's letter came as close to issuing a directive to Dowding as he dared. But his words "authoritative statement" imply precisely that that is what Dowding should do. Either Douglas knew nothing of the principles of the command structure and authority in war, or he knew only too well. Dowding had delegated to his Group AOCs almost total authority in matters of tactics, so that he could no longer issue tactical directions to them. It is doubtful whether Dowding felt he could even order a Group to use no more than two squadrons in a wing formation. The sole recourse he had, if a Group Commander's actions failed persistently to meet the AOC's expectations and strategic plan, was to replace the Group Commander.[3]

At this juncture, in early November, the time had passed. And most of Fighter Command Headquarters' energies and resources were dedicated to meeting the night attacks.

Dowding did not issue the statement as suggested by Douglas. If he had it would only have given further ammunition to the Air Staff, who would doubtless have waved the document aloft proclaiming Dowding's wilful uncooperativeness in disregarding the Air Ministry policy as laid down following the conference of October 17.

The counter-criticisms levelled by Dowding against Leigh-Mallory and Bader in his rebuttal of Balfour's report might have seemed serious enough to warrant their removal. Did this extreme measure occur to Dowding, in Leigh-Mallory's case? An answer to that speculation can never be known. It was soon to become clear that no matter what Dowding did, his days were numbered.[4]

## 4. Dowding and Sinclair — and Churchill

Dowding was invited to see Sir Archibald Sinclair, and duly had a meeting with him in the Air Ministry on November 13. From this it seems that the Air Council must have taken the decision at some time in late October or early November on a change of command at Fighter Command.

Sinclair drafted a summary of their conversation at the request of Beaverbrook and his notes are held in the Beaverbrook Library archives.[5] According to this document, Sinclair told Dowding that the Government wished to send him, Sir Hugh, to the United States as adviser on the production of military aircraft. "We believed (in Sinclair's words) that the Americans would be willing to accept the guidance of a man whose opinion and personality would command respect." Sinclair expressed to Dowding his appreciation of Dowding's great services as Commander in Chief of the Fighter Command, but he had come to the conclusion that "it was right to make the change which this new project would involve."

Dowding replied that it would be one thing if he was only being asked to undertake a temporary mission, but that he would want to return to his command at Fighter Command. The document concludes: "I replied that I must tell him that that was not in my mind and that I was proposing to appoint Air Vice-Marshal Sholto Douglas to Fighter Command. He said that he quite understood[6] but that he would want a night to think it over and that he would want to see the Prime Minister. I answered that, of course, I would not press him and that he should have time to think it over. I had no doubt that the Prime Minister would be most willing to see him; at the same time it was possible that after thinking it over he might not think it necessary to see the Prime Minister. He answered that he would certainly wish to see the Prime Minister — and so we parted."

Let us examine these statements.

Sinclair, after informing Dowding that the Government wished to send him as head of a mission to the U.S., added: "I had come to the conclusion that it was right to make the change which this new project would involve."

Orwell would have admired the double-speak: "— the change which this new project would involve." A change of command had already been decided on, i.e. Dowding's removal. Then a new assignment was thought up for Dowding. Now the logic is turned upside down, and the new project becomes the **reason** for the change. What must have stuck even more bitterly in Dowding's craw is the claim of the **'rightness'** of the change.[7]

A.J.P. Taylor's letter concludes: "Lord Beaverbrook, who favoured Dowding, was himself locked in conflict with the Air Council and therefore could not support him. He proposed the mission [to the United States] as a way out."

Beaverbrook was assuredly one of Dowding's most admiring supporters throughout the Battle. Beaverbrook was "locked in conflict" with the Air Ministry to the same degree as Dowding. Perhaps that is one reason why Beaverbrook admired Dowding: both men were independent thinkers, decisive, unorthodox in their ways, and contemptuous of shallow minds and bureaucratic obstruction.

It is therefore all the more difficult to understand Taylor's assertion that Beaverbrook "could not support him" because he "was himself locked in conflict with the Air Council." His being locked in conflict with the Air Council and the Air Staff had been a constant state of affairs from the day he had been appointed Minister of Aircraft Production on May 12th, 1940, and it had never hampered him before in his relations with Dowding. What had changed now — and apparently so suddenly — as to make him unable to support Dowding? If ever Dowding needed support it was at this moment. Beaverbrook, if Taylor's account is correct, betrayed Dowding.

That is far from all. Let us look again at the last sentence of Taylor's letter: "He [Beaverbrook] proposed the mission to the United States as a way out." As 'a way out'! A 'way out' of what? A 'way out' for whom? A way out of embarrassment for Dowding in the light of his removal from his command? A way out of an impasse for Churchill because now forced to acquiesce in his removal? A way out for the Air Council, in view of Dowding's accomplishments? None of these, we suggest, although it helped them. The proposal seems to have been Beaverbrook's. Who else would have suggested a mission to the United States, especially about the production of military aircraft? If Beaverbrook "could not support" Dowding, his proposal was a way out for himself, to save his own face and cover his betrayal of Dowding.[8] Taylor prefaces his last statement with these words: "It seems clear that the Air Council had decided to make a change at Fighter Command and that Sir Archibald Sinclair and the Prime Minister acquiesced."

There we have the truth, albeit inadvertently: "the Air Council had decided to make a change at Fighter Command". But in what follows Taylor knows not whereof he writes. Sinclair was the President of the Air Council and had wanted Dowding's removal shortly after he became Secretary of

State for Air, so acquiescence is hardly the appropriate term — though it is not hard to envisage Sinclair as wanting to **appear** to acquiesce in Dowding's removal. But the acquiescence of Churchill was, as we have seen, a *sine qua non* of Dowding's removal, and a stumbling block to his enemies' schemes and ambitions.

Before we examine the various reasons put forward by numerous writers to explain or justify the removal of Dowding from his command, it is essential to recount, and to clear up once and for all, the controversy surrounding the manner of his removal.

Dowding's removal, or dismissal, from his Command has been the subject of interminable debate. The debate and controversy centre in great part on the technicality of whether Dowding was retired or sacked, and has provoked prolonged discussion of the manner of his removal.

The controversy exists, to this day, because of the hitherto unresolved debate between the champions of Dowding and the defenders of the Air Ministry, whose official, though unwritten, policy, also to this day, as we have already pointed out, persists in denying recognition of Dowding's achievements. The Air Ministry position is that Dowding was quite properly informed that his tenure as Commander-in-Chief of Fighter Command was being terminated, and that Dowding had no complaint about the termination and the manner of its communication to him. (It must be said, however, that the Air Ministry has never issued any statement about either the fact or the manner.) Dowding's defenders insist, on the contrary, that he was sacked abruptly and out-of-the-blue by a telephone call from Sinclair, and that Dowding harboured an ineradicable resentment over this cavalier treatment for the rest of his life.

We hope to show that, unlikely though it seems, both versions have a basis in fact; and that one version is truer than the other. Such is the challenge of studying history.

We will start by quoting Harold Balfour's account of the event:

> Dowding says that in the second week of November 1940 he received a sudden phone call at his headquarters from the Secretary of State for Air. 'He told me I was to relinquish my Command immediately. I asked what was meant by "immediately" and I was told that it would take effect within the next day or so.' This version of the conversation is the foundation of the allegation that Dowding was 'sacked on the end of a telephone'. It just does not stand up."

A few pages before Balfour had written: "sacked after the Battle of Britain at a moment's notice by the Secretary of State on the end of the telephone, he certainly was not." Where do we find that Dowding was 'sacked on the end of a telephone'? Robert Wright says so in his biography of Dowding. And Wright's source of information was Dowding himself. This is his account:

> So far as Dowding knew, he was still in the position of having no time limit imposed on his appointment. . . . [He felt] that he would be given at least reasonable and adequate notice of the time for him to relinquish his Command. . . . Of what happened then, in the second week of November, Dowding stated: 'I received a sudden phone call at my Headquarters from the Secretary of State for Air. He told me that I was to relinquish my Command immediately. I asked what was meant by "immediately", and I was told that it would take effect within the next day or so. Since that was tantamount to my being given twenty-four hours' notice, and verbally at that, I pointed out that it was perfectly absurd that I should be relieved of my Command in this way unless it was thought that I had committed some major crime or something like that. But all that I could get in reply was that the decision had been reached, and that was that, with no explanation for such a precipitate step being taken.'

Before we try to resolve the mystery of the telephone call and the story of Dowding's dismissal, let us look again at another view. One of the accounts that deserve the closest attention is that given by Gough & Richards:

> After the three very short extensions of his tenure, the latest time-limit, fixed for 31 October, had on 21 August been completely withdrawn. Then, quite unexpectedly to him, he was required to relinquish his Command at a few days' notice. In later years he even told his biographer, Robert Wright, that in the second week of November he received "a sudden phone-call" from Sinclair telling him he was to relinquish his Command "immediately". . . . Sinclair, a devoted minister and the soul of courtesy, was not a man to sack a respected commander over the telephone.

Shortly after the publication of Wright's book, there was a flurry of letters in *The Times* in January 1970 seeking to throw light on 'the mystery'.

The first, on January 14, from Marshal of the Royal Air Force Sir John Slessor, gently took Dowding to task for his failure of memory. We quote almost the entire letter:

> There is one passage in Mr. Robert Wright's very interesting book, *Dowding and the Battle of Britain,* which I feel must be called in question, namely the allegation attributed to Lord Dowding that just after the real

Battle of Britain had been won, in the second week of November, 1940, he was summarily — and by implication unexpectedly — dismissed from his command in the course of a sudden and very brief telephone conversation by the Secretary of State for Air, Sir Archibald Sinclair (now Lord Thurso). No one who knows Lord Dowding would suggest for one moment that he is capable of deliberate misrepresentation of facts. I am among the many who think he was shabbily treated at the end of the Battle of Britain and has behaved with great dignity ever since. But from my own experience over a number of years of writing some military history, I know how strangely easy it is to forget completely some significant details even of really important events in which one was closely involved, even relatively few years before. And I respectfully suggest that in connexion with this event, it is not impossible that Lord Dowding's memory may have let him down. So in justice not only to Lord Thurso (who cannot now answer for himself) but also to the higher political and military direction of the RAF at the time, I have been at some pains to try to uncover the truth about Lord Dowding's retirement — not with unqualified success.

I can make no personal contribution to the solution. The Directorate of Plans, of which I was then the head, was not directly concerned with the battle; and I had no idea of what was going on within Fighter Command until — for some unaccountable reason which I can neither remember nor imagine — I was present at the famous (or notorious, according to one's point of view) conference in the Air Council room on October 17. . . . Lord Dowding h ad been at Fighter Command for a long time; he had not always seen eye to eye with the Air Ministry; and, as Mr. Wright reminds us, the question of his retirement had been discussed with him on a number of occasions in 1939 and earlier in 1940. That it should have been given even a passing thought after Dunkirk, when it was perfectly obvious that the Command he had organized and trained was soon to be put to the supreme test, passeth all understanding. That the final decision and notification to the C-in- C was made in the way described in this book is so much more incomprehensible as to be unbelievable.

I have in recent months consulted a number of the now sadly diminished band of individuals, political, military and in civil service, who were in positions of responsibility connected with these events in 1940. For the most part they have (I think understandably) no recollection of what happened in this particular connection during that period of desperate crisis nearly thirty years ago. But all agree with me that it is incredible that Sir Archibald Sinclair can have acted in the manner alleged in Mr. Wright's book.

Both Lord Dowding and Mr. Wright on his behalf took great trouble to verify the facts as far as possible from official records and Dowding's own papers. The telephone story finds some corroboration in the facts that there is no copy in the archives of any letter, which one would have expected, on the lines of the typically generous and well-deserved tribute which Sinclair addressed to Dowding after VE day. Apart from that I am informed by the responsible historical authority that they can throw no light on the story, which they think is one of those mysteries likely to remain insoluble.

There is one possible explanation — I put it no higher — as follows. One who at the time was in an exceptional position to know tells me that he has a clear recollection that Lord Dowding had one and possibly two appointments with the Secretary of State at about the relevant time. And I agree with him that it is a reasonable assumption that Sinclair then told him of the intention finally to retire him after the great strain he had undergone in his four years at Fighter Command, culminating in his victory in the Battle of Britain; and that the telephone call was merely to let him know that his retirement was to become effective in the immediate future.

However all this may be, Lord Dowding earned the everlasting gratitude of all British people as the victor in one of the most decisive battles of history. And if it should turn out that, in view of the almost unbearable strain to which he was subjected at the time, and with the passage of years, certain details of what happened so many years ago had slipped his memory, no one could hold that against him.

This letter was followed, on the 19th, by a blunt rebuttal by Robert Wright:

In his letter to you of January 14, Marshal of the Royal Air Force Sir John Slessor calls in question the description given in my book, *Dowding and the Battle of Britain,* of the way in which Lord Dowding was notified that he would have to relinquish his command.

The work that I did on this book called for an intense search over a long period of time in my effort to discover exactly what happened in this matter. The account given in the book of how it was actually done is as it was first told to me by Lord Dowding years ago, and which has been discussed by us in the numerous talks that we have had about it over the years since then. I questioned him rigorously about it; and in support of that I could find no evidence in his personal files that Lord Dowding was relieved of his command in any way other than that given in the book. As Sir John admits, there is no evidence whatsoever in the official files to support any other view.

Sir John has offered what he describes as a possible explanation for the abrupt nature of my account of the dismissal, but he bases it largely on the memory — while at the same time questioning the memory of Lord Dowding — of someone whom he does not name. He further offers the view that the whole episode is an insoluble mystery. I do not accept it as a mystery, but if there is anybody who can offer any further concrete evidence one way or the other in this matter I should be only too glad to hear about it. . . .

Whether Lord Dowding was dismissed in an interview or on the telephone, or through both, it was still done only by word of mouth, at a very short notice, and in a shabby manner. There is nothing in the record to prove otherwise. And that still leaves us with the inescapable fact that to treat him in this fashion after all that he had achieved was nothing short of disgraceful, made all the more so by the curious conduct of the Prime Minister.

There is widespread agreement that a grave injustice was done Lord Dowding in November, 1940. He is described by Sir John as "the victor in one of the most decisive battles of history". When in the name of pride, honesty and decency, is that injustice going to be corrected?

We have to ask now, in the light of the evidence presented: Who is right in all this?

Balfour and Slessor, among others, in rejecting Dowding's version of events, suggest that he must have had a lapse of memory in later years, for Sinclair was too decent and considerate a man ever to do such a thing.

Yet is it possible that a man of Dowding's mental acuity, even as late as 1970, should have imagined it, or blown it up out of all proportion to its actual message? No. There **was** a telephone call, and for it to have had the impact that it did, it must have been very much as Dowding remembered it.

Nevertheless, Wright's book shows a glaring deficiency. It makes no mention of Dowding's meeting with Sinclair. That there was a meeting, and that they discussed the termination of Dowding's tenure, as Taylor writes, there can be no doubt. Balfour confirms it — though it took place on November 13th, not the 17th as he states.

That there was a telephone call is equally no longer in doubt. Slessor's letter confirms it. And Gough & Richards confirm it: "The telephone call, saying that a change at Stanmore was to take place immediately, must have come a day or two later." No wonder that Dowding, **not having been apprised of a date by Sinclair,** was appalled, and shocked to the roots of his being.

The account given by Dowding is therefore the more accurate of the two. His discussion with Sinclair established four things: 1) that Dowding was to relinquish his command; 2) that he was to go to the United States "as adviser on the production of military aircraft"; 3) that Douglas was to be his successor; and 4) that on the completion of his mission he would not be returning to his Command.

What must be emphasized and re-emphasized here is, first, that Dowding had a document formally cancelling any time-limit to his tenure as AOC-in-C of Fighter Command; second, that Sinclair gave Dowding his marching orders by word of mouth first in person and then by telephone; and third, that neither he nor any other authority ever followed it up in writing, as formality, custom, and simple courtesy demanded.

The second point is, of course, insisted upon by Wright in his letter, when he wrote: "Whether Lord Dowding was dismissed in an interview or on the telephone, or through both, it was still done only by word of mouth, at very short notice. . . ." (We see here, incidentally, for the first time, Wright's acknowledgment of Dowding's meeting with Sinclair on November 13th.)

The third point is equally heinous. In all his, Dowding's, dealings with past and present Secretaries of State for Air and Chiefs of the Air Staff, a personal or telephone conversation having to do with Dowding's career was unfailingly followed by a letter to confirm the substance of their talk and the decision arrived at. This time there was no letter or other written communication. For one thing, as we shall see, events overtook such niceties, even on the part of such a gentleman as Sinclair. For another thing, no explanation was possible.

Without a date to go on, Dowding continued, as usual, with the task at hand, namely, the night defences.

On the night of November 18-19, Dowding got home at nearly half past one in the morning, having been on yet another visit to his night fighter operational research station.[9] He found a letter awaiting him. It was from Portal, the recently appointed Chief of the Air Staff. In the most ordinary and matter-of-fact manner, and as if nothing were amiss, the letter said:

> The Secretary of the State has asked me to consult you about the announcement and the date of Douglas's taking over from you. There has unfortunately been a slight leakage to the Press which we all much regret, and we therefore want to announce a list of appointments, of which this will be one, on Monday, 18th. Douglas cannot be made available to take over until Monday week the 25th, and what I am asking is whether you would agree to carry on in command until the later date. In the announcement the date of the hand-over would be described as in the near future.

If an almost uncontrollable indignation wells up in the mind of the reader, even 60 years after the event, he may well be excused. And those feelings have nothing to do with the contents of the letter, which are suspect enough. A "slight leakage", bad enough if there had been one, smacks suspiciously like an excuse for delaying Douglas's assumption of command lest otherwise the change-over look indecently precipitate and the Press start asking embarrassing questions. The callous, unreflecting inconsiderateness beggars belief. At the same time, Portal's letter states for the first time a precise date.

On the very next day, November 20th, *The Daily Telegraph* carried on the front page a photograph of Sholto Douglas with the caption: FIGHTER COMMAND NEW CHIEF. (And one is expected to believe that the photograph was a "slight leakage"!)

As to Douglas, he has told us of his reaction when he learnt of his new appointment. He wrote in his memoirs: "Within the space of only a few days there was a sudden and rather breath-taking development. . . . I was to take the place of Dowding, who was to retire; and a day or so later there was an official announcement about the change." (We will have more to say about this "breath-taking development" in chapter 8.)

Douglas was rushed? Dowding was a widower, and his domestic affairs were managed by his sister, Hilda, in the house provided for him by the RAF. Her recollection of the event is as follows:

> It was all a terrific rush. I had to make my own arrangements for where I was going to live. And I had to plan for the servants who had been working for us. We were working against time; and up to the very last moment we were still packing things up in order to get out as quickly as possible. And then, for all the rush, when the new man arrived he decided not to live there.

Of these few days, Robert Wright, who was Dowding's personal assistant at the time, wrote:

> "In the face of all this, Dowding was completely withdrawn. He gave very little sign, even to those who were in closest contact with him, of what he was feeling. But to the more observant, or to those who, perhaps, knew him better than he realised, it was obvious he was unhappy and bewildered. It has always been my belief that he was in a state of shock."

It was only through Dowding's will that he was able to exercise that control of self that was the signal hallmark of his command in the Battle of Britain.

> *What though the field be lost?*
> *All is not lost; th'unconquerable will, . . .*
> *And courage never to submit or yield:*
> *And what is else not to be overcome?*

> — MILTON, *Paradise Lost*

## NOTES TO CHAPTER 6:

1. Air Chief Marshal Sir Kenneth Cross (then Squadron Leader. See *Straight and Level*, pp. 116-123) was at that time Group Controller at Leigh-Mallory's 12 Group headquarters. He also says: "It was noticeable that the difficulties that existed between 11 and 12 Groups did not occur between 10 and 11 Groups since Brand appeared to accept his supporting role to 11 Group, even though he had a front of his own across the western end of the Channel."

2. When Douglas wrote this directive, which, though backed by the authority of the Air Ministry, was nothing if not impertinent, he must by then have felt pretty sure of his ground.

3. Douglas's 'telling' Dowding what he should do to resolve the dispute between 11 and 12 Groups is a sure indication that, at this stage of the game he was involved in, he felt pretty sure of his ground.

4. The critics and enemies of Dowding, notably those situated in the Air Ministry, have accentuated this difference between Park and Leigh-Mallory in order to exploit Dowding's seeming lack of control of his Command in their campaign to get rid of him. They have failed to appreciate that Fighter Command, with its unique radar detection system, at the outset of its creation by Dowding, **could only operate if the tactical control of the battle were delegated to the Groups.** Dowding, as a responsible commander, delegated this responsibility — and it was onerous — to his sub-commanders in the belief, and trust, that the Group Commanders would accept their responsibilities and operate within the strategic parameters laid down by Dowding. This the Commanders of 10, 11, and 13 Groups did faithfully. This the Commander of 12 Group set his mind against, out of a jealous hatred of his Commander-in-Chief and of his colleague at 11 Group. In the pursuit of his ambition, abetted secretly by Sholto Douglas, he seized on to Bader's 'wing' idea, as a cowardly airman shot down in combat will seize a fellow's parachute, and suborned the Officer Commanding and Adjutant of 242 Squadron to promote his ambition.

   It is no part of my intention to analyse the Park/Leigh-Mallory dispute, or of Dowding's reluctance to resolve it. These disputes, even between the closest of allies, are common enough in war. The reader will be rewarded by studying many such instances in **Appendix "E"**. My personal conviction is that, if the dispute had taken place earlier, and gone so far as to threaten the success of Fighter Command's defence against the enemy, Dowding would have got rid of Leigh-Mallory. I also think that, knowing as he did at an earlier time of the failure of the Duxford wings, he should have posted Bader and 242 Squadron to 11 Group, and had Saul at 13 Group replace Leigh-Mallory.

5. What follows is taken from a letter by the historian A.J.P. Taylor, Beaverbrook's biographer and archivist, to *The Times* of January 22, 1970.

6. How is one to interpret this? Certainly not as a meek acquiescence, and bowing to the inevitable despite his previous statement about wanting to return to Fighter Command. The mask of Irony is evident. Have the scales finally fallen from his eyes?

7. Sinclair is nothing if not a politician. Little wonder that Dowding had scant respect for politicians — as , in fact, he told Churchill the very next day at their meeting. He would have agreed with "Tizard's belief that politics is, in Roseberry's words, 'an evil-smelling bog'."

8. A brief statement in the latest biography of Beaverbrook may throw some light on this event: "Beaverbrook used Churchill **as he used everyone else.**"

9. It was Fighter Command that established the first operational research section in the RAF. (See Joubert, *The Third Service*, p. 130.)

SIR ARCHIBALD SINCLAIR
SECRETARY OF STATE FOR AIR

SIR PETER MACDONALD, MP

IRENE WARD, MP

*Dowding's Enemies and Critics:*
THE POLITICIANS

MRAF LORD TRENCHARD

MRAF SIR JOHN SALMOND

ACM SIR CHARLES PORTAL

ACM SIR PHILIP
JOUBERT DE LA FERTÉ

# *Dowding's Enemies and Critics:*
# THE AIR MARSHALS

# CHAPTER 7

# *"Dowding Has Gone!"*

A review of Chapter 2 will remind us that Dowding was kept in doubt for two years, and even up to a dangerous phase of the Battle, as to when he would be retired. Then, in mid-August, his retirement date was cancelled, so that he expected to serve indefinitely — and not just serve, but serve as AOC-in-C of Fighter Command. Then, with a suddenness which beggars belief, he was ordered to relinquish his Command and vacate his official residence at a moment's notice.

Dowding had a right to expect a word of explanation of his release from the Service. He had the right to a word — not of thanks and gratitude: he was above such considerations — but of explanation, both from the Air Minister, Sir Archibald Sinclair, and from the Chief of the Air Staff, Sir Charles Portal. In fact, he received not a word from either.

Lest, however, we fall into the risk of taking too narrow a view of this question, let us not overlook the fact that Dowding's removal is not the only issue at stake here. Park was also removed. In Park's case there can be no question of retirement. His removal from his Command was nothing less than a demotion — given a different name, of course, such as a well-earned rest, but nevertheless a demotion. The removal of Dowding and of Park, within a month of each other, cannot therefore be considered except in the same context.

Before we examine this conundrum we feel it necessary to make clear that Dowding and Park were not isolated instances of removal from their positions — albeit the most illustrious — by officials of the Air Ministry and Air Council. Other officers had suffered, or were to suffer, the same fate. Four other officers, distinguished in their fields, were removed from their appointments, without explanation. They are: Air Chief Marshal Sir Edgar Ludlow-Hewitt, Wing Commander Sidney Cotton, Group Captain 'Sailor' Malan, and Air Chief Marshal Sir Basil Embry.[1] These circumstances are recorded here in order to drive home this important principle, that men who occupied high offices of State carried out deeds of questionable honesty without being held to account for their acts.

If those four officers were removed without much of a whimper, Dowding was another matter entirely. He was the most senior officer in the Royal Air Force, senior even to the CAS. His was the genius that had created Fighter Command and its whole defensive apparatus, and then defeated the hitherto invincible *Luftwaffe* in battle. Furthermore, he had earned the admiration and the support of Churchill.

Dowding has a further claim on our regard. It is generally held that once a general or air marshal crossed Churchill, Churchill did not forgive him and that officer's effective days were numbered. That fate did not befall Dowding. Dowding was Churchill's best informed and most obdurate opponent in the agonized debate over the sending of more fighters to France. Dowding's arguments prevailed. Churchill came round to his view. But Churchill never held it against Dowding. On the contrary, he recognized Dowding's qualities, and, if we can place any trust in the documents, including Churchill's own documented statements, he became his staunchest champion. Philip Swinton corroborates this judgement: "Neither [Lloyd George nor Churchill] could easily tolerate hostile criticism or factious opposition, but when finally persuaded they were wrong they conceded without ill-feeling."

That being the case, the questions multiply. There is no doubt but that Dowding had earned his retirement. On the other hand, he was only 58. (Churchill was 65 when he became Prime Minister.)[2] A man of Dowding's vigour and accomplishments had still much to offer. To cast him aside at this critical juncture of Britain's destiny is not an act showing confidence in the wealth of military leaders available in Britain at the time. Far from it: the war was just beginning and the British forces had suffered nothing but defeat. Dowding was the one and only leader who had accomplished something — and something of such heroism that, even **at the time,** as we have repeatedly stressed, it was recognized for what it truly was: one of the most decisive battles of the 20th Century, if not of Western Civilization.

The question we have to examine is how the power-brokers on the Air Council and the Air Staff succeeded in persuading Churchill in the face of his championship that Dowding had to go.

This issue is far more complicated than the question suggests. We propose to get to the bottom of the problem, which we insist, despite contrary claims, has never been satisfactorily tackled, let alone solved. The problem invites different approaches, which themselves call for different methods. The methods we have adopted are: critical, analytical, and synthetic.

In the first, we state and expose the 'reasons' put forward by previous writers. In the second, we subject the role of Churchill in Dowding's demise to a careful examination. And finally, we present our own interpretation of the events.

## 1. The 'Reasons': Other Writers

Many writers have speculated, *en passant,* in their account of Dowding or the Battle of Britain, on the why of Dowding's removal. Only two writers have pointedly developed speculation into a thesis. They are Group Captain E.B. Haslam, who published a 12-page article in 1981; and John Ray, who wrote a doctoral thesis on the subject which he rewrote for publication in 1994.To their number we will add two other historians whose opinions carry some weight. They are Dennis Richards and Sebastian Cox. We propose to draw up a list of the reasons they severally give; then, after dismissing the irrelevant items, subject to a critical study the reasons they propose in common.

### Haslam

In 1981 Group Captain Haslam was the Head of the Air Historical Branch in the Ministry of Defence. His article was a reply to a book and a series of articles by Len Deighton on the Battle of Britain, in which Deighton repeated the account given by Robert Wright in his biography of Dowding, that Dowding's dismissal came out of the blue via a telephone call from Sinclair. Haslam refutes Deighton's account as being "both simplistic and inaccurate".

The burden of Haslam's article is developed towards the end. It is that Dowding's removal had nothing to do with the dispute over tactics and the 'wings' dispute, and seemingly little to do with Dowding's failure to resolve the personal hostility between Park and Leigh-Mallory. It had to do almost entirely with Dowding's insuccess in finding counter-measures to the *Luftwaffe's* night attacks. We will summarize.

"The situation (he wrote) was desperate and desperate action was called for. . . ." The first action was the setting up of a committee headed by MRAF Sir John Salmond, "to undertake a thorough inquiry . . . on the preparation of night fighters."

Haslam quotes Joubert, who wrote years later in his memoirs, *The Third Service:* Dowding "would not listen to those who advocated an early diversion of effort to the solution of the night interception problem."

Haslam recounts that Dowding sent a stream of reports on night interception to the Air Ministry. His reports showed his own dissatisfaction — reports that were "characteristically honest, forthright and factual. But . . ." — and what a 'but'! — Dowding "was not moving fast enough for the Air Staff." Haslam sums up in these words: "What is clear is that Salmond . . . represented Dowding as the obstacle to new thinking and progress at Fighter Command."

## RAY

In 1994 John Ray published a book entitled *The Battle of Britain: New Perspectives.* Ray acknowledges his debt to Haslam's slender article. He bases most of his case on Salmond's campaign, and buttresses it with the findings of the separate committees on night defence set up by Churchill and the War Cabinet.

In the Introduction he conveniently itemizes the 'reasons' for Dowding's removal. "One aim of this book is to show that, in reality, there were seven reasons why Dowding was replaced in November 1940. Three existed even before the Battle of Britain started." They are:

- his age ("at 58 he was an old man");
- he had been AOC-in-C of Fighter Command for 4 years and was tired, and the need for a change was felt;
- his relations with the Air Ministry had been contentious since 1937; . . . he was stubborn (and) unwilling to cooperate;
- he failed to resolve the controversy over the use of Big Wings;
- he failed to appreciate the need "for an urgent response" to the night *Blitz*;
- "a more dynamic leader was sought for Fighter Command" by the end of the year when the RAF was moving to an aggressive role;
- Churchill and Beaverbrook came to appreciate that a new man was needed.

In his discussion of these reasons Ray fails to suggest a hierarchy of importance, with one significant exception. We may, however, dismiss as irrelevant and trivial the first, second and sixth items.

## RICHARDS

Richards published his Jubilee history of the Battle in 1989. In chapter 22, "Retrospect", he mentions some of the factors that led to Dowding's replacement, but he does not address it in a direct and coherent manner, as if it were an important issue. The reader has to read through a good deal of narrative in order to identify these reasons:

- The 'big' wing' controversy play a part, though only a part, in . . . the 'dismissal'.
- "Both commanders had been under enormous strain, and Park was visibly tired."
- "He had held his post for the exceptionally long period of four years".
- "the urgent demand was for success in countering the night bombing" . . . "and then . . . for offensive operations over the continent."

## Cox

On June 25, 1990, a symposium on the Battle of Britain was held under the joint auspices of the Royal Air Force Historical Society and the Royal Air Force Staff College Bracknell. The proceedings were published under the title, *The Battle Re-Thought*. In this volume the following remarks are attributed to Cox:

- "Dowding was not a good co-operator";
- "the problem of night defence, which he was thought not to be grasping with sufficient energy";
- "the dangerous deterioration in relations between two Group commanders".

Putting aside for the time being the ill feeling and sour relations that existed but between Park and Leigh-Mallory, which we consider later, we note three substantive reasons, common to all four writers, justifying the removal of Dowding from his command. They are these: 1) Dowding was at loggerheads with and did not co-operate with the Air Ministry; 2) Dowding's tactical handling of the air battles left much to be desired; 3) Dowding's failure to counter the night attacks.

We will examine them in that order.

## I) CO-OPERATION

It is difficult to know what Dowding's critics mean by the allegation that he did not co-operate; or, to extend the charge, that he was set in his views and was difficult to move; or, to go even further, that his uncooperativeness soured the relations between him and the Air Staff and Air Council. His critics are invariably short on concrete examples, except in the matter of night defences, though doubtless they could cite others if put to it.

The criticism suggests that if the Air Staff made a strong suggestion or recommendation to Fighter Command, and if Fighter Command rejected it, the Commander would be labelled as hostile to new ideas or a difficult man to deal with.

All writers, on both sides of the dispute, have commented on the terrible relations that existed between Fighter Command Headquarters and the Air Ministry. The causes of the quarrels were, firstly, the never-ending battle that Dowding had to wage to get what he needed for his Command; and secondly, the constant intrusions by the Air Staff on highly technical matters of air fighting of which they proved they knew nothing. Dowding himself is a witness to this side of the conflict:

> It would have been easy enough to remain on good terms with the Air Staff if one had been content to accept every ruling without question, but the Home Defence Organisation had been allowed to lapse into a state of grave inefficiency and I was continuously fighting to remedy the situation while there was yet time.

There, as we have stressed, we have the origin of the "awful rows" with the Air Staff. And it now becomes clear that Dowding, in having to create Fighter Command and build up its infrastructure and equipment from scratch, with all the highly technical training of personnel implied, was fighting two serious obstacles at once: one was Time; the other was an Air Ministry that was so set in its ways, or in its inertia, that it was almost impossible to make the officials responsible understand the needs of Fighter Command or the urgency of those needs. We saw in Chapter 1 the litany of Dowding's woes; here we need only repeat the substance of the allegation made against them:

> I can say without fear of contradiction that since I have held my present post I have dealt with or am in the process of dealing with a number of vital matters which generations of Air Staff have neglected for the past fifteen years.

It is equally clear that the Air Staff took Dowding's criticisms and complaints personally and conceived of a personal dislike of Dowding which forever, not only coloured their views, but determined their decisions.

Moreover, they tried to turn the tables and accuse Dowding of the very sins they were guilty of.

We quoted Dowding as saying that he felt he was expected to "accept every ruling without question." The very notion that the Air Staff, when making a "ruling" or recommendation, should expect the Air Officer Commanding-in-Chief to accept it "without question" belongs to the order of human organization which was formerly found commonly in British military circles and which has been responsible in the past for most of Britain's worst military disasters. It is a cousin to the mentality which we stigmatized earlier as characterizing dinosaurs and ostriches. In this case it is a feature of authoritarian organizations which, by their very nature, see themselves as always right, and hence incapable of learning from events unfolding before their eyes.

There is worse. The Air Ministry appoints a Commander-in-Chief; and with the command it confers an almost absolute authority to conduct the affairs falling within the defined areas of his command in the manner he judges to be the most fitting to the occasion. That authority is conferred on him because he is deemed the best suited to carry out the operational mission of his command.

The Air Ministry proposes a course of action and the Commander is obliged to give it serious study. To do otherwise would be irresponsible. When the Commander receives a letter from the Air Staff, he does not reply offhandedly with an expression of his own views. He passes it on to his Air Staff with a request for their considered views, founded in experience and other evidence. Only then does Dowding reply with a statement of his course of action and the reasons for pursuing his own policy. Of this, of course, the Air Ministry is already fully apprised. The Air Ministry, knowing it is proposing measures inconsistent with those of Fighter Command and its Commander, has no legitimate complaint if they are rejected.

In the event that there is constant disagreement between the Air Ministry and a Commander-in-Chief, the Air Ministry has no option but to remove the Commander. That was always Dowding's position. Every Commander is in the same situation, and takes up his command knowing it. Dowding told Newall that was his position. But he added the significant rider that the Air Ministry, in removing a Commander, had better be right. It is our firm contention that the Air Ministry in its disputes with Dowding was nearly always in the wrong. When it discovered how much it had been wrong, its dislike of

Dowding festered and became a vindictiveness that, first, resolved on his removal, and only then stimulated a search for reasons to justify the deed.

There is still more to this question of uncooperativeness that has not received the attention it deserves.

The Air Staff's interest in Fighter Command and its operations — even when inspired in the minds of a very few of its officers by an ardour to help Fighter Command in its task of the defence of Britain — expressed in the form of advice, suggestions, recommendations, and even, at times, of instructions, amounted often enough in the eyes of the Fighter Command Air Staff to interference in the direction of vital operational affairs. One cannot help but ask: Why did they interfere, and interfere so much? (Let us recall the expressions of complete confidence in Dowding's direction of the Battle and of his Command uttered by both Sinclair and Newall.)

This interference takes on a peculiar colour when considered in the light of operations in Malta, in North Africa, in West Africa, in the Indian and Burmese theatres, and in Malaya. Was the Air Staff of the Air Ministry constantly looking over the shoulder of the commanders and issuing suggestions or even directives to them? Of course they didn't. Perhaps those operational theatres were too remote for them to know what was going on. But the Battle of Britain was taking place over their very heads. Not only that, but Fighter Command headquarters was only a few miles down the road from Whitehall. The temptation for the mandarins was irresistible.

Yet the principle remains the same, in peace and *a forteriori* in war: a commander is appointed to a command with plenary powers. If he loses the confidence of the ultimate authority, he must be removed. Otherwise he must be supported, aided and encouraged in every way possible to carry out his responsibilities. **Of course** the Air Staff co-operated with Fighter Command. **Of course** Dowding wrote many harsh letters to the Air Ministry. But when all is said and done, the Air Staff were signally negligent in their failure to rise above their personal prejudices and to give to Dowding and Fighter Command the full and unstinting collaboration that the situation demanded. Having neglected the air defences of Great Britain for many years, they suddenly appoint themselves experts in the field whose opinions are to be heeded.

## II) DAY TACTICS

We have already examined the controversy over tactics in Chapter 3; all that is needed here is a summary.

The 'big wing' theory of defence espoused by Douglas and Leigh-Mallory would permit the German bombers to reach their targets unchallenged, and even inflict heavy damage, provided the defenders could take such a heavy toll of the retreating bombers that they would not want to try it often.

Douglas Bader's own idea was that as soon as a build-up of German formations was detected assembling over Northern France, his wing of five Squadrons should be 'scrambled' and sent south to intercept them. This manoeuvre would give his wing plenty of time in which to gain the height judged essential by Bader to gain the tactical advantage; and it would also give 11 Group's squadrons time enough to gain height for the defence of their own airfields.

Both ideas have been dismissed as either dangerous or impracticable. In particular, the Douglas/Leigh-Mallory idea is preposterous, if not lunatic.

Bader's idea would seem to have much merit, superficially. Its defects stem from an ignorance of, or an ignoring of, the very system of radar control without which Fighter Command would have been destroyed in the first few weeks of fighting. In either case, his idea, while inspired by an admirable fervour to get at the 'Hun', was a grave error. In the first place, there was no knowing, while Bader was leading his wing south, whether the German formation over France was going to break up into a number of feints and major attacks, all headed in different directions over England. One who was there, Alan Deere, was in no doubt about the folly of such a move.

> The sober truth is that, at this stage of the war, the information from the radar chain was neither sufficiently complete nor sufficiently reliable to permit the added option of the policy with success. Although the initial build-up of a raid was quite often reported over the Pas de Calais, the strength and composition could not be accurately determined.

Secondly, once the wing had penetrated well into the 11 Group area of control, there was no way in which 11 Group sector controllers could direct the Bader wing to intercept the enemy formation or formations, since they were not equipped with the same R/T apparatus. And finally, bereft of control, Bader and his wing would be 'on their own', seeking their prey wherever they could. Incredibly, as we have seen, that is exactly what Bader wanted! He wanted to escape from the control of the ground controllers and go off as the whim took him in pursuit of an elusive enemy. This scheme of Bader's was, in the word of Dowding, when he heard of it very much later: 'Monstrous!'.

Other questions must be asked. Was Bader's wing the only wing that was to be sent south? Would even Bader's 60 fighters be sufficient to oppose, say, 300 attackers? How many other wings would be ordered south? How — this is the key question — how would they be controlled? If they cannot be controlled, how would they be prevented from interfering with each other's operations? And finally, if wings from 12 Group — and maybe from 10 Group as well — were sent to intercept the incoming raiders, what is the point of having an 11 Group, whose sole function, according to Bader, is to protect its own airfields? What would be the point of having airfields there at all?

We have already demonstrated the failure of the Duxford wings to take a toll of the enemy. That failure, allied to these objections to Bader's and Douglas's ideas, and considered in the light of Douglas's own recognition of the success of Park's handling of his resources, make nonsense of the claim that they were grounds for Dowding's removal.

These compelling arguments do not, however, mean that Dowding's rivals and enemies did not use them against him. It is in this context that we must ask the question: What were Dowding's views? Did he express an opinion? He did; and they are stated with conviction:

> I thought (he told his biographer) that the . . . discussion [i.e., the October 17 conference] about whether we should use three, four or five squadron wings was so simple and inconsequential that it hardly deserved a long statement. . . . It became obvious after a while that several people in responsible positions did hold opinions that were contrary to mine. And since, in their eyes, I seemed to be refusing to listen to what they had to say I was sentenced without trial. There's no doubt at all in my mind now that it was on that subject — the big wings — that Park and I were judged and condemned.

It is not difficult to see the impression it had produced on his mind when reflecting on it. What is more difficult to see is how, thirty years after the Battle, Dowding did not understand the role that the failure of the night defences played in his removal. It is to that issue that we now turn.

### III) THE NIGHT BATTLE

The failure of Fighter Command to mount an effective defence against the night attacks on Britain's cities in the winter of 1940-41 is, in the eyes of the writers who have dealt with the issue, the paramount reason for Dowding's dismissal. The whole question calls, therefore, for a more thorough investigation than it has hitherto received.

The case against Dowding is based mostly on the findings and recommendations of two separate committees on night defence, set up respectively by Beaverbrook at the Ministry of Aircraft Production, and by the War Cabinet — and especially, be it noted, on the first.

The former, chaired by MRAF Sir John Salmond, had three meetings, on September 16–18, and a report was completed on the 18th. A number of comments are required before we examine the report and Dowding's response.

First, Beaverbrook and Salmond deserve praise for their early recognition of the inadequate condition of the British defences against night aerial attacks, and for their initiative in taking action to remedy the deficiencies. Those deficiencies were, of course, glaring, in the light of the failure of the Air Ministry to have made any provision to meet such attacks.[3]

Second, all the nine regular members of the Committee were drawn from the Air Ministry and the Ministry of Aircraft Production, who described "the existing night fighting organisation." One wonders why a Fighter Command staff officer was not called upon.

Third, a number of officers, both air force and scientific, were invited "to give evidence" at the three meetings. Among them were the Station Commander of Drem, who was hardly engaged in the battle, and a squadron leader of a Blenheim night fighter squadron — of which more later. Dowding himself was not called until the third day; and Park did not appear at all, although AV-M Sir Quentin Brand, AOC 10 Group, did.

Fourth, it is noted that the deliberations — for that is what the meetings amounted to: they cannot be called an inquiry — occupied only 2 days, and that the committee did not see fit to visit any of the night fighter squadrons, or even the Night Fighter Interception Unit. Whereas the committee appreciated the virtue of haste, it lacked the greater virtue of thoroughness.

Finally, none of the members of the committee had any expertise in night aerial defence. These defects showed up in their report. For example, it is noted that two measures recommended improving the Blenheim as a night fighter, despite the evidence of two Blenheim pilots that the aircraft "was too slow", and "was not a good night fighter". Another recommendation urged "specialisation of existing 8-gun fighter squadrons in night work", in the face of evidence that "the 8-gun fighter was worthless [without AI] unless searchlights could usefully operate."

On the other hand, some of the committee's recommendations were eminently sensible; e.g. the formation of a special Night Fighter Staff Section within Fighter Command; the transfer of experienced night flying pilots to night fighter squadrons; and the acceleration of the development of the Beaufighter and Mark IV AI.

Salmond submitted his report to the Air Council. The Air Council, in its turn, having accepted and approved it, sent it with a covering letter to Dowding on September 25th, asking for his views. Critics of Dowding seem often to have overlooked that he had at his disposal a cadre of competent staff officers. In all such cases as the one we are examining, Dowding would pass the report to his Senior Air Staff Officer with a request for comments grounded in established facts. When he received the information he needed he would be in a position to draft a reply. Of course, Dowding frequently used the first person, because he was expressing his views, and because he had the ultimate responsibility for those views and the policies and actions based upon them. Dowding submitted his reply no less than two days later, on the 27th.

Salmond's document, entitled NIGHT AIR DEFENCE, comprises twenty-one "conclusions" in eighteen paragraphs. In preparing his reply, Dowding marked Salmond's recommendations in the margin, in blue pencil, with a tick, a cross, or a question mark; or made no mark. Some commentators, Ray among them, have suggested that these signs meant, respectively, that he agreed or disagreed with the recommendation in question, or was undecided in his own mind. A reading of Dowding's reply to the report, and a close comparison of his comments with the recommendations, show that such an interpretation is not so simple. Dowding, on his copy, has marked a cross beside ten, a tick beside three, a question mark beside five; and three are unmarked. Of the unmarked ones, Dowding's reply shows: one agreement, with modification; one disagreement; and one is deemed unrelated to the issue. Of the recommendations marked with a question mark, Dowding agrees with one, disagrees with two, finds one unrelated, and does not understand one. Of others with which he disagreed, three had to do with modifications to the obsolescent Blenheim and the use of single-seat eight-gun day fighters for night interception (two and one).

In general, it might be said that the other, non-technical, conclusions reached by Salmond's committee tended toward a division and dispersal of Fighter Command's responsibilities in matters of night defence. On Dowding's side, it might be concluded that he opposed recommendations which seemed to complicate his task; and "cordially" approved those measures which promoted the Beaufighter and AI, and aircrew training and efficiency.[4]

As Dowding marked the paragraphs of his copy of the Salmond Report, so his letter of reply was glossed by someone in the Air Ministry. Two comments are worth quoting.

Salmond's recommendation no. 13 reads: "The establishment of pilots and AI operators in night fighter squadrons should be balanced so that each officer pilot has an officer AI operator and each NCO pilot an NCO AI operator. Pilots and operators should be trained together at the existing OTU. . . ." Dowding comments thus: "I see no point in this recommendation, which would merely add to the existing serious difficulties in the production of AI operators." Perhaps Salmond and the Air Council were horrified at the idea of NCOs giving directions to officers. (Later, in Bomber Command, it became a matter of survival.) Dowding shows himself far more realistic and progressive-minded. But the marginal (Air Staff) comment is revealing. It says "Obstruction(?). Why". Dowding was often accused of being obstructive to Air Ministry recommendations, but one fails to comprehend the accusation here.

Paragraph no. 2 recommends: "The operation of filtering should be transferred from Fighter Command to Group Headquarters in order to reduce delay." Dowding replied as follows:

> The question of decentralisation of filtering was raised by Air Marshal Sir Philip Joubert in a minute dated 11th January, 1940, and was finally disposed of (I had hoped) by my letters FC/S.18082 dated 17th and 31st January, 1940. . . . At any rate my last mentioned letter terminated the correspondence. The matter has no particular connection with night interception, and the arguments which were adduced against it in January of this year still hold good. I request, therefore, that I may be spared the necessity of discussing the question afresh.

If this is an instance of Dowding's not co-operating, or of not suffering fools gladly, it is hardly surprising, perhaps, that there is no comment attached to this reply.[5]

One of the irregular things about Salmond's committee, which clearly escaped many people's approving gaze, is that the whole process occupied only two and a half days. Further, the meetings were held in the Ministry of Aircraft Production in London. Salmond committed the most egregious of the type of offences usually attributed to what is termed 'officialdom'. They carried out their assigned task in two days. One is tempted to ask: What could they find out in two days? They completed their so-called inquiries, and made judgments and recommendations which implied a certain muted criticism of Dowding and Fighter Command. Above all, they did not intimate whether their recommendations were meant to constitute a definitive answer to the problems of night defence, or only a provisional and stop-gap solution.

Salmond's committee erred, we have suggested, in not seeking the real experts' views — those of the Air Staff of Fighter Command, of the night fighter squadrons, and above all, of the scientists. This failure, in Dowding's eyes, would have constituted the gravest offence of all. For, as we have stressed before with some insistence, it is the men and women engaged in actual operations against the enemy, and the scientific minds that had helped to create this highly technical arm, who are in the best position to know their strengths and weaknesses, as well perhaps as the enemy's. The principal war function of the Air Ministry is to fulfil the needs of the operational commands and their supporting organizations. In order to do that they must constantly consult and confer with the commands. That is precisely the principle that dictated Dowding's and Fighter Command Headquarters' relations with their Groups, stations and squadrons.

It soon became clear that Salmond's report was not going to achieve the results hoped for. It was this setback that impelled Salmond to write his demanding letter to Churchill on October 5: "Recently on Lord Beaverbrook's instructions, I have carried out an inquiry into Night Air Defence, the result of which, together with what has since occurred, make a change, in my view, imperative."[6]

Churchill wanted to satisfy himself; and acted immediately to set up a new, and more authoritative, committee. But whereas Salmond's committee, and Fighter Command, were concerned solely with the means of winning the night battle, Churchill, as a politician, and above all as the Prime Minister, was driven by concerns about the morale of the people and their ability to withstand incessant night bombing. He need not have worried — at least not at this stage; but the political worries seeped, or rather poured, into the Air Ministry — after all, its head was a politician — and affected their judgment.

Churchill called his committee the Night Air Defence Committee, and it had its first meeting on October 7 under his chairmanship. The committee comprised seventeen members — Cabinet members, Air Council and Air Staff offices, and Government officials. Dowding was a prominent member and attended all the meetings.

Three other meetings were held: on October 21 and November 19 under Churchill's chairmanship, and on December 9 with Beaverbrook in the chair. These dates — two weeks, four weeks, and three weeks apart — do not exactly suggest the idea of urgency, despite the heavy raids which took place on November 6 and 7, the devastation of Coventry on November 14, and the major raid on London on November 15.

The decisions and recommendations of the first three meetings completely vindicated Dowding's views. On October 10, twelve of the eighteen recommendations dealt with radar detection and interception and AI-equipped Beaufighters. On October 21, of the twenty-nine recommendations, the first seventeen dealt with and approved the same and other related measures. On November 19, it is the same story: twelve of the twenty items approved the work done and progress achieved in the use and development of radar in the detection, tracking and destruction of enemy aircraft by fighters and anti-aircraft artillery.

These deliberations produced a number of other recommendations: wire-carrying shells, balloons carrying explosive charges released in the path of enemy bombers, aerial mines sown in the path of enemy bombers, airborne searchlights with attendant single-engined fighters, and searchlights in clusters to guide fighters.[7] These recommendations Dowding pooh-poohed. Some were implemented, but without success. However, when Douglas replaced Dowding he was required to pursue these measures. Douglas reported on them in his *Despatch*. They all proved to be will-o'-the-wisps and were progressively abandoned. Douglas failed to concede that Dowding had been right all along.

The meeting of the Air Defence Committee held on October 21 was more immediately significant. The Air Ministry reported that instructions had already been issued to Fighter Command, over Dowding's objections, that, "as an experiment, three 8-gun Fighter Squadrons should be earmarked for night fighting". The squadrons assigned by Dowding were Hurricane squadrons.

These differences of opinion between Dowding and the Air Staff and Air Council, exposed as they were personally to Churchill's view, would appear to give some substance to the Air Staff's repeated complaint about Dowding's stubbornness and unwillingness to co-operate. The reality may be somewhat different.

The pugnacious side of Churchill revelled in a good knock-down argument between opposing views in committees he chaired, up to the highest levels. More, he actively stimulated and stoked them. He provoked and welcomed opposition. But there was more to that behind his interrogations and hectoring. He used such means as a weapon to cut through waffle and to expose unpreparedness in order to get at the facts, the truth. He surely subscribed to the French dictum: *Du choc des opinions jaillit la lumière.*

There is no point in examining these committees further, for no matter what they recommended the decision had already been taken by the Air Council to get rid of Dowding.

Let us now turn to a comparison of the results achieved . We have records of both the Hurricane night fighters and the AI-equipped Beaufighters. We are also able to present the views of several night fighter aircrews, and a number of works on radio countermeasures. Two of the aircrews are a fighter pilot on one of the Hurricane squadrons, and the AI operator of a Beaufighter.

One of the three designated Hurricane squadrons was 85 Squadron. It became a night fighter squadron, in 12 Group, on October 23rd. Its commanding officer was Squadron Leader Peter Townsend, one of the most skilled pilots and accurate shots in Fighter Command at the time. Of the Hurricane itself, as a night fighter, he has this to say:

> About the Hurricane there was practically nothing that could remotely qualify it as a specialized night fighter. . . . While the Hurricane was a formidable day fighter . . . it was not designed as a specialized night fighter and would never properly perform as one. What the Hurricane did not possess told even more heavily against its suitability as a night fighter. First, it was not fitted with a radar set. Had it been possible to install one, there would be need as well for a radar operator. But the Hurricane was a single-seater. Single-engined too, which put it at high risk in case of engine failure at night.

After several months as leader of his squadron on night interceptions, Townsend himself shot down, on February 25th, 1941, the one and only enemy aircraft destroyed by 85 Squadron. A few weeks later, in April, his squadron was converted to and became operational on Havocs, a twin-engined aircraft which, like the Beaufighter, had a radar operator/navigator, was equipped with AI radar, and armed with four 20mm cannon. Townsend destroyed an enemy bomber just two days after becoming operational. After a month he sums up the situation in these terms:

Since October 1940 we had spent six months groping blindly for the enemy in the dark. . . . In the past four weeks, with Havocs, AI and GCI, we had downed two of the enemy with four 'probables' and six damaged. . . . (We) felt certain at last that we were on our way to attaining the standard set by our onetime commander in chief Dowding, who on the very eve of 85's conversion from day to night fighters, had vowed that Fighter Command would never rest "until we can locate, pursue, and shoot down the enemy by day and by night."

The implied criticism of those responsible, muted though it is, comes through clearly: "at last we were on our way to attaining the standard set by . . . Dowding." Only 'on our way': what was the situation in fact?

Townsend is writing about the events of early May 1941. Dowding had pinned his entire faith, founded as it was on the best scientific evidence and operational research[8] available until then, on the twin-engined fighter equipped with AI, armed with cannons, and guided by GCI. Despite Townsend's optimism, the actual results seemed poor. He reported that the "two horrible massacres [of April 16 and 19, 1941] were a measure of the continuing failure of the British night defence . . . to protect the civilian population."

This acknowledged failure becomes dramatic, and tragic, when we learn the result of the defences on the night of May 10/11. After seven hours of bombardment by a force of over 500 bombers against London alone, "The Luftwaffe lost only eight aircraft that night."

Some writers have blamed the failure on the defects of the Beaufighter itself. It is true that it had the teething troubles often associated with a new design. Then again, the Night Air Defence Committee heard at its meeting of October 7 that the "production of Beaufighters has been completely stopped by enemy action". But production was resumed and four or five Beaufighters were expected that same week. The problems were overcome, so that by April 1941 there were six Beaufighter night squadrons in action, in addition to Townsend's Havoc squadron.

The reasons for the failure of the defence, on the technical side, are made clear by C.F. Rawnsley in his book *Night Fighter*. Rawnsley was the radar operator of a Beaufighter of 604 Squadron, whose pilot was the celebrated John Cunningham. As early as September 1940 Rawnsley wrote: "I could not help feeling that . . . the future belonged to the man who could make the new radar sets function as they were supposed to." (The reader is invited to read that opinion again, very carefully.) In early 1941 he was bemoaning the fact that there were still plenty of problems with the airborne radar. Indeed, Rawnsley's book constitutes a record of the failure both of the AI to work as it should, from one mark to the next, and of the operators to use it to the best possible advantage. So ineffective or unreliable were the early marks of airborne radar, and so untrained the operators, that it was almost two months, from the end of September to November 20th, before Cunningham and Rawnsley had their first successful night interception. But these were early days in AI development and, let us insist, in operator training. And Dowding was toiling against insuperable odds.

The continued failure of the night defences under Sholto Douglas, from December to April, cannot be attributed to the Beaufighters or to the aircrews themselves whose devoted efforts were exemplary. It can be laid to the charge only of the AI equipment, and beyond that to the inadequate training of the operators — and that implies, may we add, lack of leadership from the top.

Denis Richards, among other historians, is emphatic in his insistence that this was the sole visible answer to the problem: "Though the Air Ministry rightly neglected no field of experiment, the real hope for the future depended, as Dowding and Pile constantly stressed, on perfecting and producing certain radar apparatus." Richards continues: "In essence, our chances of success now rested on the speed with which the new radar apparatus and the Beaufighters could be brought into service."

It cannot be doubted that the designers and manufacturers of the AI sets devoted all their skills and energies into improving the equipment. From September to November and December respectively, Dowding and Park submitted to the Air Ministry a stream of reports devoted to their efforts to combat the night raids. Douglas and Leigh-Mallory, during the worst six months of the *Blitz*, submitted none that we have been able to discover.

In his *Despatch* on Fighter Command's night operations during the time when he was the AOC-in-C Fighter Command — written in 1948 — Douglas acknowledges that the AI-equipped night fighter had the major role in meeting the enemy threat to British cities. On the other hand he is at pains to claim 'success' for his idea of using Hurricanes — while conceding that their only successes were obtained on moonlight nights.

What were the actual results? The sole figures given by Douglas in his *Despatch* are these:

Sept. - Dec.:   4 e/a destroyed by fighters (1 by AI)
March:   11 e/a destroyed by s/e fighters
11 e/a destroyed by AI fighters
21 e/a destroyed by guns & balloons
May 10:   19 e/a destroyed by s/e fighters
4 e/a destroyed by AI fighters
4 e/a destroyed by guns.

We recall that Townsend claimed that on this night of May 10/11, only eight enemy aircraft were destroyed *in toto*. Who was correct? Robert Watson-Watt, who had no axe to grind — except perhaps to put the successes of radar-equipped fighters in a good light — gives these figures, inadequately broken down (H = Hurricane, S=Spitfire, B=Beaufighter):

|  | Fighters (H/S) (B) | Guns | Balloons | Other |
|---|---|---|---|---|
| Sept.7–Nov. 13 | • 8 • | 54 | 4 | — |
| March | • 22 • | 17 | | |
| April | • 48 • | 39 | | |
| May | • 96 • | 31 | | • 10 • |

These figures are confirmed by Denis Richards in his official history, *Royal Air Force 1939-1945*, whose work preceded that of Watson-Watt by four years.

What were the real losses by the *Luftwaffe*? How many of their aircraft were actually destroyed by the defences? We have studied the day-by-day accounts given in *The Blitz: Then and Now* (vol. 2), and arrived at the following figures (S/E= single-engined):[9]

|  | Total | Beaufighters | S/E fighters | Defiants[10] |
|---|---|---|---|---|
| March | 20 | 8 | 2 | – |
| April | 47 | 15 | 5 | 9 |
| May | 73 | 22 | 2 | 13 |

These figures correspond closely to those given by Richards and Watson-Watt. But they do not correspond closely to Douglas's figures. Indeed, Douglas's figures, especially those of enemy aircraft destroyed by single-engined fighters, and the figures for the disastrous raid of May 10th, bear no resemblance to the facts. And let us not forget that Douglas wrote his account in 1946.[11]

Douglas would further have the reader believe that he, Douglas, was the architect of the successes achieved by Fighter Command in the night battle; for he manages to write his report without discussing tactics, without touching on the obstacles facing the aircrews, without dealing with the development and production difficulties experienced by the designers of the Beaufighter and AI radar, and without seemingly being aware of the training problems of AI operators.

The key to success in night interceptions, given the equipment at the disposal of the aircrews, lay in the intelligence of the AI operators. Three unchallengeable witnesses to this contention are an operational research scientist and two pilots.

The scientist is Sir Henry Tizard, who testified: "When the Service AI's were properly tested in the air, under scientifically controlled conditions, it was found that the real trouble was that they squinted, and that an aircraft which was believed, by the indications of the instruments, to be straight ahead, was in fact on the beam."

One of the pilots is Basil Embry. When he was appointed Station Commander of RAF Wittering in early 1941, one of his squadrons was 25 Squadron, a Beaufighter night fighter squadron. He knew its potential and he "took an immediate interest in its training and preparation for intensive night operations". His first discovery was "a lack of ability in certain navigators to operate the AI sets efficiently." The second was his conclusion that "more than half the success in night fighting lay in the intelligent use of the AI." This view was clinched when Embry had the inimitable Squadron Leader David Atcherley posted in as the 25 Squadron commander. Atcherley, with the Group AI technical officer, Flight Lieutenant J.H. Hunter-Tod as his set operator, "a man of exceptional intelligence and technical ability", intercepted and shot down an enemy bomber on their first or second patrol.

The sequel is pure Embry. He and Atcherley 'raided' nearby Cambridge University one Sunday afternoon and 'conscripted' a small number of science undergraduates. "We worked hard at their training, and the very first time one of them went on a night patrol, it ended with the interception and shooting down of an enemy bomber."

The second pilot, another witness to the slapdash attitude toward the training of aircrews, and especially to the attitude of some RAF station commanders, is Roderick Chisholm, a successful night fighter pilot. He wrote in *Cover of Darkness:*

> I visited fighter-training stations, and I learnt that there was another aspect of staff work. Stations had been left much to themselves to train night-fighter crews as they thought fit, and in consequence the headquarters assumption of authority to direct policy and methods was unpopular. Enthusiasts—many of them in those days inexperienced in operations—had worked out their own plans, and they did not like changing them. But some had to be changed. There was a limit to the flying hours which could be devoted to the training of each crew, and into this time had to be packed as many as possible of the lessons learnt, in this new realm, since the war began. This work was as interesting as it was at times frustrating. One station commander would listen politely and act, another would only listen, and one, I recall, would hardly deign even to listen.

This account speaks volumes about the non-existent leadership at the top, at the time of Douglas's command. It was Tizard's role, however, that was the decisive one. "The successful defence of airborne radar through a long period of disappointment was an almost personal achievement of Tizard alone." And Watson-Watt's second-in-command at Bawdsey, Dr. Edward G. Bowen, has said: "He (Tizard) was always keenly aware of the problems and clearly indicated the need for adequate training of personne . . . However, the business was plagued with a headquarters staff which was largely ignorant of the problems and requirements, and Tizard's clear view of the problem did not get across to the people concerned. This was largely the reason why the successful use of airborne radar was delayed until 1941 and 1942."

Douglas makes the assertion in his *Despatch* that "if the enemy had not chosen to pull out [in May], we should soon have been inflicting such casualties on his night bombers that the continuance of his night offensive would have been impossible (para. 51)."

Despite the disastrous failure of the defences on the night of May 10/11, (the last major raid of the *Blitz* and one of the worst raids of all on London) the successes of the AI fighters in this month went a good part of the way to justifying Douglas's opinion, even if we cannot but regard it as unwholesomely subjective.

But if subjectivity is to attain to a degree of offensiveness, in the place of the objectivity and detachment which his position called for, it is in his failure to give credit to all to whom it was due. If the figures we have culled from *The Blitz: Then and Now* (p. 249) are correct, the credit for them, the figures and the claims alike, belongs overwhelmingly to Tizard, Watson-Watt and Dowding. Yet Douglas does not give them so much as a passing mention.

These results totally vindicate Dowding's early work and insistence on the AI night interceptor to the exclusion of the other defences. Dowding toiled and battled, and was convinced that he had found the answer to the problem. He wrote in his *Despatch:* "I had to leave the development of night interception at a very interesting stage; but it is perhaps not too much to say that, although much remained to be done, the back of the problem had been broken."

We have had occasion to quote Haslam who wrote — and we repeat it: "there was no dramatic improvement in the performance of our night fighters when Sholto Douglas took over from Dowding." The reader is, however, flabbergasted by the sentence with which Haslam introduces this opinion. What he writes is: "**As might have been expected** there was no dramatic improvement. . . ." [Our emphasis.] Haslam fails to enlighten us and explain why no improvement was expected, if that was, **in his view,** the precise reason why Douglas was chosen to replace Dowding. And yet, as Haslam had written earlier, Dowding "was not moving fast enough for the Air Staff", and "the results were not coming fast enough to satisfy either the Air Staff or the politicians". Haslam, so intent on 'nailing' Dowding for his failure to counter the night attacks, is unaware of this glaring contradiction. He has obviously gone over to the political side.

The claims made by Haslam, Ray, Richards and Cox, writing long after the events we are examining, are attempts either to explain the failure of the night defences or to posit a pretext for the removal of Dowding. In the case of Salmond, his Report might now be seen, together with Douglas's hearing of October 17 into the use of big wings, as inquiries, justifiable in some respects, but in other respects conceived to the end of putting Dowding in the wrong and of discrediting his leadership.[12]

We have touched on some of the operational and technical problems which had to be solved in order to mount an effective defence. We now need to answer the questions: Who were the people responsible for the research, manufacture, testing and installation of the radar equipment? We quote a recent study:

> The technical complexity of providing for the night defences dwarfed
> those of daylight operations. Three additional weapon and detection systems
> were required. First, it was critical to have a night fighter with a two-man
> crew, capable of carrying a powerful armament. . . . Second, to guide the
> fighter to within 3 to 4 miles of its prey, there had to be an entirely different
> type of ground based radar, GCI or Ground Controlled Interception. Fin-
> ally, it was imperative that the night fighter be equipped with an airborne
> Aircraft Interception (AI) radar, capable of taking up where the GCI left off,
> steering the interceptor from 20,000 to just under 500 feet from the target.
> . . . Of these three systems, the most vital was AI radar; without it few night
> interceptions were possible.

It is abundantly clear: the testing and production of the Beaufighter and
its armament, of GCI, and of AI were entirely the responsibility of the Air
Ministry. Only the training of the AI operators fell within the jurisdiction of
Fighter Command.

The historical record confirms this assessment of the problem of night
defence. From 1936 on it had been the concerted policy agreed to by the Air
Ministry and the Air Officer Commanding-in-Chief of Fighter Command
to give almost absolute priority to the day defensive system. The decision
and the policy were, indeed, more or less dictated by technical and by
strategic factors.[13]

Technically, before 1936, there were no means of early warning, so the case
for interception did not exist. As for AI, the first successfully condensed and
compacted set — what Watson-Watt called "tabloid radar" — was constructed and flown only in mid-1939. "It was on 1 June 1939 that a complete AI set,
with all the elements substantially embodied in AI Marks I to IV, flew in a
Battle aircraft." Although the potential threat of night attack was recognized,
and though Watson-Watt and his teams at Bawdsey Manor and elsewhere
toiled to perfect and improve the equipment, they could not overcome the
immense difficulties involved in view of the lateness of the hour and the
shortness of time.[14]

Strategically, it was recognized by the most enlightened and objective
thinkers — and they include Tizard and Dowding — that Britain could be
defeated by the *Luftwaffe* in a daylight air war, but not by night assaults,
however bad the damage might be. "Failure to win the battle against the night
bomber might prolong a war; failure to win the Battle of Britain would
probably have lost one."

Night fighting received less attention in prewar years than any other
phase of aerial warfare development. This was true not only in Germany, but

also in the Allied nations. This omission was to handicap both Germany and Britain in defending themselves against night bombing from the air. Night fighting techniques were largely developed from 1940 onward, and the full significance of the night fighter force was not appreciated by the German High Command until it was almost too late.

One historian, in a recent study, has itemized the causes of the failure to mount an effective defence against the night attacks as follows:

> In large measure, the delay in developing a successful AI was the direct result of the shortage of personnel and time. With much of Bawdsey's staff devoted to completing the chain in the last eighteen months of peace, Bowen's group suffered. Nor was any outside assistance sought until it was too late to influence the course of events during the *Blitz*.
>
> The Air Ministry was equally ignorant [of the complexities of the development phase of the AI programme]. No one, not even Watson-Watt or Rowe, objected to turning Bowen's research team into what amounted to a small-scale manufacturer.
>
> [By] December 1938 it was accepted that radar research would have to be moved from Bawdsey . . . . Ironically, Bawdsey did not experience a single major attack during the war. Yet, what Watson-Watt did instead was perhaps as destructive as the most devastating air attack. Watson-Watt decided that . . . the radar researchers should move to Dundee and use the existing university college facilities. . . . The move from Bawdsey crippled AI research at a critical moment and ended any chance that an effective night defence system would be in operation during 1940.
>
> On 10 November [1940] Tizard met with Rowe and Watson-Watt at Dundee and suggested that they enlist the aid of GEC Research Laboratories, and perhaps some other industrial research laboratories.
>
> Watson-Watt disparaged the capabilities of the private companies [to conduct primary research] and Tizard did not disagree. But the latter told Dowding, in his report of the meeting: "You may have guessed rightly that one of my objectives in suggesting this plan is to provide some much need-ed competition to DCD [i.e. Watson-Watt] and his staff . . . ." Dowding concurred with Tizard's recommendation because he saw his chief trouble at the moment as being the complete stagnation in the fitting of AI, and added EMI to Tizard's list of manufacturers to be brought into the AI picture. This exchange of correspondence marks the turning point in AI research; for it would be EMI that would eventually make the improvements that would turn the radar device into an effective weapon system.[15]

To sum up, the Air Ministry had no policy relating to night defence, and hence had provided for no means of aerial defence againt night attacks, beyond a few antiquated anti-aircraft guns. In its failure to give to Dowding the backing and support that he needed in this crisis, the Air Ministry betrayed its country's, and the Royal Air Force's, most devoted servants, and exposed itself for its own woeful insufficiency.

If an explanation of this betrayal be sought, it can only be found, we suggest, in their collective fear of their political masters or in the personal ambition of some of Dowding's enemies and critics. In either case, the betrayal adds to the Air Ministry's tarnished reputation a further mark of dishonour, and reinforces the suspicion that they were ready to go to almost any questionable lengths to get rid of Dowding.

Months after Dowding's and Park's departure, while the *Blitz* was still raging, it is difficult to form an idea of what Sholto Douglas and Leigh-Mallory were actually doing, i.e. how they actually spent their days and hours. Douglas's *Despatch* gives few clues to what occupied him; and his auto-biography is no more helpful. And yet, not a word of reproach is levelled by Portal at Douglas's head for a failure, from December to May, which makes Dowding's work a shining example of energy and rightness.

## 2. The Role of Churchill

Dowding's biographer refers in his account of his subject's dismissal from Fighter Command to the Prime Minister's "curious behaviour". For the fact is that Churchill, from being Dowding's most stalwart champion in October, allowed himself to be swayed into acquiescing in his sacking a few weeks later.

Did the Prime Minister have to be persuaded? Yes, and no. No, in the sense that the Secretary of State for Air and the Air Council had the constitutional authority to promote, move, retire any officer they chose, without consulting the Prime Minister. However, the Prime Minister had also appointed himself Minister for Defence, albeit he was "careful not to define (his) rights and duties." Churchill was known to be a strong supporter of Dowding's; and it would have been a very brave or desperate Minister and CAS who risked the explosion sure to come if they retired Dowding without Churchill's consent. It was for that reason that all the assaults against Dowding were addressed to Churchill. That fact alone suggests a certain collusion.

The question we must now answer is, What had happened of sufficient gravity to implant in Churchill's mind the persuasion that Dowding had to be replaced? Or rather, what arguments did the Secretary of State for Air and the Chief of the Air Staff muster — for it must have devolved upon those two men — to persuade Churchill that Dowding had to go?

Not only that. As we have seen, on August 12 Newall wrote to Dowding to inform him that "the time limit to the period of [his] appointment" as C-in-C Fighter Command had been cancelled. We have no doubt but that that conmitment would have been honoured for so long as Newall remained CAS. Did Portal know of it? Would he have felt himself bound by it?

The early campaign against Dowding had had no effect. It was the accumulation of attacks on Dowding by Macdonald, Balfour and, especially by Salmond that took their toll and weakened Churchill's confidence and judgment to the point that one last volley was enough to push him over. We have no doubt but that it was Portal's appointment as Chief of the Air Staff on October 25 that brought matters to a head and precipitated events. Sinclair, we have seen, had wanted to get rid of Dowding as early as July. It was therefore Sinclair who made sure that he appointed as Newall's successor not only an anti-Dowding man, but an anti-Dowding man who would act.

It is clear that there must have been a confrontation between Sinclair and Portal, on the one hand, and Churchill on the other. It is not difficult to imagine the arguments they must have put forward forcefully enough to persuade Churchill, *à contrecoeur*, that Dowding had to go. We envisage Sinclair the politician taking the stand of the aggrieved Minister complaining that Dowding was a man totally stuck in his ways and impossible to deal with. And we relish the irony of Portal, the out-and-out bomber man, advancing technical arguments about the tactical use of fighters.

We are fortunate to have Dowding's own reaction to his fate. He reports on his meeting with the Prime Minister on the day following his interview with Sinclair.

> Churchill told me that I was to be replaced as C-in-C Fighter Command. He told me of his surprise that this recommendation should have been made "in the moment of victory", but did not indicate any personal opposition. It seemed natural enough to me: the Air Council had been anxious to be rid of me since before the start of the war, and this seemed to be an appropriate moment.

We need not speculate on Dowding's grievous disappointment and sense of having been let down and abandoned by the Prime Minister. We do wonder why Churchill did not allow Dowding the chance to hear the accusations made against him by Salmond, Trenchard, Sinclair and Portal. It is likely that Dowding would not have been in a mood to defend himself. His record was his defence.

Salmond met Churchill shortly after Dowding had gone, and wrote: "(Churchill) said I was right — D. had gone, 'but it nearly broke his heart'."

This is not the end of the saga. Churchill came to realize that he had been duped. In the first six months of the new commander-in~chief's tenure at Fighter Command, he saw a worsening of the night attacks and little energy displayed by him or his new 11 Group commander in perfecting the defences to counter them. He saw no preparations for the expected renewal of the daylight battle. And he saw very severe losses of precious fighters and their pilots in futile so-called offensive sorties over France, carried out without any discernible purpose.

Even after Dowding's return to the United Kingdom from his mission to the United States, from which he was recalled, Churchill tried to have him appointed to other operational commands.

In September 1986, *The Times* published a number of letters about Lord Dowding and the inadequacy of the recognition accorded him for his great services. On October 13th there was a further letter, from Martin Gilbert, Churchill's biographer, who wrote to say that a number of people had asked him whether it was not Churchill's hostility to Dowding "that was responsible for Dowding's eclipse." He gave the following account of Churchill's efforts to have him brought back:

> In November, 1940, when both Sinclair and the Air Staff unanimously urged Dowding's removal, Churchill had no alternative but to accept their advice. In doing so, he stressed to Sinclair his admiration for Dowding's qualities and achievements, and seven months later urged Sinclair to bring Dowding back to an operational command. This proposal was rejected by Sinclair and the Air Staff. In June, 1941, immediately after the fall of Crete, Churchill urged that Dowding should be recalled to active service as Commander-in-Chief of the Middle East Air Services. This too was rejected. In September 1941, Churchill wished Dowding to replace Air Tedder in the Middle East. He was confronted once more by the total refusal of Sinclair and the Chief of the Air Staff to give Dowding any active command.

No testimony could refute more convincingly the arguments of the anti-Dowding camp that Dowding was removed from his command for professional reasons.

All the efforts Churchill made to bring Dowding back to an operational rôle in the war serve to prove that his acquiescence in Dowding's removal must have been reluctant indeed, and that a very few short months later, despite all that the two men disagreed about, Churchill had more than second thoughts about the wisdom of Dowding's retirement from active service.

There is further testimony in favour of Dowding. In 1944, Air Chief Marshal Sir Wilfred Freeman, who served throughout most of the war as Portal's right-hand man, wrote to Portal: "Why did we get rid of Dowding, who did something, and retain a number of inefficients a little junior to him who have nothing whatsoever to their credit?"

In his book, *Right of the Line,* John Terraine quotes this query, and asks: "The phrase 'we get rid of Dowding' is interesting: who are 'we'? The great collective Air Ministry 'we' — or is the meaning rather more personal?" Terraine almost answers his own question by adding that Freeman "went on to suggest that it might be time to 'get rid of Sinclair'."

Freeman's question is assuredly rhetorical: it is clear he was revolving the question in his mind, and the answer — which he knew well enough — now, some years later, seemed to have bothered him. But Terraine's response to the question is beside the point. The whole point lies in the phrase, repeated, 'get rid of.' For, sure as God made little apples, 'get rid of' Dowding they did. Summarily and unceremoniously. And now, as we have said, some years later, Freeman looks back, and finds only a suspicious question mark hanging over what they had done to Dowding — 'they' being himself, Portal and the others — notably, Sinclair and Douglas. Freeman, who in 1940 with Portal was an anti-Dowding man, looks back with the benefit of distance in time, which has a way of dissipating the corrupting fog of the passions felt then, and sees events and personalities, finally, as through a glass clearly.

## 3. The Motives

In our preceding examination of the factors that lay behind the removal of Dowding from his conmand, we have demonstrated as fully as possible, and just short of proof in the absence of documentary evidence, that the explanation is not to be found in a simplistic statement of 'reasons'. There was something much more behind the decision than shortcomings of a technical nature. The criticism of day tactics became a machiavellian device used to justify Leigh-Mallory's wings by the dishonest ploy of relying on an outdated report filled with exaggerated claims of enemy aircraft destroyed.

The charge of failing to counter the night *Blitz* was a classic case of fingering a scapegoat for the Air Ministry's own myopia and neglect. Churchill's repeated attempts in 1941 to get the Air Ministry to appoint Dowding to another operational command — and we repeat: an operational command — proves beyond doubt in our eyes that he no longer accepted Sinclair's and Portal's version of events, and continued to hold Dowding in the same high esteem and admiration for his achievements. Finally, Freeman's rather guilty question to Portal confirms Churchill's scepticism.

Our first section addressed the question: What reasons did the Air Council and Air Staff have to replace Dowding? — or rather, what reasons did later writers claim they had? — for assuredly no contemporary authority even put pen to paper. The second section answered the question: How will we convince Churchill that Dowding must go? In this final section we pose the only remaining valid questions: who were the people who wanted to get rid of Dowding? What were their motives? In the absence of concrete and credible evidence to justify Dowding's removal, we have no recourse but to seek the answer to the riddle in the one area generally avoided by historians: the personal factor. We start by harking back to Haslam's article, from which we cull these observations:

He [Dowding] was not one of the intimate circle to whom Trenchard turned for advice.

Trenchard suspected Dowding of being 'a dismal Jimmy' and obsessed by fear of casualties.

He was a known 'stuffy' character, difficult to work with and often at loggerheads with the Air Ministry.

Neither Salmond nor Freeman were (sic) friendly towards or admirers of Dowding's.

These opinions are of no value in themselves; but they point the way to the answers to the missing pieces in the puzzle: that is, they are of a personal nature. Dowding himself would have concurred. In his typescript *Notes for a Biographer,* he conceded that he was not popular within Air Ministry circles, and that, as we have just seen, "the Air Council had been anxious to be rid of me before the start of the war". We also saw, in chapter 2, that he had furious arguments with officers on the Air Staff. Now, his unpopularity had become such that, at the height of his powers and triumphs, his greatest achievement was swept aside by others who revealed themselves incapable of rising above their personal aversion, even in their country's interest, and even when the prospect of defeat had not been entirely vanquished. The sole possible motive then was that he had been a constant thorn in their side with his incessant demands and not a few complaints.

It is not difficult to demonstrate, even in the absence of documentary evidence, that the critics and enemies of Dowding were spurred by passions and other powerful emotions, such as dislike, fear, jealousy, ambition, spite, hatred, and inferiority, to identify some of the strongest. We will consider the principal agents and their likely motives.

## A WEAK LINK

This document is conspicuous for the defective judgement shown by its author, even while he claims to use judgement. Nowhere is this lack more in evidence than when he claims that the replacement of Air Chief Marshal Ludlow-Hewitt by Air Marshal Portal as C-in-C Bomber Command was "an outstanding improvement". This assessment is made without evidence, i.e. it is a personal opinion. All competent opinion sides with Ludlow-Hewitt, and would only prefer Portal because he was 'cooperative', whereas Ludlow-Hewitt was, like Dowding, a thorn in the Air Ministry's side — and for all the right reasons.

The writer's assessment of Fighter Command is wildly biased and erratic, and his opinion of Dowding is distorted by a palpable antipathy. He must have felt that he would benefit from Neweall's removal, having been passed over for promotion; and that Dowding's elevation to CAS would not be to his advantage. How easy it is to find arguments to conceal one's true motives!

## WARD AND CLARRY

These bit-players in a dark drama, who involved themselves while acknowledging that they knew nothing about the issues and that it was no business of theirs anyway, are deserving only of scorn. And of our contempt, if their involvement had any effect on the outcome. As was their intent. Whether they had hoped to benefit from their meddling is impossible to judge.

## MACDONALD

Macdonald's offence, and it was egregious, was to put loyalty to his squadron commander, and perhaps to his group commander as well, above that to his commander-in-chief. Loyalty of a personal nature is a bond stronger than a loyalty to a remote and unknown authority. Moreover, Macdonald's political interests would induce him to put personal loyalty above 'party' loyalty, as he demonstrated when lobbying Churchill. In politics, one furthers one's career and fortunes by building networks of personal relations. It is conceivable that Leigh-Mallory urged the action on him — and he knew about and worked the system of personal relations. In an earlier and less squeamish age Macdonald's treachery would have been met with condign punishnent.

## SALMOND

This high ranking and prestigious officer carried great weight in the councils of the Air Ministry. In early September he authored a report on night defences which was flawed from so many points of view, and showed so little understanding of the real problems of successful defence against night bombing, that one cannot but conclude, as we have already suggested, that his report was motivated by his keenness, and the desire of others, to undermine Dowding's position. Salmond had nothing to gain personally from Dowding's going, except — and is this a negligeable factor in human psychology? — the intense satisfaction of helping to remove from a position of authority someone you dislike, and, even more, of finding oneself able to assert influence even when no longer in an official position of authority. He had already met with success in his intrigue against Newall. This success encouraged him. That he was motivated by a visceral dislike of Dowding is beyond dispute.

## TRENCHARD

Trenchard's hostility to Dowding was of very long date. His animosity was based on at least two fundamental differences. The first was that of humanity. Trenchard, like other First World War commanders, sacrificed the lives of the soldiers and airmen under his command with gross unfeeling, while accusing men like Dowding of being 'dismal Jimmies', and, later, of lacking humanity.[16] These personal slurs suggest a difficulty in accepting contrary views with good grace. Secondly, Trenchard was the personification of aggression and attack, and did not understand fighters and the need for defence. This fundamental difference of strategic outlook between the two men was resented by the authoritarian figure, who brooked of no opposition to his doctrine, and, like all authoritarian military commanders, conceived of a personal dislike of any man who challenged him. Trenchard was pleased to find a like-minded colleague only too willing to let him, Salmond, take the heat and beard the lion in the den.

## Sinclair and Portal

We now turn to a consideration of the highly placed officials who were personally, by direct or indirect means, interested in, and working for, Dowding's removal.

The very question, and the idea of the need for it, introduces a disturbing note. If senior officers and politicians determined to get rid of another, especially one who has accomplished prodigious tasks, notably in the face of contrary advice and opinions, observe a total silence in explaining their decision and action, and subsequently either leave it to later writers or even coach them to come up with explanations for his removal, there will appear eventually visible and ever-growing discrepancies between the silence and the explanations. When the discrepancies are subjected to literary and psychological analysis, the perpetrators of the dismissal will be found inevitably to be involved in intrigue and deceit.

We begin our inquiry with the question: Who was the authority with the ultimate decision to get rid of Dowding? There are only two candidates: Sinclair and Portal. If there had been disagreement between them, Portal's view would have prevailed. However, both men were so indisputably in the anti-Dowding canp that disagreement was not at issue. Moreover, if we enter the Salmond factor into the equation, it is equally clear that his efforts would not have prevailed without support — and perhaps encouragement — from the Air Council. Indeed, Portal's — and Sholto Douglas's — antagonism towards Dowding may well have been one of the key factors in Portal's appointment by Sinclair as Chief of the Air Staff.

First, do we know anything of Portal's hostility to Dowding? Portal was a cagey man: he gave nothing away. But it is possible to glean a clue from

Dowding's fate. The crucial decision was whether to offer Dowding another appointment or to retire him. Dowding's outstanding qualities and his great achievements demanded a position in which they could continue to be devoted to the service of his country. Portal's decision to retire him, despite the official cancellation of his retirement date, was tantamount to declaring that he wanted no part of him in his Air Force.

Britain was still alone, and only at the beginning of a war which was going to be long and hard. A new CAS might have put his country's need ahead of his personal antipathies, and invited Dowding to meet him, alone, the two of them, in a series of conferences in order to reach a *modus vivendi*. No such initiative was taken. This silence, this failure, is eloquently expressive of a personal hostility.

We come now to a grievous injustice in the perpetration of which Portal was the principal malefactor. We have insisted that Dowding's dismissal cannot be considered in isolation from other events. Air Vice-Marshal Keith Park, the Air Officer Commanding 11 Group, was also removed from his command. All the 'reasoned' explanations of Dowding's removal break down further when Park's demotion is factored into the complex equation we have been constructing. They are inseparable. If Park had been promoted, and then moved to a less demanding appointment, one's suspicions might not have been aroused. But his removal by Portal, without promotion, after his victorious tactical role in the daylight battle, raises a red flag of alarm.

Park was posted to an appointment in Training Command on December 23rd, one month after Dowding's departure, having occupied his command for only seven months. No writer has gone so far as to suggest that he was removed for technical or professional reasons. Only one 'reason' has been put forward for Park's removal, namely, that he was extremely tired after his exertions and needed a deserved rest. Park himself was not consulted about it.

A better 'reason' exists: if Dowding went, Park, his loyal lieutenant who shared Dowding's ideas, had also to go. Their joint dismissal would seem to give point to the contention that they were removed for 'professional' reasons, that is, their tactical mismanagement of the battle. This logic is only understandable in the light of what follows. The true explanation becomes clear when his and Dowding's replacements are known. They were, respectively, Leigh-Mallory and Douglas.

## LEIGH-MALLORY AND DOUGLAS

Leigh-Mallory's hostility to both Dowding and Park has been documented by Park's biographer.

> One day in February 1940, while Park was still at Bentley Priory, Leigh-Mallory "came out of Dowding's office, paused in mine and said in my presence that he would move heaven and earth to get Dowding removed from Fighter Command." Dowding only learnt of this episode many years later, and it came as a shock that Leigh-Mallory had harboured such bitterness toward him — an enmity provoked, no doubt, by Dowding's having rebuked Leigh-Mallory for professional lapses. Later in that year Leigh-Mallory "made it quite clear to me [Park] that he was very jealous of my group, which was in the front line [after Dunkirk]."

Leigh-Mallory would not, of course, have been successful without substantial help and cooperation from others better situated to give it. The chief of them was Douglas. One writer, who witnessed what he wrote, informs us that Leigh-Mallory and Douglas were in frequent contact by telephone. The fact of their conferring together — conspiring is the more accurate word — behind Dowding's back to gain their ends, shows a deceit common enough in political circles but rare in the higher reaches of the Royal Air Force. Park summed up his feelings in later years: "To my dying day [he told his biographer] I shall feel bitter at the base intrigue which was used to remove Dowding and myself as soon as we had won the battle." And he was not shy in revealing the names of the plotters when declining an offer to write his biography: "No doubt the intriguing that Joubert and Douglas did at the Air Ministry in collaboration with Leigh-Mallory would make exciting reading, but it would not enhance the reputation of the Royal Air Force."

Douglas was in cahoots with Sinclair from the beginning of the latter's appointment as Air Minister, who, as we have seen, sounded Churchill out in July about getting rid of Dowding. What did Sinclair know so soon about Dowding? Nothing. Or rather, what he heard in Air Council meetings; and above all what Douglas fed him.

## SINCLAIR AND DOUGLAS

Sinclair's treatment of Dowding in November when informing him he was to to leave Fighter Command "immediately" was a gross violation of every form of decency. Dowding's views of his removal distinguish between 'reasons' and 'manner'. He informed his biographer that if the Air Ministry had decided that he and Park were wrong in their handling of the battle and

Leigh-Mallory and Douglas were right in their views, "they were right to get rid of me." But they had to be right. And in all the important matters they were demonstrably wrong. It was the manner of his dismissal by Sinclair that was offensive and hurtful. It was almost as if Sinclair was settling a score.

Today no informed person will argue that the Air Staff were right and that Dowding and Park were wrong. But being right or wrong cut no ice with ambitious, jealous and vengeful people.

The relations between Douglas and Sinclair were decisive in Dowding's fate. And here we have a spark of evidence which we can fan into an illuminating flame.

When Sinclair retired from his ministerial post on May 28th 1945, a few weeks after D-Day, Douglas wrote to him. In his reply Sinclair said, among other things: "Many charming letters softened the blow of my departure from the Air Ministry but none which I shall treasure more than the one which you sent me. You were my first friend at the Air Ministry. . . . You helped me enormously in those early days. . . . I felt as though I had won a battle when I got Fighter Command into your hands — and, looking back, how right I was!"

How much a simple-seeming statement can reveal! Douglas occupied a high position on the Air Ministry totem pole, and exercised both authority and influence. Hence Sinclair's naïve, and heartfelt, tribute lends itself to some interesting conclusions: i) Douglas went out of his way to ingratiate himself with the new Air Minister while helping him into his job; ii) Sinclair, accepting Douglas as a friend, and relying on him for advice in a job which he never mastered, came under Douglas's influence; iii) Douglas exploited this influence to his own ends; iv) two of those 'ends' were to aid and abet Sinclair in dethroning Dowding, and to get the command of Fighter Command; and, crucially, v) Sinclair got Fighter Command into Douglas's hands as a reward for a friend, and with total disregard for his qualifications to replace the incumbent.

Douglas was not a discreet man. He gave the game away. We have had occasion to relate the relations of Sidney Cotton with the Air Ministry. When Cotton first met Douglas, in March 1940, Cotton was having his usual difficulties in getting authorization for his actions. Cotton wrote of that confused time:

> It was consoling to know that I wasn't the only one who was fighting on two fronts — the Germans and the Air Ministry. Another man — Air Commodore Douglas Colyer, then the British Air Attaché in Paris — advised me to handle the Air Force machine much as a good mechanic

would handle a troublesome motor-car engine; keep tickling he carburettor, and if one spanner didn't fit, try another. Sholto Douglas, whom I met about this time, told me much the same thing. The RAF, he said, was full of regulations which had been thought up over the years by people with nothing better to do, and which gave those who studied them the chance to delay and sabotage anything they could get their hands on "But take my advice, Sidney," he added, "learn how the machine works and you can beat them. You can rise to any heights if you study the machine and use it properly." Cotton adds sardonically: "It seems he knew what he was talking about, for he subsequently became C-in-C Fighter Command, C-in-C Coastal Command, and C-in-C British Forces in Germany.

It is clear that the crucial key to the enigma of Dowding's sacking was his unpopularity with the Air Council and in the Air Staff — though 'unpopularity' is a mild word, to say the least — and Dowding's unpopularity boiled down inevitably to personalities, that is to personal feelings and aims. As the French, when confronted with a crime, advise the investigator, 'chercher la femme' in the case, so it is essential in prying into human decisions, in matters both great and small, to seek out the personal factor.

It was Spinoza, in his *Ethics*, who taught that no man ever acted on pure reason. Man is a creator of ideas; but no man ever acted on ideas alone, no matter how noble they might be. He needs something more: he needs a stimulus. An idea is of no account unless it moves to action. Hence, a man is always moved to act. He is motivated, that is swayed by emotional forces. The factors that motivate him are intensely personal, either existing already within the person, like a seed awaiting germination — and it may be a poisonous or a beneficent seed — or existing in the incompatible chemistry of two beings.

Now it happens that in regard to the well-springs of human conduct, Dowding and his enemies constitute an instructive study in contrasts. His stepson, David Whiting, who knew him well, has said of him that he was a man to weigh evidence, never to be swayed by his emotions. "I never saw him make an error of judgment or a bad decision. He had the ability to brush away surface things and see even beyond the solution. He had an orderly mind — essentially he was a mathematician."

Dowding came to his overall strategic ideas by study and thought, that is by the light of reason; and thereafter, moved by the conviction of their soundness, sought to realize them with a passionate intensity, directed and controlled by a steely will.

Those who differed from Dowding and opposed him reached their ideas rather by the murky and erratic path of sentiment and emotion; and readily found plausible arguments and 'reasons' in which to cloak them. A classic case is Trenchard's faulty strategic view of the power of the bomber to bomb an enemy into submission, a view, translated into entrenched Air Force policy, devoid of evidence, but followed slavishly by succeeding generations of air marshals.

It is one of the commonest facets of man's nature, the perverse side, which is an inexhaustible resourcefulness in inventing pretexts and 'reasons' for acts and decisions whose motives are often unworthy. And there is no idea, no matter how patently ridiculous or unjust, that does not find a hundred 'reasons' to justify and defend it.

These same forces are at work in the final stage of the evolution of the relations between Dowding's enemies and their victim. They were all motivated by personal factors. And they had no difficulty in finding, and advancing, plausible 'reasons' for their conclusions and actions.

Among the real motives were dislike, ambition, jealousy, and even fear. So that, not content to charge him with professional shortcomings, his enemies resorted to personal vituperation, accusing him of defects which would have a professional impact: a stubborn attachment to his ideas and rightness; a refusal to try out new ideas; a slow brain; a persistent refusal to cooperate with higher authorities; unimaginativeness; and even — heaven forfend! — a lack of humanity.

Is it possible that air marshals and others, men who had reached the top of their professional ladder or who were well up it, could be swayed by emotions like jealousy and ambition — "green-eyed jealousy" and "tyrant ambition, the tyrant of the mind"? Then you have not read the Old Testament and Shakespeare!

The suggestion that some air marshals might actually have been motivated by fear of Dowding, on the personal level, is not hard to imagine or believe. It was said, for example, that Newall was intimidated by Dowding. But the fear went beyond the personal. Some were very afraid of what would almost certainly happen, to themselves and to their policies, in the event that Dowding were appointed to replace Newall as Chief of the Air Staff. They were not sure what his policies would be, but they were sure that he was not a disciple of Trenchard and an out-and-out bomber man; and that if he became Chief of the Air Staff there would be an unprecedented shake-up and weeding-out of the Air Staff. In a word, heads would roll. His appointment had to be prevented at all costs, and by any means. We have seen how shabby and underhanded those means were. And we have seen how, progressively, from June to November, the stakes were raised bit by bit against Dowding. We will see, in chapter 9, the measure of their vindictiveness, when we discuss Dowding's claim to promotion to Marshal of the Royal Air Force.

An occurrence of far-reaching significance was the appointment in 1937 of Sir Thomas Inskip as Coordinator of Defence. It will be recalled that the Government of the day accepted as national defence policy his urgent recommendation that the Royal Air Force turn away from its insistence on bombers and plan more energetically for an effective defence and the production of fighters. Many years of planning overturned in a trice! Someone would pay! Inskip and colleagues were out of reach. But there was a handy target for their bile nearby.

We must recall other events, closely inter-related, which may well have struck deep at the heart of the powers-that-be in the Air Ministry. When the German *Blitzkrieg* met with such bewildering success and shattered the Allied armies; when the humiliating Dunkirk evacuation took place; and above all when France collapsed, and Britain, without a single ally and close to bankruptcy, faced the prospect of imminent invasion, a wave of panic ran through Whitehall and swept the nation's leaders into a paralysis of indecision. Even Churchill was not unaffected. There was one man, however, who never wavered.

As early as May 16th 1940 Dowding wrote to the Government that historic letter in which he laid it down that, in the event of the defeat of the Allied armies in France, "there is no one who will deny that England should fight on, even though the remainder of the Continent of Europe is dominated by the Germans." Many there were who did deny it, high in Government circles, who favoured seeking terms with Hitler. It was the new prime minister's second great trial, after trying to bolster the French and keep them in the war, that of facing down the peacemakers in the War Cabinet, notably Halifax, and of carrying his other colleagues with him. Dowding's letter was presented to the War Cabinet at their meeting on the 18th.[17] Churchill must have been impressed. He was unquestionably impressed only two weeks later when Dowding, intimately informed of the situation in France, went as close as he dared in the War Cabinet meeting of June 3rd to refusing, against

Churchill's intention, to send further fighter reinforcements to aid the failing French, in order to have some strength remaining to fight the expected onslaught. Finally, when Churchill found his true voice, in his speech of June 18th on the fate of Christian Civilization, he expressed in it something of Dowding's steely resolve.

Dowding, with his Fighter Command, was the immovable obstacle against which the irresistible force of the *Luftwaffe* cracked.

How would the men of Whitehall feel now? More to the point, how would they feel when Dowding prevailed against the enemy? The good men, the fair men, the strong men, would rally to his side. The weak and fearful, consumed with envy and hatred and ambition, would seek his removal. And, sad to say, the latter were not only more numerous but, with the one notable exception, held all the places of power.[18]

We referred at the beginning of this chapter to the removal of Ludlow-Hewitt, Cotton, Embry and Park from their commands. They were men of intelligence and initiative who fretted at apathy and obstructionism, and, impatient of red tape and lesser minds, had a marked proclivity for getting things done in their own way. Unorthodoxy is a 'crime' which the entrenched bureaucratic mind cannot understand, and even less tolerate. It thrives on red tape, chains of command and conformity, as weeds thrive on dung-heaps. Its inferiority finds comfort and security in the tortuous corridors wherein it has its being; and in its constituted authority, howsoever modest, it finds a necessary protection. And nothing so alarms and activates its vindictive juices as the spurning, the violation or the by-passing of its authority.

That is not all. It not only jealously guards its rights and prerogatives; it is also maniacally sensitive to criticism or to any challenge to its plans, policies and decisions. Bluntness, outspokenness, and honesty in the expression by others of their views, and a decisiveness in taking actions without consulting 'the mandarins', are guaranteed to see the invocation of Nemesis sooner or later. The fate of Ludlow-Hewitt, Cotton, Embry, Park and, signally, of Dowding, gives point to the contention that, no matter how brilliant, successful and high-ranking an officer is, he will become *persona ingrata* if he doesn't play according to the unwritten rules laid down by the mandarins, inferior people though they may be, who wield the power; just as the 'triumph' of Douglas and Leigh-Mallory makes it clear that inferior people, if possessed of ambition, wiles and malice, will prevail if they know how to turn the rules to their advantage and to ingratiate themselves with the power-brokers.

## NOTES TO CHAPTER 7:

1. Consult the Bibliography for the references to Ludlow-Hewitt and Embry. For Malan and Cotton, see Appendix "D".

2. It may be worth repeating, in this context, that Air Chief Marshal Sir Robert Brooke-Popham was not only recalled to active service at the age of 61, but was actually sent to Singapore as the Commander-in-Chief of the British land and air forces in Malaya in October 1940.

3. At the second War Cabinet meeting of May 28, 1940, the "various possibilities now under development of countering night-bombing were referred to", but it seems the matter was not followed up. (See Lukacs, *Five Days in London*, May 1940, p. 181.)

4. One feature of Dowding's reply is that, whereas the Salmond paper addresses problems of night **air defence**, Dowding refers mostly to night **interception** and night **operations**. This subtle distinction makes it clear where Dowding's thinking and priorities lay.

5. The arguments against the transfer of filtering were again dealt with by Dowding in his *Despatch*, and explain his irritation. He wrote, in particular:

"In order to avoid waste of flying effort and false air raid warnings it was obviously very necessary to differentiate between friendly and enemy formations, and this was the most difficult as well as the most important task of my Filter Room." He goes on to explain the essential functions of Command, Group and Sector, which required that filtering be done at Command.

Incredibly, the Draft Conclusions of the Air Council meeting of October 2nd contain the assertion that the Air Officer Commanding-in-Chief of Fighter Command and MRAF Sir John Salmond had reached agreement "on all the points which were in issue following the Council's letter dated 25th September, 1940, to AOC-in-C., Fighter Command". Of those points, the first reads as follows:

"(a) the decentralisation of filtering to Group Headquarters: this arrangement
    would not come into operation until IFF equipment had been fitted into
    all fighter aircraft."

This paragraph has been heavily scored through with three lines of black pencil. Dowding's views are corroborated, and justified, 17 years later, by Basil Collier, when he wrote (p. 256): "As for devolution of the filtering and air-raid systems, they would take some time to put into effect, and in any case had little bearing on the immediate issue."

This is far from the end of the dispute. On October 1st, Sinclair called a meeting to thrash the problem out. Joubert and Dowding were again at loggerheads. We are jumping ahead in our story, but this is the place to continue and end it. At the War Cabinet meeting of October 7th, where the controversy was raised again, Churchill instructed Dowding to submit a statement of his views of the matters at issue. When Churchill approved the Salmond Report, with the omission of the filtering recommendation, the Air Council objected. Churchill then wrote to Dowding, on a personal level, and asked him to state his case again. Dowding replied the following day, on October 24th, as follows:

The Secretary of State's minute contains a few inaccuracies, only one of which
is important and that is the statement that it is really an undoubted fact that time is
saved in getting squadrons into the air by filtering at Group HQ — it is substantially untrue. Plots are told to Group HQ from my table without delay with the average
lag in transmission of a plot less than 15 seconds.

> The metaphorical edifice which you have seen in my Filter and Operations Room has been built up brick by brick under my own eye during the last four years. My predecessor, Joubert, had left the Fighter Area as it was, without having made the slightest effort to tackle what had been in fact one of the gravest problems of the defence, by the differentiation between friendly and enemy aircraft. . . . The system that I have devised might not be perfect but it cannot be improved by the disruptive criticism on the part of people who do not understand it as a whole. I started with the idea of decentralisation of filtration and abandoned it in favour of centralisation. My greatest grievance, however, is the matter of expenditure of my time in arguing with the Air Staff of every intimate detail of my organisation. Surely the C-in-C should be left to manage his own affairs if the general result is satisfactory. As the Secretary of State says, I agreed to decentralise under strong pressure because it is not a matter that is going to lose the war and I have to fight the Air Staff over so many important issues. . . . I feel that we shall pay £100,000 in material and labour in order to secure a slight reduction in efficiency.

In the end the issue of decentralisation was taken out of everyone's hands by the inexorable march of events. The Filter Room at Fighter Command HQ was simply swamped by the mass of information coming in from the CH stations and the lack of physical space to handle more people round the plotting table. I quote Bragg (p. 236): "Centralised filtering that had appeared to Dowding in 1938 as the most effective and economical way to conduct air operations had been rendered almost unworkable by the sheer quantity of information coming in from the chains which had doubled in size in less than a year and were continuing to increase."

6. This letter of Salmond's is one of the most crucial, and revealing, in the whole campaign of vituperation against Dowding, and in the drama of his removal from his command.

The date of the letter tells all: it is October 5th, that is to say, a mere **eight days** following Dowding's reply to the Air Council. Salmond was obviously wasting no time. He, and Trenchard, had made up their minds, and were going to pull every string possible to get rid of Dowding. Salmond's committee, whereas justified by the circumstances, if its true aim was to render help to Dowding in his battle, must now be seen for what it was, a red herring. It was a device calculated to elicit from their victim the replies that Salmond knew he would receive, and show Dowding in the light that would enable his enemies to 'hang' him.

What is also equally clear is that Salmond must have known in advance that he was going to get all the support he needed from the key members of the Air Council. That was almost certainly Trenchard's role in the drama.

7. The first three of these measures were dreamt up by Frederick Lindemann, Churchill's personal scientific adviser, a position he held throughout the war. The Air Ministry Scientific Committee's "all-important preoccupation with radar meant nothing to him. . . . Sometimes he argued that the parachute mine deserved higher priority than radar." Joubert wrote: "It is sad to have to record it, but there is no single authenticated instance of any of these methods having brought about the destruction of the enemy, although the minefield laid by one aircraft may have been successful. What did happen was that the entire countryside became littered with wire to which bombs were still attached, and all these had to be cleared up laboriously by the Bomb Disposal Squads." *The Fated Sky*, p.187.) It is **sad**? Why?

Lindemann's views on the area bombing of German cities, the use of 'windows' to throw off German radar, and the use of anti-submarine aircraft in the Battle of the Atlantic, were equally wrong-headed and dangerous, and cost thousands of Allied lives.

8. It was Fighter Command that established the first Operational Research Section in the RAF. (See Joubert, *The Third Service*, p. 130).

9. The differences between the totals for each month and the aggregate of the other three columns — respectively 10, 18 and 36 enemy aircraft destroyed — are accounted for by anti-aircraft artillery, balloons, engine failure, and unknown causes. In some cases the agency is stated as "shot down by night fighter" without specifying. These latter cases have not been counted.

The results for January and February are, respectively, 8 e/a destroyed (2 by fighters) in a month of 14 major or heavy attacks; and 5 e/a destroyed (6 by fighters) in a month of 11 attacks.

The devastating raid on London on the night of May 10-11, the last night attack against the capital, is revealing about the defences, and disheartening for the citizenry. "During the night 571 sorties were flown by German long-range bombers over Britain, together with 24 by long-range fighters . . ." over the period 2250–0515 hours. Fighter Command sent up 325 fighters, and claimed 28 enemy aircraft destroyed. The Germans lost, in fact, 11 aircraft, 5 of which fell to Beaufighters.

10. The successes of the Defiant are striking. This aircraft, and its crews, suffered cruel casualties as a day fighter.

11. The true figures could not have been known at the time, or even by 1946, because it was impossible to know how many enemy aircraft crashed in the sea or on return to Occupied Europe after combat over Britain. On the other hand it was possible to know precisely how many were destroyed over Britain; and even more to the point it was known how many sorties were carried out and how many interceptions were made. The following figures, given in Appendix XXXIV of Basil Collier's *The Defence of the United Kingdom,* are revealing:

ANALYSIS OF BRITISH NIGHT-FIGHTER EFFORT, JANUARY - MAY 1941

SE = single-engined fighters; TE= twin-engined fighters; AI = resulting from airborne radar

| | SORTIES | | DETECTIONS | | COMBATS | |
| Month | SE | TE | AI | Visual | AI | Visual |
| --- | --- | --- | --- | --- | --- | --- |
| January | 402 SE | | — | 34 | — | 9 |
| | | 84 TE | 44 | — | 2 | — |
| February | 421 SE | | — | 33 | — | 9 |
| | | 147 TE | 25 | — | 4 | — |
| March | 735 SE | | — | 34 | — | 25 |
| | | 270 TE | 95 | 20 | 21 | 10 |
| April | 842 SE | | — | 45 | — | 39 |
| | | 342 TE | 117 | 10 | 50 | 5 |
| May | 1,345 SE | | — | 154 | — | 116 |
| | | 643 TE | 204 | 13 | 74 | 6 |

These figures of enemy aircraft destroyed in March, April and May are confirmed by Michael Bragg, p. 259. They tell everything when comparing claims with the actual numbers of German aircraft shot down over this period, as shown above. Bragg introduces his table with these words: "The great success of GCI is best shown by the statistics of night fighting, all the more remarkable as only five night-fighter squadrons were equipped with AI, plus a further eight squadrons known as 'cat's-eye' fighters, which were directed by GCI but had to continue their search visually: they were very successful especially during moonlit nights."

12. Henry Probert, in his book on the high commanders of the RAF, says of Salmond: "One of his most significant tasks was to chair in 1940 the committee which investigated the performance of the night air defences."

Our gloss is brief:

> When needs he must, yet faintly then he praises;
> Somewhat the deed, much more the means he raises:
> So marreth what he makes, and praising most, dispraises.
>
> — PHINIAS FLETCHER, *The Purple Island*

13. There is another view. One historian, in reporting on the fruits of a meeting called by Trenchard in 1923 (whose decisions, in his view, "would set the seal on the design of the RAF for certainly the next ten years and probably on into the future"), wrote: "There was not much discussion on the need for night fighters presumably because an enemy was supposed not to have any night-flying ability. This left the way for the *Luftwaffe* to drop 20,000 tons of bombs on London in 1940 . . . and suffer precious few casualties in the process."

14. The official, unpublished, Air Ministry account entitled *Air Defence of Great Britain. Vol.iii, Night Air Defence,* entirely supports this view. (See AIR 41/17, 1-E.)

15. See Zimmerman, *Britain's Shield,* pp. 214–226.

16. Moreover Trenchard knew it was not true. When he, with Churchill and T.E. Lawrence, devised the policy of passing the responsibility for the control and policing of the desert tribes of Arabia to the RAF in the 1920s, this was done successfully, and very economically, by dropping a few bombs on the villages of offending tribesmen. "This policy was adopted but later modified due to pressures applied by Lord Dowding", who insisted that the villages be warned in advance by the dropping of leaflets. This humane measure was found to be equally effective.

17. See P.H.M. Bell, *A Certain Eventuality,* p. 19.

18. A six-page letter written by Robert Wright to Tom Gleave on July 28th, 1967, a copy of which was sent to a grateful author by John Young, historian of the Battle of Britain Fighters Association, in September 2001, contains the following paragraph:

> The troubled relationship between Stuffy and the Air Staff at the Air Ministry . . . has not been studied in sufficient depth, but it is an important chapter in Air Force history, and in the country's history in relation to the Battle of Britain. He was always forthright and fearless . . . and entirely right. There are those who cannot take that: their own personal ambitions warped their thinking and eventually Stuffy was treated very badly. And by certain political elements he was treated despicably, even during the battle, and although Stuffy was always absolutely correct towards the politicians — for all that he might have thought of them — the same cannot be said of their behaviour towards him.

# Part III

# The Aftermath

# CHAPTER 8

## *The Successors*

Dowding and Park having been removed from their Commands — Dowding retired, without thanks or reward; Park dismissed and demoted to a lesser command — and replaced, respectively, by Sholto Douglas and Leigh-Mallory, we must now ask: What were Douglas's and Leigh-Mallory's qualifications and competence for their new, and much more important, appointments?

Douglas was appointed as the Air Officer Commanding-in-Chief of Fighter Command by the Secretary of State for Air, Sir Archibald Sinclair. Was it also the recommendation of the new Chief of the Air Staff, Air Marshal (soon to be Air Chief Marshal) Sir Charles Portal, who had taken over from Newall in October?

We have already seen that Sinclair was a Douglas man. One would like to know what Portal thought of Douglas, and whether he deemed him fit for this vital command. The official biography of Portal, despite the author's evident sympathy and admiration for his subject, is a fine, albeit regrettably uncritical, account; but it accords not a word to what is, in 1940, a crucial strategic appointment. One of the latest and, by virtue of the authors' reputation, most authoritative judgements is that offered by Hough and Richards in their *Battle of Britain:*

> Sholto Douglas and the Air Tactics directorate were keen to experiment with the 'big wings', and if these were to be tried there was much to be said for having an enthusiast, Leigh-Mallory, directing the Group which would put most of them into the air. As the senior Group commander, in charge of 12 Group since its inception, Leigh-Mallory had excellent qualifications for the post.

That is all: Douglas was "keen to experiment"; Leigh-Mallory was "an enthusiast", and one who had "excellent qualifications". Let us look at these 'qualifications'.

First: Experiment. Had there not been enough experimentation? And had it not failed? We think we have proved the failure. 'Keenness' and 'enthusiasm': not exactly the most inspiring recommendations for commanders in whose hands rested "the fate of the British people." And what were those 'qualifications'? We will examine them separately.

# I. Sholto Douglas

We begin by quoting Hough and Richards again:

> Now that the daylight battle was dying down the urgent demand was for success in countering the night bombing and then, looking further ahead, for offensive operations over the continent. Dowding seemed to the Air Staff, at this juncture, the wrong man for either task. He was having no obvious success against the 'night *blitz*', and he would certainly resist the use of his fighters over France.

The facts that the attempted night interception of German bombers was carried out by single machines, not even squadrons or flights let alone wings, and the new commanders had absolutely no experience whatsoever in night fighting, seem not to occur to the authors.

Who had already decreed that Fighter Command was to be used for "offensive operations over the continent," for sending "fighters offensively over France"? Nowhere in Hough and Richards's book is there any discussion of it. Is that what the 'big wings' were to be used for? But the only discussion of 'big wings' — as opposed, for example, to smaller wings — had been in the context of the Battle of Britain. This battle had been entirely a **defensive** battle.[1] When the changes in command were effected in late 1940, the greatest dangers lay in the continuing of the night attacks against British cities, and the renewal, in the spring of 1941, of daylight assaults against Fighter Command in preparation for more determined plans for invasion. These were the two compelling menaces which occupied all informed and responsible minds in the winter of 1940-41. Douglas knew that. He wrote of his appointment:

> I was naturally pleased and proud that I should have been selected for such a responsible post, and I had sufficient confidence in my own ability to believe that I could make a good job of it. But at the same time I could not help feeling a little overawed by the importance of such high command. To a large extent the fate of the British people would be resting in my hands.

Douglas may have had a basic grasp of the nature of his responsibility. Whether he had the ability equal to his task — **to make a good job of it** (!) — is another matter.

In 1938, when he was Assistant Chief of the Air Staff, he tried to defend the order by the Air Ministry for 450 Bolton-Paul Defiants and to foist them onto Dowding. Dowding protested both against this aircraft, and against the decision taken to order them without consulting him. The Defiant was similar to a single-engined fighter except that it had a four-machine-gun turret behind the pilot. This turret could fire only abeam and aft; consequently, often the pilot had to fly without being able to see the intended target. Douglas's defence was that this kind of air fighting had been very successful in the First World War.

Dowding reserved their use in the Battle to the fewest occasions possible. And when the Germans cottoned on to this new type, the poor Defiant crews suffered terrible casualties. Their unexpected success at night was materially better, on moonlit nights.

A measure of Douglas's intelligence and grasp of things as they were was made manifest on September 7, 1940. On that Saturday — a fateful day as it turned out — Dowding had called a conference at Fighter Command HQ for the purpose of deciding on the best ways of preserving his fighter strength in view of the grave losses being suffered, especially by 11 Group, and of rebuilding his strength when the opportunity presented itself. Present were Dowding, Park, Evill and Nicholl of Fighter Command, Douglas, who was accompanied by a Group Captain, and a corporal shorthand-typist. Dowding, supported by Park, used the expression "going downhill". Douglas questioned the pessimism of this view; and he was rebutted by Dowding, Park and Evill. Discussion turned on the losses, and on the training of fighter pilots. Douglas tried to insist that Fighter Command had far more pilots than they did; and he bewildered Dowding and Park when he showed a lack of understanding of the differences between a pilot who had normal flying abilities and a 'blooded' pilot with actual experience of air fighting. Further ideas and problems were aired, each seeming to reveal yet again Douglas's failure to understand both the situation as it existed and the necessary, minimum remedies.

On the 9th Evill sent Douglas a copy of the draft minutes of the conference. Douglas replied on the 14th in these terms. They reminded him, he said, of a music-hall act involving two knock-about comedians, Mutt and Jeff, one of whom was cast in the role of the 'patsy' who asked foolish questions. Douglas protested that the minutes portrayed him in that role and as such misrepresented him. "However, life is too strenuous . . . to bother about the wording of minutes." Evill, in his reply of the same day, rejected Douglas's implied suggestion that the minutes had been faked. They reproduced, he said, almost verbatim the remarks made by the participants.

It is strange how writers allow themselves to be seduced by the temptation to denigrate one man in the idea that such belittling will enhance the stature of their subject. Bill Newton Dunn's biography of Leigh-Mallory indulges in that vice — perhaps in retaliation against Vincent Orange's hatchet-job against Leigh-Mallory. Writing of this conference, Dunn says: "he (Dowding) was tired after the strain of the Battle and his readiness to admit defeat, expressed at the conference on 7 September, could have been interpreted as a lack of will to win." Interpreted by whom? By Douglas? Or by Dunn?

This writer's interpretation of the situation and of Dowding's attitude is that Dowding had the intellectual integrity and the courage both to see the situation as it truly was and to make preparations to meet it, without for one second attempting to gloss it over or to escape the fact of his ultimate responsibility. No one who has read Dowding's letter of May 16th, 1940, could conceivably entertain the notion of his ever being ready "to admit defeat".

We have no intention of rehashing the tactics of the day battles of 1940. However, the thinking of Douglas about the interception of enemy bombers is worth looking at one last time.

Collier quotes Douglas as holding the view that "it does not matter where the enemy is shot down, as long as he is shot down in large numbers". Collier continues:

> Soon after assuming his new post [as AOC-in-C of Fighter Command] he made his attitude still clearer by announcing that he had never been very much in favour of trying to interpose 'fighter squadrons between enemy bombers and their objective'.

The origin of this thinking is significant. Before the advent of the early warning system there was no way of detecting bombers at night or above cloud, nor in daylight if they flew at high altitude. Air Exercises carried out in 1933, including fighter vs. bomber interception, proved — at least to the satisfaction of the referees, who rode in the bombers — that the bomber always got through. The post-mortem concluded that the only chance of interception was after the bombs had been dropped; for then it was possible to calculate the probable course of the bombers as they headed for their home bases, and fighters could be sent up for visual interception.

In this instance Douglas, in common with so many senior officers on the Air Staff, were backward-thinking and reactionary. He was among the conspicuous dinosaurs of the inter-war years who had so deadening an influence on air war doctrine.

One wonders, finally, whose hand may be seen in the notorious Air Ministry pamphlet of 1941 which made the preposterous claim, rebutted angrily by Dowding and Park, that Fighter Command was stronger at the end of the Battle than at the beginning. At least Douglas 'corrected' this misinformation in his *Despatch,* published on September 16, 1948:

> At the beginning of November 1940, the first-line strength of Fighter Command stood nominally at 67 squadrons. Outwardly, therefore, the Command was stronger than at the beginning of the Battle of Britain, when 58 squadrons were available. In reality it was weaker. After several months of intensive fighting some of the squadrons had only a few pilots fully up to operational standards, and the first-line strength was backed by insufficient depth. At the height of the battle the supply of new pilots had failed to keep pace with losses and it had been necessary to improvise measures to avert a crisis.

How much that Douglas was to learn after he assumed his new command he was to display as if he had known it all along! And, as in the excerpt reproduced here, without giving credit to the officer principally responsible for the "necessary . . . measures" to produce more pilots, measures he mentions in the following paragraph.

Douglas's *Despatch* on "Air Operations by Fighter Command in 1941", published as a Supplement to *The London Gazette* in September 1948, devotes six pages, of a total of twenty-one, to defensive night operations, even though claiming that the defeat of the night bomber was his "main task".

Apart from the sections dealing with abortive measures, which we mentioned in Chapter 7, the report deals with the most effective measures: antiaircraft guns and fighters.

The account of the results achieved by fighters makes dismal reading. In the seven-month period December to July, only sixty-six enemy bombers were destroyed by fighters. (We will have more to say about this.)

A reading of Douglas's *Despatch* reveals no energy or ardour on his part. Despite Dowding's efforts and real achievements in laying the foundations essential to combatting the danger, Douglas, who knew the record, gave the credit to some others — as was of course their due — while denying to Dowding his. In his autobiography, *Years of Command,* he wrote:

> I had known from the outset, and from the experience that I had gained while I was at the Air Ministry, that Fighter Command in particular was going to have to make the greatest possible use of radar. But the details of its technical development so far as the night fighters were concerned were dealt with directly by the specialist officers on the Headquarters staff at Bentley Priory, and to them and to the scientists with whom they were associated must go a great deal of the credit for what was achieved. Two of those who had been on the Headquarters staff for a long time and who were directly and intimately concerned with the use of radar in Fighter Command were Wing Commander R.G. Hart and Squadron Leader W.P.G. Pretty. . . . They had both become specialists in radar, and they were to continue to exert a great influence in developing still further the refinements in its use.

About the fighters themselves, and the arguments for and against the single-seat fighter and the radar-equipped Beaufighter, Douglas tergiversates and tries to make himself out to be at one and the same time the champion and the critic of both fighters.

> Some answer to this night bombing had to be found, and it had to be found quickly. . . . (A special committee) had decided on a number of urgent measures, . . . one of them being the recommendation that all possible use should be made of the single-engined fighters. So strongly had Dowding come to believe in his radar-equipped fighters that he had become a little blinded, I felt, to the more simple hit or miss, trial and error, use of the single-engined fighters. I agreed that it was a primitive effort to throw what were really day fighters into the darkness of the night skies in the hope that they would be able to see something. But I felt, and in this I was supported by the other members of the committee and the Chief of the Air Staff, that the effort had to be made, and despite his strenuous protest Dowding was given instructions to make more use of his 'Hurricanes' and 'Defiants' at night.

It is typical of Douglas that, though junior in rank and position to all the other members of this committee, he does his best to make it appear that the idea was his and that his superiors fell in with him. Of course, that the very idea was "primitive" and "hit and miss" would for that reason be dismissed by the precise and scientific mind of Dowding. Douglas continues:

> I could never agree with Collier's statement in his official history of *The Air Defence of the United Kingdom*: ". . . the prevailing opinion was that the slender chance of intercepting bombers in the dark with ordinary day-fighters scarcely justified their diversion from normal duties unless conditions were exceptional." That is being wise after the event, and as was shown by the findings of the Salmond Committee, "the prevailing opinion" at the time was just the opposite.

Douglas cannot have it all ways and hope to come up smelling roses. Collier's statement about "the prevailing opinion" referred to opinion — that is, to informed and expert opinion — in Fighter Command. And in that he is correct. The "prevailing opinion" which Douglas finds to be "just the opposite" was the opinion of Salmond's committee. (And no reader will fail to notice how Douglas, after having intimated that the idea of the single-engined fighters was his, now leans heavily on "the findings of the Salmond Committee" to support him.)

This clear statement of views was far from "being wise after the event". It was Dowding's view at the time. Once again, as in nearly every difference of views, Dowding was right and Douglas and the Air Staff were wrong.

What of the Beaufighter? After stating that "Dowding had made it clearly understood that he much preferred the idea of a more powerful radar-equipped twin-engined night fighter with a pilot and a navigator", Douglas switches sides and now wants to be seen aligned with those who were right. "The idea of this special night-fighter and crew," he says, "had appealed to me from the beginning. . . ."

There is not the slightest scrap of evidence to support this statement. During 1940 he sat on the fence until he saw which side the Air Ministry top brass would come down on, then hastened to declare himself. Later, when it became obvious that the pundits were wrong, he discovered the benefits of hindsight wisdom — and incorporated it into his memoirs.

The space devoted to fighter sweeps over France amounted to five pages of twenty-one. These sweeps, termed 'Rhubarbs' or 'Circuses', were justified

by Douglas on the grounds i) of "wresting the initiative from the Germans";
ii) of providing "valuable experience for pilots, operational commands and the
staffs of the formations concerned", and, after June, iii) of inducing the enemy
"to bring back fighters from the Eastern Front" so as to alleviate some of
the pressure on the Russian defences following Germany's attack against the
Soviet Union. Almost as an afterthought was added "the primary object" of
these fighter incursions as "the destruction of enemy aircraft."

Douglas writes that there was no way of knowing the German losses. He
concedes, however, that the RAF's were serious. The losses, from January to
July 1941, amounted to 226 fighters and pilots. Of these no fewer than 184 were
lost in June and July.

Douglas claims that the first and second objectives were achieved —
though he fails to elaborate on what advantage, if any, was taken of "wresting
the initiative from the Germans". The third objective failed. As to our losses,
Douglas is careful to begin by saying : "It would be unwise to attach too much
importance to statistics showing the claims made and losses suffered by our
fighters month-by-month throughout the offensive." Very unwise — and
downright embarrassing.

It was a minor 'Battle of Britain' in reverse. Douglas and Leigh-Mallory
had apparently learnt nothing from the *Luftwaffe's* experience. Finally, one
must ask what these futile incursions had to do with the serious waging of
war?[2]

If this use of Fighter Command seemed ill-advised and turned out to be
both costly and pointless, the second most important task of Douglas's
Command, that of preparing to meet a second invasion attempt by the
Germans in the spring, merits a scant sixteen paragraphs at the end of his
Despatch. Whereas the report is entitled, 'Air Operations', one recalls the
author's avowed task on taking over his Command in late 1940: "To a large
extent the fate of the British people would be resting in my hands." The pilots
of the offensive sweeps unquestionably gained valuable experience as operational fighter pilots — the surviving pilots, that is — but his Command was
manifestly weaker in July 1941 than it had been the previous December. And,
whereas the squadrons had been reorganized for tactical air fighting by adopt-
ing the flights of two and four aircraft which had already been introduced by
some of Park's Squadrons — though Douglas fails to give credit to them —
there is not a word to suggest that the Groups carried out any exercises in air

firing and air fighting, in tactical exercises, in sector control, in cooperation between the Groups, in exercises with Bomber Command, by way of training for a renewal of the Battle of Britain.

Douglas's report on his two-year stewardship as Commander-in-Chief of Fighter Command does not indicate a single idea or initiative originating with him. All the measures tried for meeting the night attacks had been proposed before he took over. The idea of fighter sweeps, according to Douglas, had been suggested, of all people, by Trenchard to the Air Ministry, who instructed Douglas to confer with his Group Commanders about it. As for preparations for invasion, or liaison with and between his Groups, nothing.

On the other hand, his *Despatch* is larded with expressions such as the following: "I was instructed by the Air Ministry"; "I received a letter from the Secretary of State"; "on receipt of the Air Ministry's letter"; "a formal directive required me to"; "obtain from the Air Ministry a clear statement". There were no fewer than twelve such directives in the first thirteen months of his command.

The second volume of Douglas's autobiography is entitled, *Years of Command.* This volume, and his *Despatch,* together suggest that he would not move without prior, and specific, orders from the Air Staff, and that he **commanded** not at all.[3]

There is something more to Douglas's two volumes of autobiography that calls for comment.

The reader is disagreeably struck by the author's constant practice not only of repeating his own rank and position at every opportunity as if to impress, but, worse, of giving thumbnail sketches of every person he mentions, with particular emphasis on how high they rose and how important they were. One example will suffice:

> Of an even closer link with those days of 1917, and a far more personal one, is the well-known political figure Harold Balfour, then a Captain, who came to join me in No.43 Squadron as one of my Flight Commanders. During the second war, Balfour was Under-Secretary of State for Air. To-day, an old friend of long standing, he is better known as Lord Balfour of Inchrye; and he is a member of the Board of British European Airways.

Such boastful asides interrupt the narrative many dozens of times. Yet in the preface he had asserted: "I shall do my best not to incur in the telling of my story the charge of 'shooting a line'." This is far from a negligible objection. That this man, who had reached the rank of Marshal of the Royal Air Force, should feel the need to indulge in multifarious name-dropping throughout his memoirs suggests a certain psychological defect, if not indeed a moral inferiority.[4]

In support of our case, we will conclude by quoting, and analysing, an episode recounted by Douglas in the second volume of his memoirs. In early 1941 Douglas wrote to the Air Ministry complaining that the Spitfire II was inferior in performance to the improved Messerschmitt Bf 109F and asked that something be done about it. A few days later he was asked to go and see Lord Beaverbrook. When ushered into Beaverbrook's office, the latter shoved a copy of his letter across his desk at Douglas asking him whether he had written it.

Douglas's avowal that he had written it sent Beaverbrook into a frenzy of anger — whether real or feigned, it is impossible to say. "The little man started to roar and shout and wave his fists in the air, and for several minutes he set about roundly abusing me, Fighter Command, and everything to do with us."

All very interesting and informative — especially about Beaverbrook's attitude toward Douglas. However, the telling thing is Douglas's reaction to this tirade. Douglas took it in silence for a time; but then he began to feel that Beaverbrook was going too far. "All said and done, I reminded myself, I was the Commander-in-Chief of Fighter Command and a high-ranking officer in the Royal Air Force. . . ." He also reminded himself that his letter had been perfectly justified, and one simple question came to him: "Why the hell should I take this outburst lying down? With that I promptly lost my temper . . . and started thumping Beaverbrook's desk with my fist and shouting back at him."

We will not dwell on the contrast between the way Beaverbrook treated Douglas and the way he had treated Dowding; nor on Douglas's outburst. What is particularly telling is that Douglas had to **remind himself** that he was the Commander-in-Chief of Fighter Command and a high-ranking officer. In other words, he was utterly lacking in that personal authority a commander **must have.** He was no Trenchard, no Tedder, no Harris. He was above all no Dowding. He was playing a role, a role for which he portrays himself as being singularly unfitted and unequipped.

## II. Leigh-Mallory

The appointment of Leigh-Mallory to command 11 Group is, in itself, a curious and contradictory posting. He wanted the opportunity to muster big wings of fighters. But Park's experience with 11 Group had proved conclusively that there was simply not enough time in which to assemble a wing of three or more squadrons. The Air Ministry conference of October 17 had confirmed the rightness of Park's tactics and leadership. Moreover, the claims of enemy aircraft destroyed put forward by Leigh-Mallory, even in the more favourable conditions prevailing for 12 Group's squadrons, we have been shown to be wild exaggerations. How then was he going to succeed in 11 Group when he had failed in 12 Group? — that is to say, how could he assemble wings of five squadrons in time to 'see off' the much larger attacks expected in the spring of 1941? In a word, what were his 'qualifications' for the position which Richards referred to?

Leigh-Mallory was appointed AOC of 11 Group a full month after Douglas had been installed as AOC-in-C of Fighter Command, and of his new lieutenant's appointment Douglas has this to say: "At the time when I was appointed C-in-C of Fighter Command it was decided that there should be some changes in the Group Commanders. Since I was such a new boy I had nothing to do with these decisions..." This statement is revealing. It reveals three interesting things. First, since some changes in the Group Commanders were being considered while Douglas was still the VCAS, and knowing of his imminent appointment to Fighter Command, he did and said nothing to ensure that Park stayed where he was or was even moved to a more responsible position; and therefore he acquiesced in his removal and demotion. Second, he most certainly did know about the decisions; and the Chief of the Air Staff (Portal) would most assuredly have consulted him about them. Third, by his use of the term 'a new boy', he tries to 'act the innocent' and to suggest that he was not important enough to be consulted on the matter. We might add  that, in saying that he had nothing to do with these decisions he tries to suggest that he had no direct and official hand in them. That may be technically correct; but the statement is dishonest because he it was who was one of the chief instigators in Dowding's removal and in the changes which he both engineered and approved of.

Confirmation of Douglas's knowing of Leigh-Mallory's new command — and hence of his mendacity — and indeed of Leigh-Mallory's knowing of it himself even before Douglas's new appointment, is provided by an officer serving at 12 Group Headquarters at the time: "The telephone conversations between Sholto Douglas and Leigh-Mallory continued until one evening Sholto Douglas confirmed that he was to replace Dowding as C-in-C of Fighter Command. Leigh-Mallory congratulated him and said, 'I am glad that I am to be closely associated with you in my next appointment.'" Note: 'in my next appointment.'

We have had occasion to review some of Leigh-Mallory's defects as a tactical commander and as a man. The following episode, recounted by Park's biographer, and which did not come to light until 1968, buttresses that judgment.

> An alarming instance of Leigh-Mallory's unfitness was seen on 29 January 1941 when he decided to conduct a paper exercise using the circumstances of an actual attack on Kenley, Biggin Hill and Hornchurch on 6 September 1940. His intention was to prove correct his opinion on the use of large formations. The exercise was carefully set up and Leigh-Mallory totally mismanaged it. The raid was not intercepted inbound and both Kenley and Biggin Hill were 'bombed' while their aircraft were still on the ground.... When Lang[5] explained Leigh-Mallory's several mistakes to him, he replied that next time he would do better. In fact, there was no next time. He later told Lang that 'if there are any more major battles over England I shall control all of them.' He went on to declare, echoing Douglas, that if a large-scale raid approached, he would permit it to bomb its target and intercept it in force on the way back to France. The enemy, he believed, would be so badly mauled that there would be no more raids.

Leigh-Mallory's deficiencies were well-known long before this. In chapter 3, discussing tactics, we mentioned 12 Group's failure to defend its own region against a heavy attack on August 15th. This attack, by fifty unescorted Ju88s across the North Sea, was precisely the kind of attack for which 12 Group had been prepared. What happened? On that day Leigh-Mallory was absent from his Headquarters on a visit to Wittering. His place as controller was taken by a wing commander who, when the raiders were plotted, took the unusual step of sending most of the fighters to protect the major industrial cities instead of on a direct interception vector over the sea. As a result the fighters made no contact and two RAF aerodromes, Driffield and Leaconfield, were heavily damaged.

We do not know what Leigh-Mallory would have done. The point is that he had put a controller in charge who he must have known was inexperienced. Leigh-Mallory was the longest-serving Group Commander in Fighter Command, having been in his command since 1937; but he had not seen to the efficiency and training of a deputy Group Controller.

A direct cause of Leigh-Mallory's failure as a fighter commander operating within the Dowding system may be found precisely in the manner he had of directing operations. His biographer, Bill Newton Dunn, writes: "During the battles, L-M sat 'in the chair' in his Group's Operations Room and conducted the battle himself. Having carried out the most pre-war practices, Cross [Squadron Leader Kenneth Cross] considers that L-M had become the best Group commander." [Dunn means: L-M having carried out the most exercises, not Cross.][6]

Of Park's direction Dunn says, amusingly, though without amusing intent: "By contrast, Park at 11 Group walked up and down his Operations Room, giving advice to other people who were sitting in the chairs and having to take the responsibility."

Churchill visited 11 Group Headquarters on September 15th. In his war memoirs he wrote a graphic, and dramatic, and admiring account of what he witnessed:

> The Group Operations Room was like a small theatre, about sixty feet across, and with two storeys. We took our seats in the Dress Circle. . . . Presently the red bulbs showed that the majority of our squadrons were engaged. A subdued hum arose from the floor, where the busy plotters pushed their discs to and fro in accordance with the swiftly-changing situation. Air Vice-Marshal Park gave general directions for the disposition of his fighter force, which were translated into detailed orders to each fighter station by a youngish officer in the centre of the Dress Circle, at whose side I sat. Some years after I asked his name. He was Lord Willoughby de Broke. (I met him next in 1947, when the Jockey Club, of which he was a Steward, invited me to see the Derby. He was surprised that I remembered the occasion.) He now gave the orders for the individual squadrons to ascend and patrol as the result of the final information which appeared on the map-table. The Air Marshal himself walked up and down behind, watching with a vigilant eye every move in the game, supervising his junior executive's hand, only intervening with some decisive order, usually to reinforce a threatened area. In a little while all our squadrons were fighting, and some had already begun to return for fuel. All were in the air. The lower line of bulbs was out. There was not one squadron left in reserve.

At this moment Park spoke to Dowding at Stanmore, asking for three squadrons from No.12 Group to be put at his disposal in case of another major attack while his squadrons were rearming and refuelling. This was done. They were specially needed to cover London and our fighter aerodromes, because No. 11 Group had already shot their bolt. The young officer, to whom this seemed a matter of routine, continued to give his orders, in accordance with the general directions of his Group Commander, in a calm, low monotone, and the three reinforcing squadrons were soon absorbed. I became conscious of the anxiety of the Commander, who now stood still behind his subordinate's chair. Hitherto I had watched in silence. I now asked: "What other reserves have we?" "There are none," said Air Vice-Marshal Park. In an account which he wrote about it afterwards he said that at this I "looked grave". Well I might. What losses should we not suffer if our refuelling planes were caught on the ground by further raids of "40 plus" or "50 plus"! The odds were great; our margins small; the stakes infinite.

This description underscores two of the magisterial features of the Dowding system. First, the important role played by every individual, who was well trained and to whom was delegated the responsibility and authority necessary to his task. Second the system of reserves. The remark of Park's, "There are none", has been misunderstood. He was referring to his own Group. But the squadrons of 10 Group, 12 Group, and 13 Group were in a very real strategic sense reserve squadrons ready and waiting to be called to the scenes of action and to replace tired squadrons in 11 Group. This feature is demonstrated by Park's call to Dowding.

Returning to Leigh-Mallory, we wonder whether it was then, after the débâcle of the mismanaged exercise, that he grasped at the straw of the idea of offensive fighter sweeps? All that has been said of Fighter Command's task in the year 1941 in discussing Douglas's role is equally relevant to Leigh-Mallory, for this officer was the commander of the group which provided most of the squadrons for the sweeps.

Peter Wykeham, in his *Fighter Command*, devotes the better part of two chapters to the tactics of 'leaning forward into France'. On the other hand, *The Luftwaffe War Diaries*, and Air Vice-Marshal J.E. 'Johnnie' Johnson in his authoritative *The Story of Air Fighting*, give them not a single line, obviously considering them as inconsequential and militarily insignificant.

But what of the wings themselves, which Leigh-Mallory championed so enthusiastically? Johnnie Johnson, who flew Spitfires in the European theatre throughout the War and took part in these sweeps, wrote in his *Wing Leader* that the wings "were difficult to control in action because the pilots got in each other's way." He learned from his experience that "Park had been right : three squadrons could be worked together, more could not, and a pair was the ideal formation."[7]

Leigh-Mallory's opportunity for fame presented itself on August 19th 1942 when instructed to provide fighter cover for the Dieppe raid. It turned out to be the greatest one day air battle of the war.

> Control of the air operation was entrusted to Air Vice-Marshal Leigh-Mallory, and a force of fifty-six fighter squadrons — Hurricanes, Spitfires and Typhoons — was placed at his disposal. . . . Caught by surprise, the German Air Force could at first challenge us only with fighters; but these appeared in growing numbers — twenty-five, fifty, a hundred. Then, at 1000 hours, the enemy's bombers came on the scene. Under strong escort they repeatedly strove to pierce the protective canopy of our fighters. As repeatedly they were driven off. . . . On the more general issues, it was realized at the time that the close support provided by Leigh-Mallory's squadrons was not entirely effective. . . . On the other hand, the all-important task of protecting the raiding troops and the vessels off shore was performed with outstanding success. Our soldiers fought completely unmolested from the air.

This operation does merit a comment in *The Luftwaffe Diaries* — a succinct two lines : "The British and Canadian landing attempt at Dieppe, bloodily repulsed and with the loss of 106 British bombers and fighters." The Germans lost forty-eight fighters.

The preceding paragraph in this book records another major episode in this period : "The successful break through the Channel, aided by strong air cover, of the battleships, *Scharnhorst* and *Gneisenau,* and the cruiser *Prinz Eugen* on February 12, 1942." Wykeham describes the scene thus from the British side:

> Fighter Command was caught off guard, more than at any time in the war. No. 11 Group radar began plotting the German fighter umbrella from 8:30 a.m. onwards, but for some reason decided that it was an enemy air/sea rescue operation, and it was not until 10:20 a.m., when the plot was seen to be moving at 25 to 30 knots, that Leigh-Mallory's controller concluded that it might be a convoy. Leigh-Mallory himself was taking part in a parade at Northolt. The weather was bad and a pair of Spitfires sent to investigate saw only the E-Boats on the fringe of the fleet. While the pilots were making

their report the radar stations on the south coast informed No. 11 Group that attempts were being made to jam them, and shortly afterwards they actually detected ships off Le Touquet. Yet with all these indications the first sighting report came from the merest chance.

Group Captain Beamish, Station Commander at Kenley, had decided that the weather was ideal for a 'Rhubarb', and had obtained permission to fly one in company with his Wing Leader, Wing Commander Boyd. They hoped to pick up a stray Messerschmitt over the French coast, and in this they were eminently successful, for at 10:30 a.m. they bumped full tilt into the fighter escort of the German naval force. Unable to dogfight owing to the low cloud they speedily quitted the scene, only pausing to rake with their cannons an E-boat which appeared in the mist and rain below. As they turned away from it they saw the screen of German destroyers creaming along on a north-easterly course, and behind them the looming bulks of capital ships, forging through the sea in line ahead.

Churchill was furious. It was a black eye for Fighter Command. The offensive sweeps, night fighting failures, Dieppe, the *Scharnhorst* and *Gneisenau:* these are the consequences of Leigh-Mallory's 'qualifications' for his command. He sought to entice the enemy into the air and engage them in battle; and he succeeded, to our cost. Fighter Command was on the offensive; the defending Germans inflicted heavy losses on our pilots. That should have told a great deal to Leigh-Mallory and Douglas about either the relative odds, or the relative standards of training. The results indicate that Leigh-Mallory and Douglas had neglected the advanced fighter training of their pilots to a degree that should have set off alarm signals in the Air Ministry. But the Air Ministry seemed to give Fighter Command the licence to do what they liked.

What of renewed assaults against Fighter Command and invasion in 1941? Douglas opined in his *Despatch:* "I believe that if the Germans had delivered a second daylight offensive in 1941 . . . Fighter Command would have given as good an account of itself as in the previous Summer." It is a cautiously hesitant and tentative opinion. The opinion of most experts is not at all hesitant. And it is not in the least complimentary to Douglas and Leigh-Mallory. Neither officer produced a single idea by himself. Every 'idea' ever put forward by Leigh-Mallory — such as the 'big wing' idea — originated with someone else, and was appropriated by him and advanced as his own. The policy of 'leaning forward into France' was costly and achieved little. Dowding "would certainly resist the use of his fighters offensively over France". Precisely!

We have an eye-witness account of the futility of these incursions into France, in particular those requiring close fighter escort to bombers. In them, the new leaders of Fighter Command show they had learnt nothing from the Germans' mistakes of 1940. Leigh-Mallory used to hold regular conferences at Northolt, attended by the leaders of the fighter wings and the bomber leaders. At one such conference the fighter leader Johnnie Kent, who was commanding officer of 303 (Polish) Squadron, questioned the purpose of these operations. He first stated that the small bombers used in such small numbers had no visible effect on the enemy industry. He then continued:

> If the bombers were merely there as bait to bring up the fighters so that they could be destroyed then we should restrict our radius of activity to that which would permit us to fight without the nagging fear of running out of fuel. This mental obstacle seriously interfered with a pilot's fighting spirit and it was my opinion that we had already lost far too many first class men because these factors were not receiving sufficient consideration.

Kent goes on to say that at this challenging of his policy, Leigh-Mallory looked taken aback, and turned to his Group Operations Officer for reply. This was Group Captain Victor Beamish, an experienced and successful fighter leader. To Leigh-Mallory's bewilderment, Beamish agreed with Kent. Leigh-Mallory then turned to another of his staff officers, one who had had no operational experience in this war, and presumably got an answer, fatuous though it was, that satisfied him: "My answer to Kent is — we've done it!" Kent got angry and flung back some "rude remarks". "The AOC," concludes Kent, " preferred the second opinion and we continued to go to Lille and lose good men, all to little purpose."[8]

"Worse even than the fact that these operations were virtually useless from a military point of view was the fact that they dominated all thinking about fighters." This stultifying effect on progressive thought at the highest levels can be seen in its woeful influence on the two strategic arenas in the immediate present and in the near future.

Firstly, the effect on overseas operations was disastrous. There existed no air defence system in India or in the Far East, and none even in the Middle East, where decisive battles were being fought out. While a thousand Spitfires, with all their equipment, armament, pilots and ground crews, did next to nothing in Britain, the Middle East had to make do with Hurricanes, which were not adequate opposition to the Me109s. It appears that Douglas refused to release any of his squadrons. And Portal sat on his thumbs, despite urgent and repeated pleas from Tedder throughout 1942. It was not until late 1942, about the time of Alamein, that Spitfires began to reach the Desert squadrons. So much, once again, for the 'global strategic view' of the Air Ministry.

Having excoriated Douglas and Leigh-Mallory for their incompetence, unfitness and consequent bungling, and exposed Portal for his failure of strategic vision, we must properly ask: What else could Fighter Command have done? An excessive amount of Fighter Command's resources and of its commander's energies and time were devoted, wastefully, on the useless operations over Northern France. As a result, the development of a first-class night-fighter and controlling system, and the perfecting of the daytime defensive network of groups, squadrons, and controllers, were grievously neglected, especially during the first seven months of Douglas's and Leigh-Mallory's commands.

AIR VICE MARSHAL
TRAFFORD LEIGH-MALLORY
AOC 12 GROUP

AIR VICE MARSHAL
WILLIAM SHOLTO DOUGLAS
VICE-CHIEF OF THE AIR STAFF

## The Schemers who benefited the most from Dowding's removal

Perhaps these tasks would not have occupied their resources and energies fully after May 1941. There was, however, one over-riding requirement which Fighter Command and the Air Ministry reprehensively ignored. That was the development of a long-range fighter. The pilots and squadrons complained endlessly about the limitations of their fighters — exactly as the German fighter pilots had complained about theirs during the Battle.

All too often the Air Ministry, perhaps because "an unwieldy and cumbersome administrative machine", seemed to function in a vacuum, remote from what was going on at the Commands and squadrons. Its record, both during the War and again, lamentably, in the post-war years, in the matter of the development of realistic strategic plans and of the equipment, especially of aircraft, to carry them into effect, is calculated to inspire disillusion and cynicism.

The failure to develop and exploit the manifold uses of the de Havilland Mosquito — in Embry's opinion the finest aeroplane to be produced in the War — is well-known. The failure to develop the jet engine before the Germans, who accomplished it two years before the RAF, despite the intensive bombing campaign against their homeland, was a disgrace. Their joint failure to recognize that the offensive fighter could be effectively — and in the event, **was** — a pre-eminent **strategic** weapon of the War, can be attributed to their inward looking habits and their endemic failure to see ahead.

This judgment is not hindsight. There were in the 1930s airmen and strategists, admittedly few, but who saw that the next war would be dominated and decided in the Air. Most of the few, it is true, thought only in terms of attack, and the bomber. But the concept of 'supremacy in the air' must have led, eventually, to its corollary, namely, that command of the air — i.e. of one's own airspace as well as that of the enemy, which was the whole point of the Battle of Britain — could only be won by fighters. To think such thoughts, to look ahead, to learn lessons from the past, whether distant or close, well, isn't that the whole purpose of staff colleges and defence colleges? Is it not indeed one of the major reasons for existence of the Air Staff of the Air Ministry?

After the proving of the Messerschmitt in Spain, and the success of the Hurricane and Spitfire designs in 1936, and especially after the demonstration of radar, there was no excuse for looking for guidance to the past. For lessons, yes; but not for precepts for policy and action. The failure to recognize this fundamental reality both before and, signally, until at least 1942, is one of the gravest strategic shortcomings chargeable to the CAS and the Air Staff.

The fighter was essential for protecting and escorting bombers to their targets. The long-range fighter was essential to the perfecting of a long-range bombing strategy. The Americans rejected the RAF's night-bombing strategy. Portal denied for three years the need to develop a long-range fighter. Eventually the Americans produced the P-48 Thunderbolt and the P-51 Mustang — the latter with British help and, especially, with a Rolls-Royce engine.[9] Thanks to these magnificent long-range fighters, and especially to the Mustang, the USAAF were finally able to escort their bombers wherever the bombers went, and thereby established domination of the German airspace. Without this supremacy, the invasion of Normandy in June 1944 would not have been possible.

There is little doubt but that Portal's failure here was a grievous one. John Terraine has summarized the dispute between the British and the Americans in Appendix "G" of his book, *The Right of the Line*. Terraine has been criticized by the pro-Portal, and hence the pro-Air Ministry, faction in this controversy. But Terraine's evidence, documented and impeccable, is beyond dispute. We will recapitulate the salient points; and conclude by contributing an item which may have escaped the notice of both Terraine and his critics.

When the Americans entered the war and engaged in discussion with the RAF on strategic bomber policy, they determined on daylight bombing as the best way of achieving positive results. They thought that massed boxes of their heavy bombers, with their gun positions covering every possible angle of enemy fighter approach, would 'see off' any possible *Luftwaffe* attack. They were sadly mistaken. Their losses were terrible. They concluded that the only way in which they could maintain their strategic bombing offensive by daylight was for their bombers to be escorted by fighters. Long-range fighters, that is, capable of fighting on equal terms with the *Luftwaffe* fighters which had the advantage of range and warning.

The Americans — in particular, their Commander, General H.H. Arnold — looked around and saw the Fighter Command of the RAF virtually unemployed. "He found the spectacle of a fighter force which Portal stated to consist of 1,461 aircraft with crews remaining inactive while his bombers were being shot out of the sky both incomprehensible and unacceptable."

Portal persistently opposed the idea that a fully operational long-range fighter could be produced. Terraine produces none of the evidence buttressing Portal's arguments. But he quotes the official history of the aerial campaign against the German heartland with telling, and conclusive, effect.

In 1941, 1942, and even 1943, Portal was blind and obdurate. On May 27, 1941, he told Churchill: "The long range fighter, whether built specifically as such, or whether given increased range by fitting extra tanks, will be at a disadvantage compared with the short range high performance fighter." Portal repeated this view one week later, when Churchill insisted that everything be done to increase the operational range of fighters.

In 1942, the Air Staff, under Portal's direction, viewed with considerable scepticism — perhaps because of their 'superior' experience! — the preference of the United States Army Air Force for carrying out the bombing of Germany by daylight. It was preferred precisely because of the greatly increased likelihood of accurate bombing of targets correctly located and precisely identified.

> The clear realization of the limited offensive potential of Fighter Command did not result in efforts to extend the range of that force. Indeed, Sir Charles Portal was convinced that the production or modification of an aircraft with the range of a heavy bomber and the performance of an interceptor fighter was a technical impossibility. In 1943 there was an acrimonious exchange of letters between Arnold and Portal. But Portal remained obdurate. Webster and Frankland conclude their analysis of the situation in these terms : Sir Charles Portal saw no prospect of engaging the Royal Air Force Fighter Command effectively in the POINT BLANK campaign [i.e. the coordinated bombing of Germany industrial and military targets by the RAF and the USAAF]. He had never accepted the proposition of a long-range fighter which could effectively engage opposing short-range, or interceptor, fighters.
> . . .

Arnold had no difficulty in proving Portal wrong by having a number of Spitfires disassembled, crated and shipped to the United States, where they were modified — "specially equipped" — and then flown back across the Atlantic non-stop to England. Even that demonstration failed to convince, or move, the RAF's top thinker.

In fact, Arnold did not need to do that. The feat had already, and long before, been accomplished. We have already seen that Sidney Cotton, having acquired two Spitfires from Dowding in early 1940, managed to strip and equip them so as to give them a range of 1,250 miles — which was 1,000 miles more than their normal range. He did better. In consultation with Supermarine's, who fitted extra tanks, he got Spitfires capable of a range of up to 2,000 miles. This was in February 1941.

It is true that these long-range, reconnaissance Spitfires were stripped of all armament and superfluous weight. But how much ingenuity at Supermarine's was required to extend the combat Spitfire's range by two or three or even four times its normal fighting range, provided only that the drive to do so was exerted from the top? Did Portal know about Cotton's achievements? Of course he did. His was the decisive hand in Cotton's dismissal. Portal's failure to promote the development of a long-range escort fighter for the Royal Air Force is one of the most egregious sins of the Second World War.[10]

If the RAF had pioneered the long-range fighter, several consequences would have flowed from it : 1) Bomber Command would have been able to carry out an infinitely more accurate, sustained and scientific assault against Germany's war industries; 2) the war might well have been shortened; and 3) Bomber Command would have been spared its terrible casualties.

The notion of the fighter as a war-winning strategic weapon is hard for some people to grasp. It was obviously hard to grasp for an avowed 'bomber man'.

The answer to 'Hap' Arnold's problem was found in the Mustang, once it was fitted with the Rolls-Royce Merlin 66 engine — which combination in itself was a happy product of coincidence. "When the sturdy little Mustang first appeared over Hanover, Goering refused to believe the reporting centre and censured its personnel; but when he was finally convinced he simply said, 'We have lost the war!'"

Goering's insight is fully corroborated by the US Strategic Bombing Survey, one of whose conclusions was that their daylight bombing campaign, with fighter escort, effectively destroyed the *Luftwaffe's* defensive arm. This result, albeit a by-product of the campaign, permitted the Allies to establish the supremacy of the air but for which the Normandy landings could not have been carried out.

The offensive fighter/interceptor thus proved to be one of the major strategic weapons of the war, for it determined the outcome of land and sea battles as well as strictly aerial battles. Few people understood this. Certainly no one in the Air Ministry understood it. Neither Douglas nor Leigh-Mallory, and not Portal either, three accomplices blinded by their ignorance of fighters and their hostility to Dowding, were even remotely capable of grasping that central fact.

We have demonstrated time and again in the course of our inquiries that the Air Ministry and its planners were incapable of thinking of any other concept than that of strategic bombers. After the Battle of Britain they had a fighter arm which kept on growing, in size if in nothing else. Now, with the battle won, they did not know what to do with it. Dowding's and Park's successors were not fighter men. They bungled the night defences; and when the night *Blitz* came to an end, they lamely continued their useless and wasteful sorties over France, for the sole reason that they did not have the imagination or leadership to envisage any other use for the fighter.

Douglas lasted for two years as chief of Fighter Command, and one wonders why. Leigh-Mallory, for his part, succeeded Douglas as  Air Officer Commanding-in-Chief of Fighter Command, and the same question shouts itself aloud.

Is it possible for a man to rise so high, without the personal and professional qualifications necessary for the job?

The public are accustomed to seeing this scandal take place around them all the time in the domain of politics, for there are no established qualifications and no formal training required for political office.

But even in spheres of life where applicants and incumbents are appraised constantly — in the armed services, in universities, in the civil service, in industry, for example — it happens even there all too frequently. Men are poor judges of others. The good judge of character and hidden motives is a rare person. Why? Because men are not what they seem. It is the first lesson — and a lesson which nearly drove him out of his mind — that we see Hamlet learn : "Seems, madam !" he replies to the Queen. "Nay, it is; I know not 'seems'."  And three scenes later, in referring to the King, the perfidious Claudius: " O villain, villain, smiling, damned villain! . . . That one may smile, and smile, and be a villain".

Unmerited advancement is accomplished by means of a diverse armoury of attributes and wiles, including flattery, bluff, charm, glibness, dissimulation, mock indignation, off-loading work to subordinates, taking the credit for other's work, falsification. In a word, they have mastered the art of appearances, of concealing what they are and appearing what they are not. It is too often assumed that what rises to the top is cream. Ambitious men will do anything to reach the top. But can others be readily misled and duped ? Listen: "I reaffirm my impression that U.J. is the goods — sincere, simple and big."

U.J., or Uncle Joe, is Stalin. The impression is Portal's. And of Portal his biographer wrote : "In small things as in great, Portal had a habit of being right." And did not Portal **know** for a positive fact the horrendous record of Stalin as a mass murderer? Surely Stalin was, and was known to be, one of the most evil men who ever added suffering beyond all calculable measure to a suffering humanity. Portal, who thought him 'sincere, simple and big', was not the only man-at-the-top who was taken in, or who allowed himself to be led by the nose.

This entire question of appearances and ambition, aims and achievement, is a variation on the theme of justice itself. The moral problem of justice analyses the relationship between good and evil, and reward and punishment, and wrestles with the notion that the virtuous will be rewarded and the wicked punished. Men feel intuitively that it is only **right** that such a moral order should exist. Religions teach the inexorable workings of the moral law. But then they spoil things by adding the rider: "Well, if not in this world, in the next." Rationalists posit a natural law which also promises a universe governed by an immutable moral law which is discoverable by reason alone; but the rationalists do not have the comfort of being able to fall back on an afterlife if things don't turn out according to one's hopes; and when they discover that both experience and observation of real life have a disconcerting propensity for demonstrating time and again that 'good things happen to bad guys'; that crime can pay; and that 'good guys come last'.

In eighteenth century France the hitherto accepted moral order had been, apparently, so thoroughly turned inside out that de Sade wrote a number of brilliant — and yes, prurient — philosophical novels whose central theme is an extended elaboration of the thesis that 'no act of kindness goes unpunished.' Conversely: "Being bad can be a good career move. Discarded principles can hasten a climber's ascent. The most popular people may be skilled deceivers or flatterers. A ruthless competitor may be safer from retribution than one encumbered by principles and pity." Ambition, jealousy, malice, revenge: these sins compound the equation. There will be no end to people reaching the top because they were opportunists and good dissimulators to boot.

Sholto Douglas is characterized by Gough and Richards as being "cleverer and more worldly" than Dowding. A comparison of the two men's achievements and character suggests that 'cleverer' means 'more calculating', and 'more worldly' means 'ready to put ends before means'. Such a man would know the art of dissimulation. He accomplished nothing that might be called memorable. His biography confirms this assessment. The style is a measure of the man. The methods of literary analysis reveal his writing to be ordinary, featureless, unoriginal, and pedestrian. To compensate, he is given to boasting, to fudging, to name-dropping, and at times to outright mendacity.

Douglas was not as discrete as Portal. When Sidney Cotton first met him, in March 1940, Cotton was having his usual difficulties in getting authorization for his proposed actions. Cotton wrote of that confused time, in France:

> It was consoling to know that I wasn't the only one who was fighting on two fronts — the Germans and the Air Ministry. Another man . . . Air Commodore Douglas Colyer, then the British Air Attaché in Paris . . . advised me to handle the Air Force machine much as a good mechanic would handle a troublesome motor-car engine; keep tickling the carburettor, and if one spanner didn't fit, try another. Sholto Douglas, whom I met about this time, told me much the same thing. The RAF, he said, was full of regulations which had been thought up over the years by people with nothing better to do, and which gave those who studied them the chance to delay and sabotage anything they could get their hands on. "But take my advice, Sidney," he added, "learn how the machine works and you can beat them. You can rise to any heights if you study the machine and use it properly."

Cotton adds sardonically: "It seems he knew what he was talking about, for he subsequently became C-in-C Fighter Command, C-in-C Coastal Command, and C-in-C British Forces in Germany". Sadly, this writer would place more credence on this word of Sidney Cotton than on the sworn testimony of ten air marshals testifying for Douglas.

Leigh-Mallory, similarly, accomplished little in 11 Group or Fighter Command. He was out of his depth and knew nothing of fighters and their potential.

After Leigh-Mallory's death in a flying accident, 'Johnnie' Johnson wrote an appreciation of him, in which he said: "L-M was very much a 'fatherly' figure and at his best when he held conferences with his young 'wing leaders', because he did not pretend to know about fighter tactics and relied on us to keep him up to date."

The statement beggars belief! This was 1944. Leigh-Mallory had been in Fighter Command since 1937 — that is, for seven continuous years — yet "he did not . . . know about fighter tactics"! At least that is believable! Johnson is altogether too kind.

In the summer of 1942, the Chief of the Imperial General Staff, General Sir Alan Brooke, had the invidious task of going to Egypt to tell General Auchinleck that he was being relieved of his command. The Prime Minister wanted Brooke to take over. Brooke, despite his burning desire to have an operational command again, had a number of reasons for declining. The clinching reason, as he explained in his diary, was the following: "Finally, I could not bear the thought that Auchinleck might think that I had come out here on purpose to work myself into his shoes." Sholto Douglas and Leigh-Mallory had no such scruples.

The Royal Air Force is an unparalleled creation. In a real sense its foundations were the work of one man, Hugh Trenchard. In 1928 T.E. Lawrence wrote to him: ". . . the RAF is the finest individual effort in British history. . . . the RAF is your single work, and it's thanks to your being head and shoulders greater in character than ordinary men that your force even in its childhood surpasses the immemorial army and navy."

An essential ingredient of that creation is high ideals. The Royal Air Force has attracted, by that very virtue, thousands of men and women of the finest character and ability. Sholto Douglas and Leigh-Mallory were not of their number.

## NOTES TO CHAPTER 8:

1. The crest of Fighter Command, which is reproduced on the front cover of this book, bears the motto: OFFENCE - DEFENCE. One wonders where in the Air Ministry this devise was dreamt up. To place 'Offence' before 'Defence' is to put the cart before the horse, in defiance of the first principle of war, and Fighter Command could never prove itself as an offensive arm in any event.

2. Douglas's career shows us that he took over Fighter Command after all the real work had been done; that he then went to the Middle East Command after the battle had been won; and that he then became AOC-in-C of Coastal Command after the U-Boat had been mastered in the Battle of the Atlantic. Nothing in the chapter on Douglas in Henry Probert's book, *High Commanders of the Royal Air Force,* justifies any change in this section of chapter 8.

3. Robert Wright, who wrote much of Douglas's memoirs, complained later, regretting that he had been hoodwinked into the job of co-author, because he found that he had written things for Douglas that were demonstrably untrue.

4. ACM Sir Kenneth Cross, *Straight and Level,* p. 122. Cross recounts that later in the war, after meeting Douglas for the first time, "I heard (him) described as 'the Goering of the RAF'." (p.78.)

5. Wing Commander Thomas Lang, one of the senior controllers in 11 Group.

6. A careful reading and search of the relevant chapters and sections of Cross's autobiography discloses no such opinion on the author's part. It is wishful thinking by Dunn. But then, Dunn was Leigh-Mallory's nephew.

7. For Park's views of wings, see Appendix "B".

8. J.A. Kent, pp. 165–166.

9. A full account of the development of the Mustang is to be read in *Wilfred Freeman,* a biography by Anthony Furse, chapter 14.

10. It is pertinent to wonder whether Dowding had any views about the possibility of a long-range fighter. The answer is that he did. In his *Twelve Legions of Angels* (ch. 3), he wrote (in 1941):

    > It is not possible to make a fighter which can accompany bombers to Berlin and back unless you make it nearly as big as the bomber, and then it would lose its handiness and manoeuvrability and be at a disadvantage against enemy fighters.

    To this he added: "We have so many specialised types already that we do not want to add to them." The Dowding admirer is disappointed to read this short-sighted view. But one wonders whether he would have changed his mind as the war progressed, if he had remained in the Royal Air Force — especially if he had remained as C-in-C of Fighter Command, or become the Chief of the Air Staff.

WINSTON S. CHURCHILL
PRIME MINISTER

LORD BEAVERBROOK
MINISTER FOR
AIRCRAFT PRODUCTION

HAROLD BALFOUR
UNDER-SECRETARY OF
STATE FOR AIR

*The men who let Dowding down at the end*

# CHAPTER 9

## *Recognition Denied*

We suggested at the beginning of our investigations that the achievements of Dowding were of such magnitude and far-reaching consequences that his name should be as illustrious as any other great commander of the 20th century, or even of Western Civilization. That it is not can be attributed to a number of factors.

In our Introduction we stated our conviction that the Battle of Britain could have been won without Churchill: it could not have been won without Dowding. Yet, ironically, it was Churchill, despite his admiration of Dowding, who was partly to blame for denying to Dowding the public fame that was rightfully his.

We have no need to add our mite to the universal recognition of Churchill's leadership and oratory in galvanizing British resistance to Hitler's threats, aggressions and numbing victories. His was the dominating presence, not only in Britain but, thanks to radio, throughout the free world — and parts of the world that were less than free — that focused attention on the Battle and its true import.

General Montgomery, later, had all the time in the world to exploit his situation. Dowding, after his retirement in 1942, was in no comparable situation to capitalize on his achievements, any more than Wavell was, for the reason that the war was still far from won, and men's minds were turned inexorably to the present and the future, not at all to the past. Future historians would look after the past. At the successful end of the war, Dowding had been virtually forgotten. But Montgomery was still very much a public figure — and a revered public figure, because of his stream of reported victories from 1942 until the end of the war. Then again, in 1940 the interests of security were paramount, whereas three and four years later there was greater scope for personal publicity.

Could Dowding have publicized his achievements after the war in order to gain public recognition? We believe that he could have done so, and by the same means as those exploited by Montgomery, namely, by encouraging and sponsoring the organization of rallies and reunions of Battle of Britain veterans, both aircrews and all other personnel involved, at, for example, the Albert Hall. But there lies the difference between the two men. Montgomery was a self-publicist. (It is only fair to say that that was his style: he made himself known **and seen** by all his officers and men. During the Battle of Britain Dowding hardly ever visited his squadrons. But his presence was felt throughout Fighter Command nonetheless.)

Dowding was not a public figure. He was, strange though it may seem, a retiring man. When confronted by the needs of a nation in mortal danger, he fought as no one else fought. But that was behind the scenes. And yet, I for one have no doubt but that, had he been called upon to do so, he would have stepped into the full glare of the public light to rally the nation or the Royal Air Force. (For he knew there was no other high officer, not even Trenchard himself, who possessed the same dynamic conviction and articulateness.) But the call was not needed. And when the time came for him to retire, as it did in 1942, he was content to withdraw into an almost total obscurity.

The Air Ministry was also, not only content, but relieved, that he should do so. And therein lies the gravest obloquy attached to its name. When the Air Ministry was under the most solemn obligation to make known the illustrious accomplishments of one of its two greatest air marshals, and of its greatest operational air commander as the saviour that he was, it embarked on a policy of wilful denial.

Of course, within the Air Ministry it was widely held that it was right and fitting that official recognition of the victory that was won by the Battle of Britain, and that an official record, if necessarily brief and provisional, of what was accomplished by the men and women who had played the major roles in the Battle, should be published.

This was done in the spring of 1941, and took the form of a slim paperbacked anonymous booklet entitled: *The Battle of Britain. An Air Ministry Account of the Great Days from 8th August–31st October 1940.* The narrative concluded with these words: "Future historians may compare it with Marathon, Trafalgar and the Marne."

No one would question this claim. There are none who would challenge the inclusion of this Battle on the same scale of national and global significance as Marathon, Trafalgar and the Marne. One writer has judged that all subsequent battles and victories in the Second World War, and all leaders who subsequently rose to fame in it, did so by the grace of Dowding and the Battle of Britain. Anyone who would dispute these claims has only to consider the consequences to the world if the Battle had been lost. The immediate consequence would have been the invasion, defeat and occupation of Britain and the British Isles. Hitler would then have embarked on his assault of the Soviet Union. With no aid possible from or via Britain, as was in fact pro-vided throughout the war, the Soviet Union would have been defeated and her political and military leaders would have been liquidated, as well as the *intelligentsia,* to the last man and woman.

Similarly, with no reinforcements reaching North Africa or the Middle East from Britain, as in fact took place throughout 1940 and 1941, those regions would also have been overrun. A link-up of the German armies from north and south on the east side of the Mediterranean basin would have given Germany all the oil of the Middle East, and would have isolated India, Burma and China, and eventually, Australia and New Zealand.

Imagine, in this global situation, the position of the United States. Would Japan have still attacked Pearl Harbor, or taken some more decisive action? Would the strategic and political decisions of the U.S. have been the same? (Let us remember that, in this hypothetical global chessboard, many South American states were very unhypothetically pro-Nazi.) Or would the U.S. have retreated into a Fortress America until . . . until Germany and Japan, each dominating half of the world, went to war against each other? . . . Or until the U.S. were able to develop and produce atomic weapons with their delivery systems before their enemies?

But all that, or some similar course of events, did not take place. And that it did not take place we look to the Battle of Britain and its outcome. A penetrating look will convince the reader of the likely truth of the global prognosis outlined above. Churchill did not exaggerate when he proclaimed, and warned, on June 18th in a characteristic prophetic voice: "What General Weygand called the Battle of France is over. I expect that the Battle of Britain is about to begin. Upon this battle depends the survival of Christian civilization."

It is true that in this speech Churchill was the politician appealing to the United States, with an implied threat, to enter the war, or at least to provide Britain with the weapons and armaments she needed in order to resist Nazi

Germany. But the speech was also that of a statesman with olympian vision. Dowding agreed with Churchill's evaluation of the situation, and wrote to Churchill to tell him so.

The victory in the Battle of Britain meant that the British Isles became the unsinkable platform and armed camp from which was launched the eventual onslaught against Germany, by air from 1941 and by land in 1944, which resulted in the destruction of the Nazi régime and the liberation of Western Europe.

Marathon, Trafalgar, the Marne: decisive battles indeed. Yet it is not too far-fetched to suggest that two other battles, whose outcome was of equal, and perhaps of profounder import for England and Europe, and hence for the world, are notable for their omission: Hastings, and the Armada. These two conflicts, unlike the others, were actual or intended invasions and conquests.

There is, however, an even more startling omission from the Air Ministry account of the Battle of Britain.

Is it possible to conceive of an account of Marathon, however brief, without mention of Callimachus? Of Trafalgar without mention of Nelson? Of the Marne without mention of Joffre (and Gallieni)? Having established the global importance of the Battle of Britain, we note next that this battle was fought by the Fighter Command of the Royal Air Force. Should not the chief of Fighter Command, Air Chief Marshal Sir Hugh Dowding, have merited a passing mention, even in a pamphlet of a mere thirty-two pages? Yet that is a simple and stark fact. The name of Dowding is nowhere mentioned or even alluded to.

It is important to discover why no mention is accorded to this man, the architect of the victory; whereas, on the other hand, the authors see fit to mention Goering, the chief of the *Luftwaffe*, fairly frequently.

This pamphlet, let us note at the onset, was an official publication of the Air Ministry. The omission of Dowding's name must therefore have been deliberate and not a mere oversight on the part of the authors. Nowhere in the pamphlet is the reason for the omission given, nor the name of the writer. It can only be assumed that he was following specific instructions, and not acting in his own name. That is why we have said not only 'authors', but also 'writer'.[1]

We shall have to seek elsewhere for the answers to these disturbing questions. It appears that the matter was allowed to disappear from the public awareness after its publication — perhaps because the booklet itself sold out quickly and disappeared from the bookshelves.

It is only recently that this twofold issue has been raised again, and this in works published to observe the 50th anniversary of the Battle in 1990. We will examine two such publications.

In *The Battle of Britain: The Jubilee History,* by Richard Hough and Denis Richards, we read: "The pamphlet, which cost the Air Ministry £50 in fees to the author and sold six million copies, mentioned no names at all on the British side except that of Churchill, and only two on the German — Goering and Goebbels. The Air Ministry's Department of Public Relations at the time was trying to discourage the press from building up fighter 'aces'. This was because adulatory reports about certain individual pilots or squadrons in the early days of the war had tended to create ill-feeling among others equally valorous but less well publicised."

On June 25th, 1990, a conference was organized at the RAF Staff College, Bracknell, by the Staff College in conjunction with the RAF Historical Society. In the course of open discussions following the invited papers, this matter was raised. "Dr Orange had said that the Air Ministry had suppressed the name of Dowding in the first accounts. It was not suppressed, said Richards. The story was written up on the basis of blanket instructions from the Department of Public Relations, which was determined not to create personal heroes. In World War I a lot of ill-feeling had been caused by blowing up the reputations of certain 'aces', when these chaps had done no more than others in their squadrons, so when World War II started the view was that we shouldn't personalize. There was trouble in France with a New Zealander named Cobber Kane, because the press (Noel Knights, of the *Daily Mail)* got hold of his story and blew it up. This caused some ill-feeling amongst the rest, so they decided to operate under this limitation. In that pamphlet, therefore, no individual was mentioned on the British side, and only Goering, he thought, on the German. There was no desire to do down Dowding, but the man who wrote it was told to leave out personalities."

These explanations, such as they are, cry for comment.

Denis Richards implies that the question of anonymity was a decision taken by the Air Ministry's department of public relations. This department was not autonomous; it acted as an agency of the Air Ministry, and necessarily followed policies laid down by the Air Ministry. The pamphlet is in fact "an Air Ministry account." Therefore we are forced to conclude that the Air Ministry itself — that is, a highly-placed authority in the Air Ministry — ordered the writer "to avoid the personality cult" and to avoid "building up fighter 'aces'."

Dowding, as Commander-in-Chief, was not in the latter class. And by no stretch of imagination could it have been construed that a mention of Dowding, that giving even passing credit to the Commander-in-Chief for this famous victory, amounted to a "personality cult."

But even if we accept this explanation, how do the authors of the Air Ministry booklet, or Denis Richards, account for the many mentions of Goering? (One entire section is entitled: "London *versus* Goering".)

We must question another statement made by Richards. We have quoted him as saying that the creation of 'aces' caused "ill-feeling among the rest, so they decided to operate under this limitation." Is it possible? If the Air Ministry and the Air Staff air marshals allowed Air Force policy to be dictated by the supposed discontent of a few junior officers and NCOs, the occasion would have set a record unique in Air Force annals both for the influencing of policy and for solicitude for juniors' sensibilities on the part of the Air Ministry, not to mention the setting of a precedent. And we shall have something to say later about the matter of precedents.

Does the claim made here by Gough and Richards hold water? It is true that, in quoting pilots' combat reports, the author of the pamphlet omits their names. But there is one conspicuous exception. He quotes at length one combat report by a Squadron Leader who makes frequent reference to his 'Wing' and his 'two other squadrons.' The author is readily identifiable: the report in question can have been written only by Douglas Bader, whose exploits as the leader of a wing of three, four or five squadrons were being reported at that time.

The claim to attempt to avoid "building up fighter 'aces'" must be seen as a red-herring. The public demanded 'aces'. The people needed heroes, especially in that perilous time. Consider again: the booklet came out in the spring of 1941. The Battle of Britain had been over for six months. The names of dozens of fighter pilots were already household names. And the Air Ministry itself was compiling the 'scores' of individual fighter pilots. More than that: the Air Ministry was actually issuing periodical lists of the top fighter 'aces'. The list of the end of March, 1941, put Sergeant 'Ginger' Lacey in the top place with 23, Tuck fourth with 22, and Malan sixth with 20. (In the June 30 list, the rankings were: Malan, first, 29; Tuck, second, 26; Lacey, third, 23. It is hard to resist the suspicion that the Air Ministry, having once embarked on this course, continued it to ensure that a mere sergeant no longer occupied the top place.)

There is still more. The Air Ministry maintained the long accepted practice of singling out aircrews for decorations. Nearly every day *The Times* carried an announcement such as this: "The King has approved the following awards in recognition of gallantry in flying operations against the enemy...." In that same spring of 1941 the people of Britain were fully expecting a renewal of the air battle and were bracing themselves to face again the threat of invasion.

Again, can this claim be taken seriously when we find the Air Ministry appointing official war artists? The eminent names of Eric Kennington and William Rothenstein come to mind, men who were commissioned to paint the portraits of our air heroes. Kennington made notes about his sitters. The note he made about Flight Lieutenant R.A.B. Learoyd VC is the following: "This portrait was drawn in the gallery at the top of the Air Ministry in September 1940. Learoyd knew better than I that Hitler was going all out for a quick breaking of Great Britain. Distant bombing grew so close and intense that I asked him if it was not unusual. He took one stride and threw open the door. There were about 120 bombers, almost above. He only made one remark, "What rotten formation." The docks were a furnace, and I asked if we should go to the dug-out or continue the drawing as watching helped no one. He strode back and sat. I found his courage contagious." Note: "in the . . . Air Ministry" — and "in September 1940."[2]

In his *Jubilee History* Richards had the grace to concede the blunder. "This curious omission quickly evoked the ire of the Prime Minister.... On 12 April 1941 Churchill wrote to Sinclair: 'The jealousies and cliquism which have led to the committing of this offence are a discredit to the Air Ministry, and I do not think any other Service Department would have been guilty of such a piece of work.'" Churchill's letter continued, and concluded, thus:

> What would have been said if the War Office had produced the story of the Battle of Libya and had managed to exclude General Wavell's name, or if the Admiralty had told the tale of Trafalgar and left Lord Nelson out of it! . . . It grieves me very much that you should associate yourself with such

behaviour. I am sure you were not consulted beforehand on the point, and your natural loyalty to everything done in your department can alone have led you to condone what nine out of 10 men would unhesitatingly condemn.

In concluding his account of this episode, Richards notes: "In applying a policy of anonymity in *The Battle of Britain* pamphlet . . . the Department had clearly taken leave of its senses."

In the RAF Staff College conference held a year after the publication of his book, Richards made no such concession, and repeated the same untenable explanation.

Dowding's name not suppressed? If the instruction to leave out personalities is not suppression, the word has no meaning. The word 'suppression' may mean merely, 'deliberate omission'; it can also convey the notion of 'withholding due credit'. And that is the whole point of the indignation of Dowding's champions and of his critics' disclaimers.

If it were only a matter of the suppression of all mention of Dowding's name or allusion to him, the offence would be serious enough. There is worse. This narrative is totally lacking in any suggestion of the existence, in Fighter Command, of overall leadership, of a directing strategic mind, of a central authority controlling the defensive forces and of thinking ahead to anticipate changes in the disposition of his forces to meet various contingencies on this chessboard of destiny. The nearest the pamphlet comes to any such notion is in saying: "The Sectors are grouped together under a . . . Group Headquarters which in its turn comes under the general control of Headquarters, Fighter Command." No suggestion here of one man exercising this "general control": on the contrary, 'Headquarters' suggests many people, all apparently working together on their own initiative and without need of direction.

Goering's aims and plans and changing tactics are discussed repeatedly; but never a word or allusion to indicate the presence in Fighter Command of a chief, a commander, countering Goering's moves. The omission of Dowding's name, we have seen, was deliberate. The failure by the writer — and by the authors — to include a mention of Hastings and the Armada was, I suggest, equally conscious. Hastings and the Armada took place on or close to our shores. They were not only close in geography: they are still close in the collective national memory. Everyone knows what happened in 1066 and 1588. How many can say where Marathon, Trafalgar and the Marne are, and describe the issues or the outcome or name the commanders?

(Well, Trafalgar, perhaps: at least the victor, if not the location and the issues.)

The omission, especially, of the Armada, and the suppression of Dowding's role in the Battle of Britain seem to be of a piece: to deny to Dowding all recognition for his role in this heroic victory.[3]

There is more to the story of suppression. In 1946 Dowding published a book entitled *Twelve Legions of Angels*. Written in 1941, it analysed the strategic, tactical, material and logistic requirements for the successful prosecution of the war. But it also speculated on the ways and means whereby statesmanship might prevent wars in the future. When it was published in 1946 Dowding added a Foreword, which begins thus:

> This book was written more than four years ago. . . . The fact is that when the book was submitted for censorship in due course, the powers that be (or rather the powers that were) refused to pass it for publication. When you have finished the book you may wonder what it contains which could not have been given to the world at the time it was written. It contains no military secret and . . . as a matter of fact, the veto was not imposed on account of anything in Part I of the book.
>
> I do not feel at liberty now to disclose the reason given for the suppression of the book, but it is one which I think few people would guess if they did not know it.

The word used by Dowding in this context is 'suppression'. Whether it is in the same class of 'suppression' as the Air Ministry booklet, we leave it to the reader to judge. The facts are that Dowding met with Churchill on several occasions in 1941 to urge him to read his book and give his approval for its publication. Churchill had Brendan Bracken read it and report to him on it. As a result Churchill refused to give his consent to its publication.

In 1969, Robert Wright published his biography of Dowding. In chapter 15 he gives a full account of this suppression. The reasons for it can be summarized in the following terms.

In Part II of his book, Dowding examined the causes of war, and, horrified by its cost in human lives and misery and in material destruction, proposed a number of measures designed to prevent it, so far as possible, in the future. Churchill did not like it at all. He considered that war was a necessary process in the development of the vigorous and manly qualities in a race. Stalwart defence of one's homeland cannot be achieved at too high a price. If attacked, energetic and ruthless counter-attack is the only answer.

Sport is all very well, even relatively dangerous sports. But they are no substitute for war. War alone can bring out the best in a race. Without it, a nation's youth degenerates into slothful habits, indolence and effeteness, and ends up good for nothing — good not even for sport, daring enterprise, and business adventurism.

In an article which Dowding published in the *Sunday Chronicle* of December 13th, 1942 (and which is appended to the text of the book in question), he returns to this theme. "Is war a Good Thing, or not? This is not a purely rhetorical question, because there are those who think that war and training for war are necessary for the virility of the race, and that periods of continuous peace lead to softness, luxury and decadence."[4]

This is not the end of the tale of suppression.

On Dowding's return to Britain from his mission to the United States and Canada in 1941, he was asked to write a *Despatch* on the Battle of Britain. This he did. When, in June that year, Germany invaded the Soviet Union, all likelihood of a renewed assault on Britain by the *Luftwaffe* disappeared. There was, therefore, no obstacle, by reason of national security, to the publication of Dowding's *Despatch*. Its publication was, however, also withheld or delayed until 1946. Justification there may have been for this deferral: it appears that all such operational reports were published only in 1946.[5] However, Dowding had a genuine grievance when he learnt that his *Despatch* was not even circulated to the parties within the Air Ministry and Fighter Command who would have benefited from its study.

We have seen that the writer of the Air Ministry pamphlet was instructed to suppress all mention of Dowding and his leadership. We have demonstrated that the 'reason' given, by someone obviously in the know, strains the credulity. We are, perhaps, permitted to wonder who precisely in the Air Ministry gave such instructions. The search would be limited indeed. Whose was the final responsibility? There is no question or doubt: it was Sinclair's. Hence Churchill's angry and indignant reaction. But could a pamphlet about the Battle of Britain have been written and published without Portal's knowledge? Absolutely not! Could such a pamphlet have been produced without Freeman's knowledge and approval? No! On the other hand, could it have been done without Sinclair's knowledge? Possibly; but not likely; and in any event most unwisely.

Portal's and Sinclair's joint responsibility in the matter is clear. The next question which imposes itself on one's mind is: Why should Portal want to deny to Dowding the recognition that was due to him for his heroic accomplishments?

This question of denial of recognition has been the subject of commentary and discussion for over 50 years — from the time of Dowding's removal to the present moment. It is so classic a case of injustice that it cannot be suppressed; it will not go away.

The deliberate denial to Dowding of recognition in the Air Ministry pamphlet of 1941 is not a minor matter. Richards's explanation is so absurd that it reveals, by implication, more than it conceals. When Richards fails, in his authorized biography of Portal, even to mention Dowding's removal, it would appear that he is concealing, by his silence, some unpalatable facts about him.

There is more. And it is equally disturbing.

Ever since Dowding's victory over the *Luftwaffe*, certain admirers of Dowding's achievements have promoted the idea that Dowding should have been elevated to the highest rank, that of Marshal of the Royal Air Force. The Air Ministry apologists have argued that it would have created a precedent. In the past, they explained, only those officers whose careers had culminated as Chief of the Air Staff had been promoted to the highest rank.

The counter-arguments are more impressive.

The first counter-argument is that, of all the past Chiefs of the Air Staff, whose accomplishments were so signal as to warrant the highest promotion? The answer is, of the five Chiefs of the Air Staff, from Trenchard to Newall, probably not more than two.

The second argument is, of course, related to Dowding's achievements. We will repeat again that Dowding was the architect of Fighter Command and the directing brain which out-thought and out-fought the *Luftwaffe*. His leadership of Fighter Command in its victory, against heavy odds, in one of the decisive battles of the world, saved Western civilization from a murderous tyranny which would have known no end and no bounds.

And let us stress another important fact. Today, some people are apt to look back and say that the outcome of the Battle of Britain, and the winning of the war even, were foregone conclusions: they were inevitable. That thinking is hindsight history at its worst. We have presented the scene as it appeared to the British people and their Government and, especially, to the

Air Force, at that time. Was the nature of Dowding's heroic accomplishment known at the time? Of course it was. If ever a custom or tradition called for breaking, and a precedent to be set, it was by his over-arching heroism. Beyond all these arguments and reasons, however; beyond the customs and traditions we have paraded, there exists a final explanation of the denial to Dowding of the coveted promotion. What follows is of the nature of speculation. Perforce: for no authority implicated in this denial would have dared to commit to paper so much as a syllable which risked revealing the truth.

The rank of Marshal of the Royal Air Force, by virtue of its exalted character and rarity, carried with it a prestige, a *cachet,* which conferred upon its holder certain prerogatives. Among them was the privilege of giving advice, and of offering the fruits of mature reflection, on any weighty matter affecting policy and strategy — and indeed on any Air Force issue — to the Air Council, whether invited or not. Indeed, the dignity of Marshal of the RAF gave to its holder a permanent *ex officio* membership of the Air Council.

Imagine the situation: Dowding henceforth, and for all time, an un-invited member of the Air Council . . . of the Air Council which had sacked him! They had no fear that Dowding would abuse his new position to the end of justifying his direction of Fighter Command and demolishing his critics. They knew Dowding too well. What they did fear was his command of facts, his remorseless logic, his unparalleled knowledge of air fighting, his unequalled experience, his sharp tongue and superior intelligence.

Had each and every member of the Air Council been scrupulously honest with themselves, they could not fail to have conceded that Dowding had much sage counsel to offer on the equipment and training of the Royal Air Force and the direction of the air arm. But, sad to say, they permitted their personal antipathies to cauterize their reason and judgment.

The top members of the Air Council were Sinclair, Balfour, Portal and Freeman — anti-Dowding men all. Of the others — Gossage, Courtney — in fairness to them we remain silent, not knowing their views. The seventh man was Garrod, a personal friend of Dowding's of long-standing.

There were two other men, and they carried a great deal of weight. They were none other than Trenchard and Salmond, the only two retired officers of the rank of Marshal of the Royal Air Force, who, as we have seen, were both active in the affairs of the Air Force and the Air Council, and in the forefront of the campaign to remove Dowding. ·

In the total absence of an official statement, the explanation that comes closest to one is, as we have seen, the word of Denis Richards, who has written that the promotion of Dowding to the rank of Marshal of the Royal Air Force would have created a precedent. It appears that Richards had forgotten that the policy had in fact been broken, and the precedent created, even at the time of his writing.

On January 1st 1946, Air Chief Marshal Sir Arthur 'Bomber' Harris was promoted to Marshal of the Royal Air Force without having been Chief of the Air Staff. This was a propitious moment and an unequalled opportunity to make amends to Dowding and to promote him at the same time. Portal and the Air Council pointedly let the moment pass.

This same date was marked by the recognition of another air marshal who had not been Chief of the Air Staff. No less an unworthy figure than Sholto Douglas was promoted to Marshal of the Royal Air Force with Harris. Who dares compare Douglas's achievements with those of Dowding! Douglas's elevation can be regarded as nothing other than a conscious and wilful insult to Dowding on the part of Portal and the Air Council.[6]

Dowding **was** honoured, however, when he retired definitively from the Royal Air Force in 1942 — with no thanks to the Air Ministry. He was created a baron, and took the suitable title of Lord Dowding of Bentley Priory.

A gratifying irony is attached to this honour. In his copy of the correspondence between Salmond and Trenchard which we have quoted at length, Salmond wrote this personal note, as if to himself: "Had the PM not agreed [to Dowding's removal], I had decided to appeal to HM [the King]." It was the King himself, aggrieved at the lack of recognition accorded to Dowding, who initiated an inquiry which culminated in this honour.

On October 13th, 1987, Edward Bishop ran a letter in *The Daily Telegraph* on the subject of the statue of Lord Dowding which was to be erected in London — again with no contribution from the Air Ministry. We reproduce two paragraphs from it:

> It is sad that the official diminution of Dowding should persist at a time when commemoration of the 50th anniversary of the Battle of Britain is being prepared for 1990. As far back as 1942, King George VI was deeply concerned about Dowding's treatment. The monarch's view was made clear in a letter from his private secretary Sir Alexander Hardinge to Sir Archibald Sinclair, Secretary of State for Air, to "raise with you the question of his being promoted to Marshal of the Royal Air Force on retirement."

In 1942 the King, being obliged to accept Sir Archibald Sinclair's assurance that Dowding would be rewarded at the end of the war, replied through his private secretary that he was "quite satisfied to know that his services will come up for consideration of one kind or another at the end of the war."

Although Dowding received a barony, he was denied the marshal's baton which he so richly deserved. Sinclair's assurance of reward turned out to be worthless.

The official history of the Royal Air Force during the Second World War concludes with a chapter entitled, 'The Balance Sheet.' In it four air marshals are distinguished as leaders whom the "Royal Air Force was singularly fortunate in possessing". They are Portal, Tedder, Dowding, and Harris. All were honoured with the rank of Marshal of the RAF except Dowding.

There can be little doubt but that if Dowding had been an Army or Navy man he would have been so honoured. Especially, if he had been a Navy man, there would be a second monumental column in Trafalgar Square, and his name, like Drake's and Nelson's, would reverberate down the halls of history's noblest pantheons.

## NOTES TO CHAPTER 9:

1. "It was written, we are now allowed to say, by Hilary St.George Saunders, of *Red Beret* and *Green Beret* fame." See *The Battle of Britain* (London, Wingate-Baker, 1969), which reprinted the Air Ministry pamphlet. St. George Saunders was, of course, the co-author with Denis Richards of the magnificent, official history of the Royal Air Force in the Second World War. St. George Saunders was therefore the writer of the pamphlet; whereas the authors were those others, of the Air Ministry, responsible for some of its contents and for its omissions.

2. Private publication (np, nd) presented to the author by Eric Kennington.

3. The Air Ministry issued a second booklet in August 1943, Air Ministry Pamphlet 156, entitled also *The Battle of Britain*. It is a fuller story, and in many ways superior to the 1941 pamphlet, and

it does mention Dowding. On the other hand it falls as short as the earlier one in not doing justice to the two chief victors of the Battle. Not only in the text, but conspicuously in the illustrations. There are full page or half page photographs of Portal, Bradley, Pattinson and Bowhill, of whom only the last had even the remotest role in the Battle; and of Dowding that faintly ridiculous one, with his bowler hat, dark suit and furled umbrella, on the occasion of the second anniversary reunion with eleven of his pilots. And the list of names beneath contains no fewer than eight errors.

4. Perhaps both Churchill and Dowding were in error. Consider this judgment by a professional soldier, Sir John Hackett, who wrote: "Mussolini said in the early 1930s: 'War alone brings all human energies to their highest tension, and sets a seal of nobility on the peoples who have the virtue to face it.' This is rubbish, and dangerous rubbish at that. War does not ennoble . . . But the interesting thing is that although war almost certainly does not ennoble, the preparation of men to fight in it almost certainly can and very often does."

5. An exception was the publication of Lord Ramsay's report on Operation Dynamo, the account of the naval evacuation of the British and French armies from Dunkirk. Why one and not the other?

6. On September 20, 1986, *The Times* published a letter from the (now late) son of Lord Dowding in response to a proposal to give belated recognition to his father by the creation of a statue. He wrote:

   "I read with great interest and welcome, of course, today's letters from Dr Brian Porter and Air Commodore Chisholm, and have some grounds for hope that a suitable permanent memorial will one day soon be forthcoming.

   "I write to protest mildly against the evident English belief that recognition, 16 years after death, in some way compensates the individual concerned for the ingratitude shown to him during life.

   "I think that my father, Air Chief Marshal Lord Dowding (1882-1970), would like to have been promoted "Marshal of the Royal Air Force", and this indeed would have carried concomitant financial advantage.

   "But in the event this considerable public figure was retired on a pension not far exceeding £1,500 PA, and this in days preceding indexation. His later years were clouded by financial insufficiency. . . . Indeed this country, 140 years previously, had granted the family of Lord Nelson £5,000 PA in perpetuity. This only came to an end in 1951.

   "As a nation we cannot really expect people of the right calibre to come forward for public service if this is the treatment they can expect. Things are better arranged now, I know, but this particular piece of bureaucratic meanness should not go unrecorded and unpublished."

# CHAPTER 10

# *Dowding on War:*

# *Strategist and Visionary*

Little has been written, here or elsewhere, about Dowding's supreme qualities as a commander. Even more surprising, in view of his notable victory in 1940, nothing has been written about Dowding in terms of what Clausewitz called "the conduct of war".

Tribute has been paid to Dowding's "genius for organization" in the creation of Fighter Command. This genius has been nowhere more precisely and accurately detailed than by Hough and Richards in the first three chapters of their *Jubilee History of The Battle of Britain.*

Tribute has been paid, by no less an authority than Churchill, to Dowding's "genius in the art of war." Tribute has been paid in handsome measure, by every perceptive writer who has commented on Dowding's personality, to his luminous integrity, his questioning mind, and his moral courage.

Here, in a three part summing-up, we begin by putting the case for the visionary — a quality as rare as oxygen at 40,000 feet. In the second part we examine Dowding's dominant strategic idea. And we conclude with a study of Dowding's conduct of the battle in terms of the art of war, under the twofold rubric: 1) The Principles of War, and 2) The Qualities of the Commander. We will thereby arrive at a fuller appreciation of this "thin inscrutable figure . . . the prophetic strategist who, as Chief of Fighter Command before the war, shaped the invincible lines of Britain's air defence."

## I. The Visionary

It is by no means far-fetched to consider Dowding a 'prophetic strategist'. His strategical intelligence stemmed from his capacity to see ahead. I have called him a visionary. Lest there be any misunderstanding of what I mean by 'visionary', I will define the term as I understand it.

A visionary, in the everyday real world of power, politics and history, is a man who knows the past and who sees the significance of events as they take place; who grasps the consequences of those events if nothing is done to counter them; and who sees what must be done in order to halt their fateful evolution.

## RADAR

The first undoubted manifestation of Dowding's visionary gift of which we are aware took place — we can pinpoint the precise date: February 26th, 1935 — at Weedon, a few miles west of Northampton.

Since September 1st 1930, Dowding had been the Air Member for Supply and Research. (This position became Air Member for Research and Development on January 14th, 1935.)

At night, on the date mentioned, it had been arranged for a Heyford bomber of the Royal Aircraft Establishment, Farnborough, to fly on a regular course between Daventry and Wolverton, back and forth, whilst a team of scientists were 'bouncing' radio waves off it. Their echoes were received, and visually recorded, on a cathode-ray oscillograph.

The experimental demonstration was conducted by H.E. Wimperis, the Director of Scientific Research in the Air Ministry. Wimperis had asked his chief, Dowding, to procure funds for the development of his project.

Dowding, self-instructed as he was in scientific matters related to defence, but also heavily committed for funds for the development of the Spitfire and Hurricane at this time, had asked for a practical demonstration so that he could see for himself what he would be requesting funds for.

It is useful to understand the situation of Great Britain in military terms at this time. Britain had for centuries been protected by her Navy and had enjoyed virtual impregnability against invasion. But in 1917 and 1918 all changed for the worse overnight when London was bombed by German airships and aircraft, and hundreds of civilians were killed and maimed. The Navy was no longer the defensive shield that it had been for over eight hundred years. Beneath the bombers the Navy was powerless: not only powerless to protect, but itself vulnerable to attack. It was as if the Channel and the North Sea had dried up and ceased to provide an impassable barrier. The ringing words of Shakespeare now rang hollow. No longer was England

> This happy breed of men, this little world,
> This precious stone set in the silver sea,
> Which serves it in the office of a wall,
> Or as a moat defensive to a house ....[1]

During the twenties and thirties the people became increasingly alarmed by the prospect of indiscriminate attack from the air. Their fears were exacerbated by the production of a film based on the novel of H.G. Wells, *Shape of Things to Come*.

A happy consequence of this growing concern was that it forced the hand of the Air Ministry, who established a committee, under the leadership of Professor Henry Tizard, "to study all ideas which could provide a more effective defence system."

Wimperis had asked Robert Watson-Watt whether he had any ideas about the use of death-rays against bombers. In reply Watson-Watt suggested, rather, that radio waves might be used to detect approaching aircraft. It was decided to carry out a test.

Hence, on that night of February 26th, 1935, Dowding, with a few others, watched the cathode-ray tube with expectant fascination, not unleavened by a healthy scepticism. What he saw was beyond dispute.

The small group of men, gazing into the oscillograph, saw the radiation from Daventry depicted as a straight line. But as the Heyford entered the path of the beam, they saw the line oscillate until when the aircraft was most nearly overhead a deviation of over an inch was observed. Without specially designed equipment, without control of wave-length, and without any great transmission power, it had been demonstrated beyond doubt that electro-magnetic energy was reflected from an aircraft, and that these reflections could be depicted visually by the cathode-ray apparatus. We can only surmise what went on in Dowding's mind. But the feeble little lights on the screen before him must have been as it were an illumination. It was clear to him, as Wimperis was to write to him a week later:

> We now have, in embryo, a new potent means of detecting the approach of hostile aircraft, one which will be independent of mist, cloud, fog or night-fall, and at the same time be vastly more accurate than present methods in the information provided and in the distances covered.

Already, in his mind's eye, Dowding was envisaging a series of such detecting stations, positioned at intervals round the coast of Britain, so that approaching hostile aircraft could be tracked and followed and, if need be, intercepted before reaching their targets.

Perhaps he saw much more in the future. What he did know was the historical and immemorial position of Britain as an island. He knew also that on July 24th, 1924, the then Prime Minister, Stanley Baldwin, speaking in the House of Commons, had said:

> It is easy to say, as many people do, that England should isolate herself from Europe, but we have to remember that the history of our insularity has ended, because with the advent of the aeroplane we are no longer an island.

From 1918, with the air raids on London, until this moment, February 26th, 1935, in a field at Weedon, England was in fact "no longer an island". But the experiment which Dowding witnessed illuminated the future. He was heard to murmur: "We are an island again!"[2]

## THE HISTORIC LETTER

On May 15th, five days after the opening of the *Blitzkrieg*, the German 'lightning war' against Holland, France and Belgium, Dowding attended a meeting of the Chiefs of Staff which was presided over by Churchill. The principal item on the agenda was the French appeal for more fighters to be sent to France to oppose the devastating attacks by the *Luftwaffe* on forward elements of the Allied armies and on their airfields and supply convoys. Dowding resisted the appeal, supported though it was by Churchill. In his view, a certain minimum number of front line squadrons, including all his Spitfire squadrons, had to be kept in England for the defence of the home-land, **in the event that the worst should befall.**

Already, the day before, he had written to the Air Staff to apprise them of the desperateness of the situation:

> The Hurricane tap is now turned full on and you will not be able to resist the pressure[3] to send Hurricanes to France until I have been bled white and am in no condition to withstand the bombing attack which will inevitably be made on this country as soon as our powers of resistance fall below a level to which we are already perilously close.

At the meeting of the 15th it appeared to Dowding that he made little headway in overcoming Churchill's loyalty to an old friend in jeopardy and in convincing him both of the seriousness of the drain on Fighter Command's resources and of the ultimate futility of sending more fighters to France.

The following day, in an attempt to make his point as forcefully as possible, he composed this letter which he sent directly to Harold Balfour, the Under-Secretary of State for Air. It is reproduced here in full, a letter which can only be called prophetic:

Sir,

1.  I have the honour to refer to the very serious calls which have recently been made upon the Home Defence Fighter Units in a attempt to stem the German invasion on the Continent.

2.  I hope and believe that our Armies may yet be victorious in France and Belgium, but we have to face the possibility that they may be defeated.

3.  In this case I presume that there is no-one who will deny that England should fight on, even though the remainder of the Continent of Europe is dominated by the Germans.

4.  For this purpose it is necessary to retain some minimum fighter strength in this country and I must request that the Air Council will inform me what they consider this minimum strength to be, in order that I may make my dispositions accordingly.

5.  I would remind the Air Council that the last estimate which they made as to the force necessary to defend this country was 52 Squadrons, and my strength has now been reduced to the equivalent of 36 Squadrons.

6.  Once a decision has been reached as to the limit on which the Air Council and the Cabinet are prepared to stake the existence of the country, it should be made clear to the Allied Commanders on the Continent that not a single aeroplane from Fighter Command beyond the limit will be sent across the Channel, no matter how desperate the situation may become.

7.  It will, of course, be remembered that the estimate of 52 Squadrons was based on the assumption that the attack would come from the eastwards except in so far as the defences might be outflanked in flight. We have now to face the possibility that attacks may come from Spain or even from the North coast of France. The result is that our line is very much extended at the same time as our resources are reduced.

8.  I must point out that within the last few days the equivalent of 10 Squadrons have been sent to France, that the Hurricane Squadrons remaining in this country are seriously depleted, and that the more Squadrons which are sent to France the higher will be the wastage and the more insistent the demands for reinforcements.

9.  I must therefore request that as a matter of paramount urgency the Air Ministry will consider and decide what level of strength is to be left to the Fighter Command for the defences of this country, and will assure me that when this level has been reached, not one fighter will be sent across the Channel however urgent and insistent the appeals for help may be.

10. I believe that, if an adequate fighter force is kept in this country, if the fleet remains in being, and if Home Forces are suitably organised to resist invasion, we should be able to carry on the war single handed for some time, if not indefinitely. But, if the Home Defence Force is drained away in desperate attempts to remedy the situation in France, defeat in France will involve the final, complete and irremediable defeat of this country.[4]

We have seen where this letter was passed to. But who is not to say whether, at that crucial moment in the history of the human race, the tide of battle might not have been turned if every available aeroplane in the RAF had been thrown into the fray? Perhaps if the Poles at Warsaw and, yes, the Spanish defenders of Guernica, had had the resources of Fighter Command at their disposal, their cities might not have been destroyed.

There was something to be said for the position of those who argued for sending more help to France. After all, it was only May 16th, and the war was only six days old.[5] But Churchill was a romantic, and at times impossibly quixotic. He allowed ancient loyalties and affections to sway his judgment, and he argued vigorously in the War Cabinet for more fighters for France.

It may seem strange to some that, in these historical and biographical contexts, and in an essay purporting to show Dowding as a visionary, the author, suddenly as it were, switches registers and tries to show that Dowding was also a hard-headed realist. But that is nothing less than the truth.

Have we not already seen that Dowding always insisted on the facts, wanted to see things for himself, would not make do with less than eye-witness accounts of events? To find out what was really going on in France, he sent a scout, carefully selected.

> At this bleak juncture, as the French armies were falling back in the face of the German onslaught, Hugh Dowding . . . sent a personal emissary to France to report directly on the worsening situation. . . .The officer assigned to the task was Wing Commander The Duke of Hamilton. . . . Hamilton flew this three-day mission (17–20 May) to the battle area in a tiny Miles Magister, a light, single-engined aircraft with a top speed which would have compared unfavourably with a modern small motor car. . . .
>
> The report which Hamilton brought back convinced the C-in-C that, with the French crumbling, no further fighter squadrons should in any circumstances be sent to France.[6]

The sequence of dates will be noted: May 15, Dowding's appearance before the War Cabinet; May 16, Dowding's letter; May 17–20, Dowding sends an emissary to France.

Most writers have claimed that Dowding's decisive intervention in the War Cabinet deliberations was on May 15th. If that were so, what was the purpose of his sending Hamilton to France to find out what the situation was? No, Dowding had not convinced the Cabinet. Especially he had not convinced Churchill. What he wrote in his *Despatch* after the Battle —

> I was responsible for the Air Defence of Great Britain, and I saw my resources slipping away like sand in an hour-glass. The pressure for more and more assistance to France was relentless and inexorable

— referred to the desperate days in late May. Dowding had not given up the fight to save his precious, and irreplaceable, resources, before they were all squandered in what he saw as a futile battle. His decisive intervention occurred on June 3rd, which was also the last full day of the evacuation from Dunkirk, but when the French were still fighting, and pleading for help.[7]

Balfour testifies in his autobiography that "Dowding had insisted on personal intervention with the War Cabinet to stop any further of his meagre force leaving these shores to prop up the failing French"; and "he came to my room to appeal as an old friend that I should use any influence I had with my Air Council colleagues to this end."

There is no need to recount the events of that tension-filled encounter in the War Cabinet meeting, when Dowding, with his graph of losses thrust before Churchill's eyes and the sharp crack of his pencil as he laid it dramatically, amid the tense, foreboding silence, on the table beside the graph, won the day.

## THE TURNING POINT

Between August 15 and September 6, Fighter Command's aerodromes and, especially, the important bases with sector control stations, came under increasingly heavy assault by the *Luftwaffe*. The Germans did not know how serious their attacks were, knowing nothing, as they did, of the central, crucial function of these stations.

They knew about radar for they had operational radar stations themselves — after all, their radar had detected the RAF's bomber attacks on units of the German fleet in September 1939 early enough to 'scramble' their fighters with disastrous results for the RAF's bombers. But their intelligence was so weak that they had little inkling of the Dowding system of radar control of the fighter squadrons. The *Luftwaffe* had earlier bombed the very visible radar receiving towers on the South coast. They had put a few out of action. But they had not succeeded in destroying any of the towers; and nearly all the radar stations which had been knocked out were back in action within hours, either through repair or by replacement by emergency mobile equipment.

The Germans' intelligence was so poor, indeed, that among their targets were airfields which were not Fighter Command fields, and aeroplane factories which did not produce fighters.

The airfields attacked by the *Luftwaffe* were targeted with the twofold aim of destroying and damaging as many fighters as possible **on the ground,** and of inflicting the maximum damage on the infra-structure of Fighter Command's forward bases — hangars, with their repair and servicing facilities; fuel storage tanks; communications lines; ammunition dumps; administrative centres.

If they had concentrated their attacks on the sector control stations, and succeeded in putting them all out of action within the space of a week or so, Park's greatest fear would have been realised and he would have been left controlling "nothing but his desk."

Even so the German bomber attacks inflicted more and more damage on 11 Group's important airfields, until, by September 6th, in Dowding's eyes, the situation was verging on the desperate. The front line defensive forces of Fighter Command were reeling, and the final attacks, if delivered within the next few days with sufficient concentration, seemed certain to carry the decisive blows which would prepare the ground for airborne invasion in the southeast, and at the same time force Dowding to set into motion his emergency plan, which entailed the withdrawal of all 11 Group's squadrons north of the Thames, to stations beyond the effective range of the Messerschmitt 109 escort fighters.

In the early evening of Saturday, September 7th, Dowding was in 'the Hole', that is, the Fighter Command Headquarters Operations Room, watching with intense concentration the status of developing raids, indicated by the build-up of enemy formations over Northern France, as they were plotted on the table beneath him.

Who knows but whether his mind may have been carried back to an earlier day, a calm day in July, so long ago, when his major preoccupation was the protecting of Channel convoys — to a day of inactivity yet of anticipation, when, instead of raids being plotted below, all he saw was an empty table and a solitary crane-fly alight on the Dover Straits and start a slow march towards the Kent coast. Dowding was reported to have gazed, chin on hands, in fascination and in silence, at this 'invasion', until he was heard to murmur: "It looks like a naval engagement!"

Now, today, on this September 7th, everything was different. The fate of England was in the balance. The enemy formations increased, gained height, assembled — and began their relentless progression across the Channel. But, as Dowding watched, it soon became apparent that there was something different about this incursion.

In previous raids the enemy formations had come in at different heights; and they had split up, and headed in different directions, making it designed-ly difficult for the defenders to know where the main attack was destined for, and hence where, and in what strength, to direct the defence efforts.

There was something very different — deliberately, and sneakily, different? — about this raid. They came on, steadily, in a single stream, without varying their course, without a feint or diversion, all seemingly head-ed for a single objective.

At Fighter Command HQ, Dowding watched, and wondered. Even before this huge, single bomber force had begun to reach the out-skirts of London, he was no longer in doubt: the target was London. The *Luftwaffe* had let up from its concentrated assault on the RAF's fighter squadrons and their installations. The German High Command calculated that nothing would draw up the RAF's few remaining fighters, to their intended destruction, so surely as the bombardment of England's capital city. With the RAF's defensive forces thus destroyed, Southern England lay exposed, defenceless, and open to invasion by Germany's *Wehrmacht*. England's days were num-bered! They deluded themselves. Their shift in tactics — which was an abandonment of the crucial doctrine of maintenance of the aim — was a classic error, a fatal miscalculation. It was a blessed reprieve for Fighter Command's battered aerodromes. London could absorb all the bombing the *Luftwaffe* cared to launch against the sprawling urban agglomeration.

Dowding understood all this, and the implications for the immediate and the distant future of this German miscalculation. If the *Luftwaffe* were only to persist in its attacks on London for a week, most of the damage done to his fighter installations could be made good and the personnel of the damaged stations would get a rest. And as for the future, had Dowding not seen eye to eye with Churchill when he had proclaimed on June 18th: "Hitler knows that he will have to break us in this Island or lose the war"?

Dowding, who, throughout the Battle, was the only man in Britain to know at all times how close they were to victory or defeat, was now the first to see and appreciate this new situation as it unfolded. His mind went back to a comparable phase in the First World War, to an early battle which became a reprieve and a deliverance, and he summed it up, on the spot, this assault against London, in the prescient words: " It is the Battle of the Marne again!"

## The Prophet

Anecdotes and sketches of a personal nature which might show Dowding as a more human figure and throw an unexpected light on his personality, as opposed to the stern, unsmiling, dour, 'stuffy' figure which legend has passed down to us, are all too infrequently met with.

It was therefore with a sense of serendipity that we came across the following description of an incident recorded by Sir Maurice Dean, who must have witnessed it himself. His description provides a fitting conclusion to this section.

> We have left to last an account of Dowding's greatest service. He was always a modest man. For all his professional skills, his ability to achieve a political judgement was inconspicuous. In fact, despite everything, it fell to him to arrive at such a judgement. In the dark days of 1940 he decided that France would collapse, that our destiny depended on the survival of Fighter Command, and that if Fighter Command survived, Britain would survive. Many arguments could have been adduced against such a view. All the same, it was Dowding's view. Around the time of the fall of France he walked into the office of the Head of the Air Staff Secretariat in Whitehall and said: 'Now we cannot lose'. His face was shining. His words and demeanour would have become a major prophet ... that for practical purposes was what he was at that moment.

# II. The Strategist

Dowding's vision was pre-eminently strategic. Yet let this reservation be added: he was pre-eminently a defensive strategist. He had no ideas, and he advanced no ideas, about how the war was to be won. On the other hand, no one in Britain had the slightest idea either, in the aftermath of the *débâcle* of

France and the deliverance of Dunkirk. One of the final ironies of the saga we have recounted is that the German Air Force came within a hair's breadth of realizing the Trenchard doctrine of air power, whilst his own air arm was impotent to carry the lesson to the enemy.

When Dowding became the first AOC-in-C of the Fighter Command in 1936, he foresaw that the new Bomber Command, formed at the same time, would not be able to realize its potential in the foreseeable future; and he set about creating a force whose aim was essentially to interdict the success of the Trenchard strategy. Dowding's pre-eminent achievement, and his great gift to civilization, was to preserve the home base, and thus to prevent the losing of the war at the outset.

The security of the home base: he never lost sight of this principle, and he followed and preached it with a single-minded tenacity of purpose.

This was the vision which oversaw the building of Fighter Command's defensive organization and structure; which obliged him to oppose the fatal weakening of his fighter resources for France; and which inspired his conduct of the battle itself.

That battle won, and the immediate danger of defeat passed, Dowding turned his gaze outward and asked himself whether any other threat appeared on the horizon, or closer. Again, he saw it with his customary lucidity. It was the Atlantic Ocean and the supply-line, the very life-line, which connected the British Isles to its oversea sources of food, raw materials and war matériel. In the early spring of 1941 he was writing: "we must assume that the loss of shipping is the gravest danger which threatens our national existence today." That being the case, priority had again to be conceded to countering that danger before considering the actual means of winning the war. It was again a clear and urgent case of not losing the war before thinking how to win it. "We are as yet far from having won the Battle of the Atlantic," he wrote at the same time, "but if we can do that . . . we shall have made secure a base from which our offensive may be launched."

The brilliant German strategist, Karl Dönitz, also knew the vital importance to Britain's war effort and survival of the Atlantic. "The focal point of the war against England and the one possibility of bringing her to her knees lies in attacking sea communications in the Atlantic."

Similarly, Werner Baumbach, although an airman, had the same strategic grasp of things: "the British could be defeated only if the Motherland could be cut off from her overseas sources of supply. Her dependence on such sources was the Achilles heel of British world power." Is it not the most obvious thing in the world? "The greatest secret of war and the masterpiece of a skilful general (said Clausewitz) is to starve the enemy."[8]

In order to prove the truth of this judgment, we will content ourselves with a mere summary account of the Battle of the Atlantic. Its waging was bedevilled by jealous quarrels between Navy and Air Force and between Bomber and Coastal Commands. Allies can also muddy the waters. After June 1941, when Hitler attacked the Soviet Union, the political direction of the war decreed that all possible military help be given to the Russian Allies. This help took the forms of supplying them with war materials and of bombing Germany. When Japan attacked Pearl Harbor and the United States entered the war in December 1941, in-fighting broke out within the US Navy over the respective demands of the Pacific and the Atlantic, and squabbles erupted between the US Navy Air Arm and the US Army Air Force over the providing of long range aircraft to protect convoys.

The Battle of the Atlantic was almost lost and Britain starved into defeat and surrender, first in 1940, then in March–April 1942, and again the following year when "the Germans never came so near to disrupting our communications between the New World and the Old as in the first twenty days of March 1943."

It boggles the mind to think that it took two and a half years, following the repulse of the *Luftwaffe* in 1940, to master the U-Boats, when this threat to survival, and eventual victory, was transparently obvious to all possessed of a modicum of reason, and who were not obsessed with the offensive.

The secret to the successful waging of this war lay, first, in escorting the convoys by sea and in protecting them from the air across the entire Atlantic; and, second, in developing electronic equipment capable of detecting submarines. The crucial area lay between Greenland and Iceland, an area known as the Air Gap, and within it a smaller area which was dubbed the Black Pit.

For two years Coastal Command was to be denied the long range aircraft it needed. The Liberator proved to be the ideal plane. With the need desperate, the first twenty were delivered in June 1941. No sooner had they become operational, in September, than half of them were transferred to Ferry Command and British Overseas Airways Corporation — for the transport of top brass and politicians.

Bomber Command was pressed to bomb the U-Boat assembly plants and their bases. The results were negative. "By May 1943, when some 18,000 sorties had been made and 33,000 tons of bombs dropped the sacrifice of 882 bombers and their crews [of the RAF and the USAAF] had not stopped a single U-boat going into service."

The most heinous offence was the refusal of the RAF to lend help to the Navy and to its own Coastal Command. On June 24th, 1942, when Admiral Pound served notice on the Chiefs of Staff that "the gravity of our position at sea increases day by day", and pointed out the need for "more land-based squadrons of heavy aircraft as a matter of supreme urgency," he was met with a blanket refusal by Portal, who argued that Bomber Command needed every bomber available to it for its offensive against Germany. Portal, playing the politician rather than acting the responsible airman, opposed the demands of Coastal Command and the Navy throughout the war — unless ordered by higher authority. He was, of course, fully supported by Harris, who believed, and continued to believe throughout the war, that he could win the war on his own. Portal was even supported by Churchill until as late as mid-1943.

The story was the same with the 10 centimetre radar which began to reach Bomber Command in January 1943. Coastal Command managed to acquire an Anti-Surface Vessel (ASV) version in March; the crews were amazed, and delighted, by its capacity to detect submarines at night; and 'kills' increased at once. "If just a handful of the sets had been available in early 1943, they might have been significant in the course of the battle, but Bomber Command maintained their exclusive right to the new weapon, code-named H2S."

Coastal Command appreciated the danger and saw the need; but, in view of the denial of the right weapons and the internecine strife during a protracted period of mortal danger, one cannot but question the leadership.

During the years from August 1937 to June 1941, the Air Officer Commanding was Air Chief Marshal Sir Frederick Bowhill. Thanks to the denial of equipment we have noted, his efforts were devoted almost exclusively to the battle against surface ships. His successor, in the crucial period from 1941 to February 1943, was Air Chief Marshal Sir Philip Joubert de la Ferté. Joubert, although a radar man, lacked the imagination and force of character that were indispensable to doing battle with his own Chief of the Air Staff.

Joubert was replaced by Air Marshal Sir John Slessor in February 1943, when the battle still balanced on a knife edge. A dynamic commander, Slessor began to attack the U-boat packs in the Bay of Biscay, especially with the powerful Beaufighters and Mosquitos. His hope for a decisive blow, which depended on getting more Liberators, was dashed by disputes between the Americans; and an opportunity was missed for the lack of 72 extra aircraft.

If ever there arose an occasion when a second prophetic letter to the Air Minister, or an intervention in a meeting of the War Cabinet, was justified, both Joubert and Slessor failed the occasion. Had Dowding been appointed to Coastal Command in early 1941, history would have had a different story to tell.

## III.  Dowding and the Principles of War

The Battle of Britain was a battle unique in the history of war. It was, as has often been remarked, a uniquely aerial battle, fought out by two air forces while navies and armies looked on idly, powerless to intervene and affect the outcome either way. It was, moreover, as most battles are, an aggressive action on the one side, countered by defensive forces on the other.

The air was a new medium in war; one wonders whether the air had anything to learn from past wars. T.E. Lawrence, writing to his biographer, Liddell Hart, in June 1933, said: "With 2,000 years of examples behind us we have no excuse, when fighting, for not fighting well." But Lawrence fought a guerilla war on the ground. Could he have had the air in mind as well? Just six months later he was writing to the same military historian: "I think the general opinion is that they have greatly improved the RAF ship-bombing practice. In a few years aircraft will deal infallibly with ships."[9]

Only in four previous wars had the air played a role of any significance: in the First World War, in the Italian aggression against Abyssinia, in the Japanese invasion of China, and in the Spanish Civil War. In the Abyssinian, Chinese and Spanish conflicts, the air action, while both strategic and tactical in its operations, was totally or largely unopposed by the defenders. In the First World War the air played no strategic role: the aircraft were of primitive design and performance, and served a limited purpose in support of the land and sea forces. Even when air battles took place — and there were many, involving large numbers of aircraft — they had no bearing on the decisive events taking place below.

The Battle of Britain was a very different conflict in every respect. It was a strategic action in the strictest sense of the term. For our purposes, we accept the definition of strategy elaborated by Clausewitz, who wrote: "According to our classification . . ., tactics is *the theory of the use of military forces in combat.* Strategy is *the theory of the use of combats for the object of the War.*" Or, in our case, of the Battle. He enlarged on this when he described "the totally different activities . . . of the *formation* and the *conduct* of these single combats in themselves, and the *combination* of them with one another. The first is called *tactics,* the other *strategy.*" This distinction is important, for, as we have seen, Dowding delegated to his Group commanders the authority for day-to-day and hour-to-hour decisions within the parameters of his policy, whereas he retained in his own hands complete strategic control.

Clausewitz makes the further distinction between *"preparations for war"* and *"the War itself"*. Our study is concerned solely with "the War itself". The "preparations for War", that is the creation of Fighter Command from the ground up, is beyond the limits of this narrative.

Strategically, the Battle of Britain meant in all likelihood for the defenders either total defeat or survival: for the aggressor sought to destroy the enemy's defensive forces and thereby prepare the ground for the launching of invasion forces. Any attempted invasion would be considered and planned for by the German High Command subject only to the destruction of the defenders.[10]

The Fighter Command had been established as a separate arm of the Air Force in recognition of the fact that technical advances in aviation and weaponry had transformed the military situation of Britain: she was for the first time in her history since 1066 vulnerable to attack and defeat. Everything now was different.

The defenders had, according to some writers, little to guide them by way of past lessons of war. A.J.P. Taylor, for example, in his Introduction to Len Deighton's book on the Battle, writes: "The key to the story is that the air commanders before the Second World War had very little experience to draw on." Is "previous experience" the only factor? What of this opinion? Having stated the "five fundamental factors" in war, Sun Tzu concludes: "I will be able to forecast which side will be victorious and which defeated." Is it conceivable that an air force commander in the 20th century AD could benefit from a study of a Chinese genius of war of 500 BC?[11]

Let us first consider whether a contemporary air commander could gain any help from a study of previous aerial actions.

In Abyssinia, the Italian bombing of the defenceless and naked people induced panic, and a swift surrender. Perhaps the Italians had taken a leaf out of the RAF's book after seeing the results of the bombing of Arab tribes in the 1920s. When it came to London's turn in 1940, the Government's near-panic reaction, when faced with uncertainty over the British people's ability to "take it", is equally understandable.

In Spain, the bombing of undefended towns, especially of Guernica (1937), elicited a general outrage and horror. It would be surprising if Dowding, along with other forward-looking airmen, scientists and politicians, was not stimulated by it to accelerate his search for an effective defence. What of fighter operations in Spain? The most effective action was that taken by formations of Messerschmitt 109s of the German Air Force. It was there that Werner Molders developed the basic finger-four formation: two Rotten of two fighters each comprising a Schwarm. The Royal Air Force continued to deploy its fighters in squadrons of twelve fighters, made up of four flights of three throughout 1940. A few squadrons led by innovative leaders adopted the German practice independently in late 1940, but it did not come into general use until 1941. No one in the Air Ministry, or Fighter Command for that matter, was apparently paying attention.

We have few means of knowing to what extent Dowding made a study of the art of war.[12] Yet this whole question, whether or not Dowding had studied war, as other commanders had studied, and were to study, war, is of considerable interest. It could be shown that many great commanders of the past had not studied war, in the sense that they had read widely on what others had written about it.[13]

But they assuredly studied it in the important, and vital, sense that they devoted much thought to the military situation in which they found themselves, and to the battles or engagements to which they were sure they would be committed. And it is to their greater credit that they succeeded without having had predecessors to learn from. Dowding was pre-eminently one of them. That Dowding thought about war constantly, and thought about the role of Fighter Command in a war he was preparing it for, can be deduced from what he wrote and how he conducted the battle.

In May 1937 he gave the same lecture, slightly modified, to the RAF Staff

College and to the Imperial College of Defence. In it he outlined Fighter Command's and his own roles in the event of war. Among other things he stated that one of his major preoccupations was the defence of London as the seat of Government. But he had an open mind, and learnt from experience. For less than four years later he would be welcoming the *Luftwaffe's* diversion of its attacks away from his sector airfields onto London.

Whilst, as we have insisted, Dowding and Fighter Command faced a totally new situation in war, we feel that certain principles apply to every war; and that every great commander is possessed of certain essential qualities. These principles and qualities, which have been culled from some of the most illustrious writers on war of the past, form the subject of the following section, in the belief that they are fully applicable to the Battle of Britain and to the Commander of Fighter Command. Whether or not Dowding had read Napoleon, his strategic and tactical ideas and plans bear out the wisdom of this advice: "A plan of campaign should anticipate everything an enemy can do, and contain within itself the means of thwarting him. Plans of campaign may be indefinitely modified according to the circumstances, the genius of the commander, the quality of the troops, and the topography of the theatre of war."

In the light of these principles, it would be impossible not to subscribe to this pronouncement by General Burnod, the editor of Napoléon's *Military Maxims:* "The art of war is susceptible of being considered under two titles: the one, which rests entirely on the knowledge and genius of the commander; the other, on matters of detail. The first is the same for all time, for all peoples, whatever the arms with which they fight. From this it follows that the same principles have directed the great captains of all centuries. The matters of detail, on the contrary, are subject to the influence of time, to the spirit of the people and the character of armaments." General Burnod, whether he had read Sun Tzu or not, never knew how wise and prescient was this statement.

## Principles of War

The major principles of war that form the substance of this study, as they apply to the Battle of Britain, are the following: 1) Security of the base; 2) Maintenance of the Aim; 3) Intelligence; 4) Surprise; 5) Reserves; and 6) Morale.

## 1. Security of the Base

This is the first essential, without which nothing can be planned. And it is true of all military planning, whether concerned with attack or defence. Dowding's sole and exclusive responsibility was the air defence of the United Kingdom. This responsibility exercised his mind, engaged his powers, and directed his energies for the full four-and-a-half years while he was the Commander-in-Chief of Fighter Command. His remit was local and limited; yet his resources were huge; and his task he perceived with a global vision. For if he wavered or failed, all was lost.

Yet this over-riding principle did not seem to enter into the policies, estimates and calculations of the Air Staff during the 1930s, when they persisted in giving priority to the production of bombers — of obsolete bombers at that — well into 1938, and thereby risked losing the war before having the chance to strike offensively.[14]

## 2. Maintenance of the Aim

We have seen that one of the contributing factors to the loss of the Battle by the Germans was their failure to maintain their strategic aim. That aim was the destruction of Fighter Command. Once Britain's fighter force was destroyed, nothing could prevent the success of the German Air Force from either bombing or starving Britain into submission, or from carrying out an airborne invasion. It was the decision to switch the attacks from Fighter Command's airfields to London, in the mistaken idea that, by forcing the RAF's fighters into the air to defend the capital they would destroy what remained of them, that doomed the offensive effort.

Dowding made no such error. His every thought and deed were centred on the over-riding imperative of preserving the strength of his combat forces in being. Park and he thought and acted as one, the daily and hourly tactical operations stemmed like manifold branches from one great central strategic trunk. The trunk remained firm, constant, and inflexible. The branches were designed freely to move, waver, change, like the tentacles of an octopus, in search of its prey. In an extremity, even the trunk could be moved, to a station farther from danger, with its branches moving intact with it.

The entire system comprised an intricately meshed organization of brain, eyes and arms. The brain, at Fighter Command Headquarters, was invulnerable. The arms were the fighter squadrons and their pilots, who were equally safe from annihilation, when they were scattered throughout the realm, and while some were in the air and some were on the ground. It was only the eyes, the radar eyes, that ensured that the other two components survived to perform their tasks.

## 3. INTELLIGENCE

Intelligence has two branches, an active and a passive: the one seeks to acquire information of the enemy's plans and intentions, as well as to learn the effectiveness of one's counter-intelligence; the other takes measures to prevent the enemy from learning yours. The side which neglects or fails in either branch is the more likely to lose the war.

It is easy to show that the German Air Force possessed very scanty and imperfect intelligence of Fighter Command's infrastructure and resources in 1940. They were even ignorant of their enemy's radar system of aircraft location and reporting. Whereas they took frequent aerial photographs of the Royal Air Force's stations and airfields, they failed to interpret and exploit the information in their hands.

The RAF, for its part, did not have much or precise strategic intelligence of the German capabilities. The assault on Britain which began in July 1940 being an impromptu affair, the chaos following the French military defeat militated against the setting up of an espionage network; and photographic reconnaissance of the German airfields was woefully inadequate.[15] Moreover, the breaking of the German High Command code, known as Enigma, came too late to be of use.[16] On the other hand, there were two sources of information of priceless value, the one of a strategic, the other of a tactical nature.[17]

The strategic information was to be deduced simply from the time of year. The French surrender occurred at the end of June. German preparations for an invasion would have to be completed by early or mid September at the latest before autumn weather prevented the supplying of the invasion forces across the Channel. If the expected preliminary attacks could be met successfully for three months by the scrupulous husbandry of existing resources, Fighter Command — and hence Great Britain — would survive and be able to build up her strength during the ensuing six months and so confidently face the heavier, renewed assaults in the spring of 1941.

By far the most continuous and reliable source of intelligence was that supplied by the British radar location and reporting system. The information received, after filtering at Fighter Command Headquarters, was passed to the Groups, who in turn transmitted to each Sector Station what was relevant to their regions. The Sectors, finally, acted on the information received and 'scrambled' the number of fighters available to meet the incoming raiders. Had it not been for this radar early warning system, the RAF would have had only two recourses: i) to mount permanent standing fighter patrols; or ii) to 'scramble' interceptors only when raiders were sighted visually or heard overhead. The fatal defects of these alternatives were that i) the RAF disposed of totally inadequate resources for this scale of operations, and ii) the attempt to intercept at the last moment would have invited destruction by the escorting enemy fighters as the defenders climbed towards the higher enemy.

As the Battle unfolded throughout July, August and September, 11 Group sent to Command HQ a steady stream of reports of the enemy raids, their changing tactics, and the Group's counter-tactics. These reports permitted an evaluation of the enemy's apparent aims. Dowding and Park did not waver: together they out-thought and out-fought the enemy.

### 4. SURPRISE

To take the enemy by surprise is one of the oldest stratagems of war, and one of the most coveted by military commanders to spring on the enemy. It is a measure advocated by all writers on war, from Sun Tzu to the Doctor Strangeloves of the nuclear age. Surprise is, however, in its essence an admirable enterprise, when successful, as a strategic manœuvre. It is of limited tactical value. And in tactics its usefulness is most evident in defence.

When surprise is accompanied by a powerful offensive thrust launched in the right place, the effect produced on the mind of the defenders can be catatonic, as General Guderian demonstrated. In May 1940, his tank columns broke the French defenders by thrusting through the Ardennes Forest, and achieved a success far more decisive than even the German general had expected.

The Battle of Britain, being a defensive battle — albeit one characterized by aggressive rather than a merely passive defence — presented no opportunity for strategic surprise. It was therefore on the tactical level, in the actual interception of enemy attackers, that the element of surprise was feasible. And one manner in which the enemy might most readily be surprised was to be 'bounced' from above.

The intent is full of merit, and the defenders were right to attempt this tactical surprise whenever they could. We discussed the actual implementation of the intent fully in Chapter 3, and have no need to recapitulate the limited successes achieved.

When carried out under intelligent leadership, tactical surprise will result in appreciably greater losses by the enemy attackers. However, an equally important impact — one which did not enter into the calculations of the 12 Group enthusiasts and which 11 and 10 Groups were not able to realize for various technical reasons — would have been inflicted on the enemy morale. It is not difficult to imagine the state of mind of the hostile aircrews if they came to expect to be had at a tactical disadvantage seven or eight times out of ten when crossing into enemy territory.

## 5. RESERVES

In war the provision and deployment of reserve forces are an indispensable component of fighting.

Churchill was rightly obsessed with them. We will give two examples. In May 1940, after the Germans had broken through the Allied lines and threatened Paris, he flew to France to confer with the Prime Minister. In discussing the critical military situation he demanded to know where was the reserve *(masse de manœuvre)*. "There is no *masse de manœuvre!*"

Later that summer, on September 15, Churchill was visiting 11 Group HQ, as we have seen. When all their squadrons had been scrambled he turned to Park and asked: "What reserves do you have?" He replied: "There are none."

In the first instance we are talking about a strategic reserve; in the second it is a case of a tactical reserve. If Park needed reinforcements to buttress his defences in a specific engagement, as we have seen, he called on the resources of his neighbours, 10 and 12 Groups, for support. Churchill was to learn soon enough that Park was not at the end of his tether.

We have had occasion to point out that Fighter Command had divided the United Kingdom into four geographical regions, and that for the purposes of its defence, each region was entrusted to a Group organization. So it was that each Group, in the event of the destruction or near destruction of the forces of one Group, became in a very real sense a strategic reserve. The defensive functions of the incapacitated Group were supplied by components made available by the other Groups.

It was largely this interdependence of the Groups, and the moving around of the squadrons from Group to Group, and the intimate relationship between Strategy and Tactics as laid down by Dowding, which later so impressed Churchill that he extolled the Commander's "genius in the art of war."

## 6. MORALE

The morale of a fighting force is so vast and complex a matter that it can only be touched upon in some of its salient aspects. To discuss it thoroughly, it would be necessary to study not only the individuals who fought the Battle, and their ground crews, but also the spirit of leadership filtering down from the Command, the national feeling among the people at the time, and, above all, the moral qualities of the commander.

Let us, at the outset, define morale. We perceive it to be the fighting spirit, the will to do battle and to win, sustained by a confidence in one's superiority to the enemy shared totally by one's comrades, and by a singleness of purpose felt intensely and intuitively rather than arrived at by analysis. Morale is a moral force with roots drawing sustenance from the deepest regions of the emotive soil.

We saw in Chapter 7 the crucial role played by the emotions in human decisions. Morale belongs very much more in the area of mind governing the affective being than the cognitive being.

The distinction between them is easily demonstrated. A Battle pilot experiences only a narrow field of conflict, and cannot know the larger picture, or even where in it his piece of the action fits. On the other hand, he is keenly sensible to the moral support and encouragement flooding in like a wave to encompass him and the whole Air Force from an unseen and unheard source.

What could be the source of that flood of sympathy and benevolence?

When the French army and government surrendered, and Britain found herself alone, without allies, to face the coming storm, the British people let out a collective sigh of relief, as if disencumbered of a great burden. Overnight the people found themselves blessed not only with a rare freedom of action, but with a stark simplicity of action. They had but one thing to do, and that one thing was a matter of life and death which concentrated their minds and energies into a unified spiritual force. The people felt as one: its power and influence were almost palpable, and imbued the people with a conviction of invincibility.[18] This force communicated itself to the pilots; and they in their turn, by their exploits recounted hourly and daily to the people, fuelled their admiration and enthusiasm.

The unqualified support of the people was one thing, but it was not enough in itself. It would have availed nothing had the commander not radiated that power of example and decision which is the hallmark of leadership at its highest. By way of introducing our next section, dealing with the qualities of Dowding as a war commander, we quote the accolade of one of his pilots:

> Dowding's qualities of leadership produced high morale throughout Fighter Command, which, in my view was the most important single factor in the winning of the Battle of Britain.

## The Commander

A purely defensive battle, even though fought with the maximum freedom of action and aggressiveness, cannot fail to induce in the Commander the possibility of defeat. In Britain's case, in 1940, the consequences were so grave and far-reaching that that possibility constrained the Commander to ponder the measures necessary, if not to win the battle, at least not to lose it; and to weigh solemnly the role to be played in it by his own conduct.

He must know, down to the last nut and bolt, the extent and the limits of his resources. He will keep a close eye on them daily, and constantly assess gains and losses.[19]

The corollaries of these requirements are that, at one and the same time, he pay a meticulous attention to detail and that he have a firm grasp of the overall situation. That these essentials call for an almost limitless capacity for unremitting work goes without saying.

> "The first principle of a general-in-chief is to calculate what he must do, to see if he has the means to surmount the obstacles with which the enemy can oppose him and, when he has made his decision, to do everything to overcome them." (Napoléon)

The commander depends greatly in carrying out his campaign on his staffs and subordinates for their reliability and skills in the performance of their duties; but in many cases, where he is faced with unknown factors, the Commander will have no other recourse than to find out or verify for himself what he needs to know. The ultimate responsibility is his.

The Commander has a clear understanding of the intimate relationship between his material resources and his human resources. He neglects no measure, he misses no chance, he overlooks no opportunity, to weed out incompetents, to promote solely on the basis of merit, to encourage improvement, to foster enterprise and inventiveness. Above all, he harbours an unfailing concern for his people, especially for those who face danger, and seeks ways to communicate his concern to them.

Having schooled himself to face the possibility of defeat, the Commander must equally be prepared to face setbacks and reverses, and to know in advance how he will conduct himself in a severely deteriorating situation. He has all along shown his control of his resources, and the firmness and decision with which he exploits them. Now he must strengthen his resolve and control, and at the same time exhibit to all a calmness and confidence which belie the severity of the situation, whilst guarding against the accident that his subordinate commanders and immediate staff mistake his calmness — what the Greeks called ataraxia — for an unawareness of the danger.

We are convinced that Dowding possessed and manifested all the powers and virtues we have outlined above. It was Montesquieu, the French philosopher, who stated that the most powerful force exerted by a leader was the power of example. If that is so, Dowding, it can be proved, was the very exemplar of the highest moral strength. His luminous integrity is common knowledge. He wrote and spoke lucidly what was on his mind — his needs, his policies, his fears, his contempt for incompetents, slackers and self-seekers — and no one, from the highest to the humblest, was ever in doubt as to where he stood on any matter touching his professional life and responsibilities.

Dowding demonstrated courage of a high moral order whenever he had an imperious cause to defend or promote, and never more ardently than when Air Ministry officials should have done so and proved themselves deficient. Above all — and all his powers came to be concentrated on this over-arching demand — he showed an unwavering singleness of purpose and a constancy of aim which are among the hallmarks of genius. That singularity and that constancy were dedicated, first, to the creation of a Fighter Command which would not be found wanting when the clash of arms came, as he felt sure it would; and second, to the proper conduct of war when it was thrust inescapably upon him.

We have said little of the distinction between offensive and defensive battle. There is little to add. We wrote above, "All defenders have fallen before them." Some of the greatest battles in history have been defensive battles, and losing battles. If we discount the Spanish Armada,[20] the Battle of Britain is not only the sole uniquely aerial battle in history; it is even more significantly one of very few entirely successful defensive battles in history.

On defensive actions, Clausewitz has written: "If in military history we rarely find such great victories resulting from the defensive battle as from the offensive, that proves nothing against our assertion that the one is as well suited to produce victory as the other; the real cause is in the very different relations of the defender."

It is probably Frederick the Great that Clausewitz had in mind when writing those lines, of whom it has been written: "Single-handed he fought all the great powers of Europe in the Seven Years' War and successfully defended the national territory." While the Battle of Britain did not last seven years, there is no question but that Dowding could have defended England successfully for that period. And he knew it; for had he not written in the prophetic letter already reproduced: "I believe that, if an adequate fighter force is kept in this country, if the fleet remains in being, and if Home Forces are suitably organised to resist invasion, we should be able to carry on the war single handed for some time, if not indefinitely." And, given the global significance of the Battle and its outcome, it is not too fanciful to place these two great commanders and humanitarians in the same company.

In this conclusion I have attached perhaps inadequate importance to that mysterious and unquantifiable quality called morale. What was the Commander's role in the generation of that spirit, and how was it communicated from him throughout Fighter Command? The answer is to be found, I think, in both direct and indirect channels,

Indirectly, and by deduction or intuition, the men and women at the fighting end of the chains of communication, far though they were from the top, knew, or presumed, that the Commander was the architect of Fighter Command as well as its chief. This knowledge gave them a high confidence in their equipment and matériel, and in the organizing intelligence behind it. This confidence was enhanced by the very excellence of their fighting machines, the Hurricane and the Spitfire, which they saw as a match for anything the enemy could throw at them; and multiplied by their intimate association with their comrades, both aircrews and groundcrews.

It has often been remarked of Dowding — by some in a critical spirit — that he seldom visited the squadrons, and so on the personal level was an unknown quantity. He was, in the words of one contemporary pilot, "an invisible figure," and adds: "at the time we all felt he was rather a remote figure." He goes on to say, however: "at the time we all felt that he was fighting a notable battle on our behalf and had implicit trust in him, but he did not come 'down amongst the people' and was rarely seen. What we had in him was total faith he would do his best for us, but this was not attained by personal contact in the great majority of cases."[21]

In some cases, however, there was personal contact, and the testimony of one of their number enlarges on the above assessment. He is Robert Wright, who was Dowding's Personal Assistant throughout the Battle. In a personal letter to Tom Gleave written on July 28, 1967, he wrote this considered tribute:

> Of all the men whom I have known in my own varied and very extensive experiences, I say without hesitation that the one who has the highest integrity, who is of the greatest strength of character, whose loyalty and fortitude are unequalled, and whose friendship I value the most is unquestionably Stuffy Dowding. You of all people will appreciate that it is for those reasons that I have for him a feeling of affection that is unique in my own personal feeling.

> His courage and fearlessness have always been . . . an inspiration. I say that with a full realization that such a sentiment on my part is likely to be viewed in some quarters with cynicism; but those who are unable to feel that way and who would jeer at it are the poorer for not being able to understand, or know, what this great man can inspire in one through direct personal contact over a long period of time. I say with every appreciation of what that implies that he is a truly great man, one of the greatest men of our times.

Let the last word be from 'Johnnie' Johnson, the eminent fighter pilot and historian of air warfare, who in this summation writes from the historical perspective:

> Few men in our long history have shouldered such a burden, and Dowding was one of the great commanders of all time. During the contest the strands of leadership in Fighter Command flowed down from the Commander-in-Chief through the simple chain of command — groups, stations and squadrons — to a thousand fighter pilots and their ground crews, and produced that priceless pearl, high morale, which made men bigger than their normal selves.

NOTES TO CHAPTER 10:

1. Shakespeare, *Richard II.*

2. A recent book, *A Radar History of World War II: Technical and Military Imperatives* by Louis Brown (2000, Institute of Physics Publishing), shows, according to a review by Robert Hanbury Brown, "that the early British experiments at Orfordness . . . were turned with remarkable speed into a highly effective defence system in time for the outbreak of the war by the combined efforts of Watson-Watt, Tizard and Dowding" — at the head, let us add, of a brilliant team of engineers and physicists.

   We must also say that there is some serious doubt whether Dowding was in fact an observer present at this Daventry Experiment. The first writer to state that he was there was none other than Basil Collier, who wrote in his 1957 biography of Dowding (p.37): "After his visit to Weedon, Dowding took steps whose consequences were perhaps as decisive as any event recorded in British history. . . ." However, Michael Bragg, in his *The Location of Aircraft by Radio Methods 1935-1945*, states in the course of his description of the experiment (pp. 30-32) that only Watson-Watt and Rowe were present. In a personal communication to me on February 9th, 2003, Mr. Bragg wrote — and I quote with his permission: "There are two (sic) reasons for thinking that Dowding was not there. The first one is the account of the experiment in Watson-Watt's book *Three Steps to Victory*. If Dowding was there, it is certain that Watson-Watt would have mentioned it. Secondly, an Air Ministry official in the shape of A.P. Rowe was there as the official observer and, in his report to his superior, H.E. Wimperis, he makes no mention of Dowding, which I thought he would have done if Dowding was there. Thirdly, in the AM correspondence file there is a memo dated 4 March 1935 from Wimperis to Dowding that advises him of the result of the experiment and enclosing Rowe's report. So I came to the conclusion that Dowding was not at Weedon."

   Zimmerman also states that only Watson-Watt and Rowe witnessed the result of the test in their little van.

3. Note this significant accusation: you will not be able to resist the pressure. That should put an end to the claim by Air Ministry apologists that the CAS and the Air Staff fully supported Dowding in his efforts to block Churchill's commitment to keep supporting the French.

4. The original of this letter hangs, suitably framed, on the front wall in the imposing entrance of Bentley Priory, still a part of Royal Air Force Station Stanmore, in recognition of its historic significance.

5. This was the burden of an article by Lt-Col. Rogé entitled, "Les Aviations allemande, française et anglaise du 10 mai au 25 juin 1940" published in *Revue de Défense Nationale*, Ottawa, février 1951, but it fails to convince.

6. Lucas, *Wings of War*, p.50.

7. See Bell, pp.24-25.

8. It was also, said Churchill, his most sombre concern. But his record in the struggle did not reflect it.

9. A pity that the Air Ministry staff officers weren't heeding the prescient views of one of their aircraftmen! The "general opinion" does not seem to have penetrated their "towers of (concrete) ivory."

10. Whether or not the Germans could have launched an invasion of England after the elimination of the Fighter Command of the Royal Air Force is immaterial to our theme in this chapter. The essential thing is that the British thought so at the time, and took all necessary steps to repel

one. One may not agree with Grinnell-Milne's thesis, as elaborated in *The Silent Victory*, that any attempt by the Germans to carry out a sea-borne invasion in 1940 would have met with a complete defeat and disaster for the Germans, even if the Fighter Command had been destroyed. The one pre-condition of invasion was the elimination of Fighter Command.

On the other hand, the Germans, had they defeated Fighter Command, did not need to invade, except for purposes of prestige — and that may have carried great weight in the calculations of a man like Hitler. All they had to do was to cut off Britain's oil or to starve Britain into submission by mounting a blockade of the British Isles, and destroy the British fleet from the air. There was nothing that the United States could have done about it.

The outcome of the Battle of Britain was, therefore, of quite decisive importance. It is more than likely that Dowding realized this when he wrote his prophetic letter of May 16th, in which he made no mention of 'invasion', but only of "irremediable defeat".

11. The five "circumstances in which victory may be predicted" are these:

> "He will be victorious
>
> 1) who knows when he can fight and when he cannot;
>
> 2) who understands how to use both large and small forces;
>
> 3) whose ranks are united in purpose;
>
> 4) who is prudent and lies in wait for an enemy who is not; and
>
> 5) whose generals are able and not interfered with by the sovereign."

The last article is particularly significant: for "sovereign" read "Air Ministry".

12. His two biographers were negligent in not having interrogated their subject on this matter. We know that Dowding attended and passed the Army Staff College course at Camberley in 1912-14 when a junior lieutenant. He has told us that it was while there that he decided to learn to fly, for the reason that 'the Air' was one of the only two subjects on which the instructors were not open-minded: "I thought (he wrote) that perhaps it might be a good thing if the Army had some Staff officers who knew something about flying . . . so I decided to learn to fly, as being the best, in fact the only way of finding out." He was labeled one of the "bad boys", being a non-conformist, and decried the lip-service paid to freedom of thought, which contrasted with an actual tendency to repress all but conventional ideas. On the other hand, Dowding praised the course for enabling "the facility of marshaling one's ideas, and setting them forth logically and consecutively with a minimum of words".

13. Napoléon exhorted his generals: "Read over and over again the campaigns of Alexander, Hannibal, Caesar, Gustavus, Turenne, Eugene, and Frederic. Make them your models. This is the only way to become a great general and to master the secrets of the art of war. With your own genius enlightened by this study, you will reject all maxims opposed to those of these great commanders."

14. As late as 1938 the Air Ministry was ordering more obsolete light and medium bombers. A few examples: a total of 3,100 Battles were constructed, 5,421 Blenheims, and 1,812 Whitleys. And none of them a war-winning strategic bomber. Moreover, the ratio was still four bombers to every one fighter produced.

15. The reason for this failure was the removal of Sidney Cotton from the PR unit he had created. See chapter 6 and Appendix "D".

16. I am indebted for this information to the late Earl of Selkirk — then Squadron Leader 'Geordie' Hamilton, Chief Intelligence Officer at Fighter Command Headquarters in 1940, when I visited him at his home in Dorset on July 13, 1995.

17. There was also, of course, the third source: the intelligence provided by captured enemy airmen. This was necessarily of a tactical nature, and of very limited use, in terms of volume, accuracy, and the time factor. To our knowledge, this source has not been studied.

18. By a strange coincidence, the motto of the preparatory school the author went to in Broadstairs, Kent, was *Invicta*, meaning "Unconquered", and by implication, "Unconquerable". The motto of his next school, in Ramsgate, was *Pro Bono Vince*, which also at the time seemed supremely apt.

19. Joubert criticizes Dowding's leadership of Fighter Command by accusing him of paying too much  attention to detail and not enough to principle. Joubert is wrong. Dowding had long ago established his principles. And no commander can pay sufficient attention to detail. Indeed, attention to detail is what distinguishes the great commander from the lesser ones.

    The old adage is applicable to commanders as to corporals: 'For want of a nail, the shoe is lost; for want of a shoe, the horse is lost; for want of a horse, the battle is lost.'

20. Why discount the Armada? Because, although a resounding defeat for the invading Spanish, it can be shown that the defeat was inflicted not so much by Drake and the English fleet as by the inability of the Spanish fleet to manoeuvre, and by the weather. After putting in to Gravelines to pick up the infantry, they could not possibly have sailed across the Channel to land them.

21. I am indebted to Air Chief Marshal Sir Christopher Foxley-Norris — who was at the time a flying officer on 3 Squadron — for this appreciation. (Personal letter, June 5, 2002.)

# APPENDIX "A"

## *The Duxford Wing Operations*

### Enemy Aircraft Claimed Destroyed

|  | Sept. 7 | Sept. 9 | Sept. 11 | Sept. 15 | Sept. 18 | Sept. 27 |
|---|---|---|---|---|---|---|
| 12 Group Report[1] | 20 (5 - 6) | 21 (5 - 1)[2] | 12 (14 - 7)[3] | 26 (8 - 2)[4]<br>26 (8 - 1) | ?[5] | ? |
| The All-Canadian Squadron[6] | 20 | 18 | No action reported | 37 | 30 | 13 |
| 242 Squadron[7] | 11 (10) | 10 (11) | No action[8] | 6 (12)<br>5 (10) | 12 (10) | 5 (4) |
| CLAIMS *vs* LOSSES[9] | 103 : 41 | 52: 30 | 93: 29 | 185: 59 | 48: 20 | 133: 57 |
| Wing Action Figures[10] | 2 - 16 | 0 (6) | 0 (13) | 3 (18) | ?[11] |  |

### NOTES TO APPENDIX "A":

1. The figures in parentheses give, respectively, the number of additional enemy aircraft (e/a) claimed 'probable' - 'damaged'.

2. Three squadrons engaged — 34 and 33 fighters respectively — on the first two operations, at the cost of 8 fighters destroyed and 4 damaged.

3. Four squadrons engaged — 36 fighters — at the cost of 3 destroyed and 3 damaged.

4. Two patrols carried out, am and pm, by five squadrons totalling 56 fighters engaged in each of the two actions: 3 destroyed and 3 damaged

5. No 12 Group Report found for this or the next wing patrol, Sept. 27.

6. This report also gives the analysis by squadron as well as the total wing figures.

7. Figures of claims compiled by the author from the Squadron Operational Diaries held in the Public Records Office (AIR 27/1471-1473). The figures in parentheses are the claims made of e/a destroyed for 242 Squadron by the All-Canadian Squadron.

8. On this day S/L Bader was at 12 Group HQ conferring with Leigh-Mallory, and 242 Squadron was not engaged.

9. The two figures show the claims made by Fighter Command at the time, and the losses shown by the *Luftwaffe* in the German Quarter-Master records discovered by the Allies at the end of the war.

10. The figures shown here have been calculated on the basis of a comparison made between the 12 Group Operations Report and Ramsey's authoritative work, *Battle of Britain: Then and Now*. The former states only the area of the patrol, which could be vast; the latter, the locale where each e/a crashed or landed. If these revised figures seem drastic, they are almost certainly closer to fact than the claims. It is impossible ever to establish the exact figures for each squadron, and even less for each pilot.

11. In the absence of 12 Group Reports on the Wing actions of September 18 and 27, we give here-under the comparative figures compiled, respectively, by John Frayn Turner from the individual Squadron Combat Reports, and by this author from Ramsey's *Battle of Britain: Then and Now*.

> On **September 18** the Wing carried out three patrols, and did not encounter the enemy on the first two. On the third, over London and the Thames estuary from 1630 hrs to ca. 1730 hrs, the Wing of four squadrons claimed 29 e/a destroyed "without a scratch" to themselves. Of these, 242 Squadron claimed 12.

From Ramsey, given the time and the place of the patrol, we get 5 certain or almost certain, and 3 other possible.

> On **September 27** the Wing carried out three patrols. It had no encounter on the first and third. The second patrol, of four squadrons, was over the Dover-Canterbury-Dungeness triangle from about 12 noon. The Wing claimed 13 e/a destroyed, of which 242 Squadron claimed 4. (The Wing lost 5 fighters.) Our calculation gives 2 certain, and 6 others possible.

It is interesting to note what Turner says about this patrol:

> "Bader heard over the R/T: 'Bandits south-east of Estuary. . . .' When he could not find them, the Duxford controller told him to return. Douglas said: "I'll just have one more swing round."

Here was another instance of Bader's ignoring his Controller's instructions, and taking his Wing, uncontrolled, deep into 11 Group. It was this occurrence that elicited from Park his 'famous', and angry, complaint about 'poaching' — an unfortunate choice of words, perhaps, but indicative both of the culprit's disregard of vital regulations, and his wilful ignorance of Fighter Command's system of fighter control.

> On **September 16, 17, 21, 22, 23 and 25**, the Duxford Wing carried out nine vain patrols. These were days of relatively little activity, but on which nevertheless a total of 40 e/a were destroyed by our fighters.

# APPENDIX "B"

# *11 Group Wing Formations*

## I.

From:  Headquarters, No. 11 Group.

To:     Officer Commanding, RAF Station,
         Debden North Weald Hornchurch Northolt
         Tangmere Biggin Hill Kenley

Ref:    11G/486

Date:  1st October, 1940.

### Wing Formations:

1.   There is a feeling among pilots in some Squadrons that the only way to defeat the enemy raiders against this country is to employ our fighter Squadrons in Wings of three Squadrons. The object of this Note is to explain why such formations have been used off and on during the past five months, yet have not been made the standard method of grouping our fighter Squadrons in home defence fighting.

2.   During the operations by No. 11 Group over France and Belgium, Squadrons were originally employed singly. When the enemy opposition strengthened, Squadrons were employed in pairs. Moreover, when Squadrons could only raise three Sections each, they were employed in Wings of three Squadrons. The conditions were that our Squadrons were being operated on a pre-arranged programme and could be allotted to their task some hours in advance and were normally collected and despatched from forward aerodromes on the coast. This gave ample time for Squadrons to be arranged into pairs or Wings, under conditions which do not obtain in the defence of this country, when the enemy can and has made four heavy attacks in one day, giving only the minimum warning on each occasion.

3.   In spite of the favourable conditions during the operations over France for the employment of Wings of three Squadrons, the best results during the whole of this operation were obtained by Squadrons working in pairs. Whenever possible, two pairs of Squadrons patrolled the same restricted

area; two at high altitude to engage enemy fighter patrols, and two about 5,000 to 8,000 feet lower to engage the enemy bombers, which, in those days, did not normally employ close escorts as they were operating over their own territory.

4.  Experience in home defence during the last two months' intensive operations has shown that there are many occasions in which the use of Wings of three Squadrons is quite unsuitable, because of cloud conditions and lack of time, due to short warning of the approaching attack.

5.  Experience over many weeks has shown that when there are two or more layers of clouds, the Squadrons of a Wing have great difficulty in assembling above the clouds at a rendezvous, also in maintaining touch after passing through clouds when on patrol. Instead of devoting their time to searching for the enemy, Squadrons have frequently had to devote much of their attention to maintaining contact with other Squadrons of a Wing of three. Unless the sky is relatively clear of clouds, pairs of Squadrons have been more effective in intercepting the enemy.

6.  Quite apart from cloud interference, the lack of time due to short warning of the approach of raids frequently renders it inadvisable to detail Wings of three Squadrons. Experience has shown that it takes much longer to despatch, assemble and climb to operating height, a Wing of three Squadrons than one of even two pairs of Squadrons. Frequently Wings of three Squadrons have been attacked by enemy fighters whilst still climbing or forming up over their Sector aerodromes. It has been found better to have even one strong Squadron of our fighters over the enemy than a Wing of three climbing up below them, in which attitude they are peculiarly vulnerable to attacks from above.

7.  In clear weather when the enemy attack develops in two or three waves, there is often time for the Squadrons of Sectors on the flank of the attack, e.g., Debden, Northolt and Tangmere, to be despatched as Wings of three Squadrons to meet the third incoming wave or to sweep across and mop up the retreating enemy bombers and close escort. There is rarely time for London Sectors to get Wing formations up to the desired height before the enemy reaches important bombing targets, e.g., factories, docks, Sector aerodromes.

8.  Until we have VHF in all Squadrons, it is not practicable for three Squadrons in a Wing to work on a common R/T frequency; at least, that is the considered opinion of the majority of Squadron and Sector Commanders. Pairs of Squadrons can and do work successfully on a common frequency whenever the State of Preparedness in a Sector permits. Here again some Squadron Commanders prefer to be on a separate R/T frequency in order to have better intercommunication within their Squadrons.

CONCLUSION:

9. As a result of five months' intensive air fighting in No.11 Group, it is clear that Wings of three Squadrons are not the most suitable formations under many conditions of TIME and WEATHER. On the whole, some Squadrons working in pairs have obtained better results in home defence, especially as our practice since July has been to detail two or more pairs of Squadrons to intercept raids in massed formation. However, when conditions are favourable, Squadrons will continue to be despatched in Wings of three, but the only person who can decide whether Wings or pairs of Squadrons should be despatched is the Group Controller. He has the complete picture of the enemy's movements on a wide front from Lowestoft to Bournemouth, and must quickly decide whether the time and cloud conditions are suitable for pairs or Wing formations. Squadrons must therefore continue to study and develop fighting tactics in Wings of three Squadrons, which will probably become more common in the Spring of 1941.

10. Two copies of this Note are to be distributed to each fighter Squadron, and one copy is to be read by each Sector Controller.

(Signed) K.R. PARK
Air Vice-Marshal, Commanding,
No. 11 Group, Royal Air Force.

# II.

SECRET

From: Headquarters, No. 11 Group.

To: Officer Commanding, RAF Station,
DEBDEN NORTH WEALD HORNCHURCH NORTHOLT
TANGMERE BIGGIN HILL KENLEY

Ref: 11G/486

Date: 6th October, 1940.

WING FORMATIONS:

1. When the sky is mainly clear of clouds and the Group Controller receives ample warning by RDF of the forming up and approach of mass attacks over the French coast or from the South, some Squadrons will be despatched in Wings of three units. Moreover, this type of formation will continue to be used to bring Sectors in the North and South of London in to meet the third wave of a prolonged attack or to "mop" up raids that are retreating after having been engaged by other Squadrons around London.

2. As a result of practical experience during the last five months by Squadrons, Sectors and Group Headquarters, the following brief instructions are issued. As further experience is gained by Squadrons working in Wing formations, fresh and more detailed instructions will be issued for the benefit of all concerned. Much of that which follows applies to Squadrons working in pairs; the normal formation for reasons already stated in my letter 11G/486, dated October 1st.

## LEADERSHIP:

3. The Squadron and leader of the Wing must be decided by the Sector Commander before the beginning of daylight operations each day. After a heavy engagement it may be necessary to change the leadership, when the strongest Squadron should be appointed to lead the Wing.

## TAKE-OFF:

4. Squadrons should take off separately and not form up in Wing on the ground.

## ASSEMBLY:

5. The Group Controller will order the place and height of rendezvous, according to the cloud conditions and the proximity of enemy raids. The rendezvous will, whenever possible, be well inland, in order to enable Squadrons to join up at the height ordered before engaging the enemy. The Wing leader must report immediately the Wing assembles, and Sector Controller is to report to Group Controller, who will then detail Wing to a raid or a patrol line above the enemy raids.

## FAILURE TO ASSEMBLE:

6. If slow take-off or unexpected cloud conditions unduly delay the assembly of the Wing when enemy raids are approaching important bombing targets, the Group Controller may be compelled to detail one or more Squadrons of the intended Wing to intercept approaching raids to break up or harass bombers before they reach the target. In this event, it will be necessary for Squadrons having V.H.F. to revert from common frequency to their own R/T channel.

## RENDEZVOUS:

7. Group Controller will normally select an aerodrome or other good landmark well back from the approaching enemy raids.

## R/T FREQUENCIES:

8.   Until all Squadrons have VHF, it is not considered practicable for all units in the Wing to work on a common R/T frequency. This ruling is based on the experience of many Squadrons in several Sectors over a long period. On the introduction of vhf Squadrons will work on a common R/T frequency as soon as they assemble as a Wing. If the Wing becomes broken, Squadrons should revert to their own R/T frequency to facilitate communication with the Sector Controller.

## FORMATION:

9.   The leading Squadron will normally be lower than the two following Squadrons. Sectors, however, are to try out stepping down one or more of the following Squadrons.

## TACTICS:

10.   Before leaving the ground it is essential that the three Squadrons shall know which unit is to take on the bombers, which to attack the escort, and lastly which Squadron is to act as above-guard or screen to hold off enemy high fighter screen. As the enemy close escort may be above the bombers, in rear, or on a flank or even ahead, and on other occasions may fly weaving between the bomber sub-formations, it is not always possible to lay down rigidly beforehand which Squadrons in the Wing will attack bombers or their escort. This makes it all the more necessary for the general tactics of the Wing to be discussed and decided on the ground before a patrol.

## LOOK-OUT GUARDS:

11.   Each Squadron should provide its own look-out guards, especially for the period prior to assembly, and after the Wing has become split up by an engagement with the enemy. The Wing should normally have one Squadron slightly in rear and above to act as cover to the whole Wing against very high enemy fighters.

## PIP-SQUEAK:

12. Each Squadron is to provide one aircraft with pip-squeak to enable fixing at Sector Operations Room.

## THE SUN:

13.   The Wing formation should whenever possible patrol across the direction of the sun. Enemy fighters attacking out of the sun will then be offered only deflection shots at our fighters.

## SECTOR FORMATION:

14. When in Wing formations, Sections should normally be composed of four aircraft, consisting of two pairs of fighters. Each Squadron should, therefore, have three Sections of four aircraft.

## ASSEMBLY AFTER COMBAT:

15. It is not considered necessary or advisable for Squadrons to try to re-form Wing after a general engagement over our own territory. If, however, the engagement takes place over enemy territory or over the sea, then it may be advisable to lay down beforehand the Wing rendezvous.

## BREAKING OFF FROM WING:

16. If Squadrons are detailed to be detached from Wing formation, Sector Controller should give the order "X Squadron break away, Vector. . . .", and then inform the Wing leader that X Squadron has been ordered to break away.

(Signed) K.R. PARK
Air Vice-Marshal, Commanding,
No. 11 Group, Royal Air Force.

# III.

SECRET

From:   Headquarters, No. 11 Group.

To:      Headquarters, Fighter Command.

Ref:     11G/493

Date:   7th November, 1940.

**German Attacks on England 11th September - 31st October.**

*Excerpts*

[First Phase | September 11th - October 5th]

## USE OF WING FORMATIONS

18. When early warning had given adequate time, and cloud conditions were suitable, Squadrons were employed in Wings of three against enemy bomber formations and their close escort. Being located outside the area

normally patrolled by enemy fighter screens, the Squadrons from Debden, Northolt and Tangmere were not infrequently employed in Wings of three Squadrons. These Wings were successful in engaging retreating bomber formations, who normally lost their escort before reaching London, because of the vigorous action of Spitfire and Hurricane Squadrons working in pairs against incoming raids.

19. Experience showed that even small Wings of three Squadrons were not effective against German high fighter patrols, and the Spitfire Squadrons were, therefore, used in pairs.

## [Second Phase | October 5th to October 31st]

### USE OF MASS FORMATIONS — BIG WINGS AND "BALBOS":

61. The Air Ministry held a Conference on October 16th (sic) to examine a proposal that Wings should be adopted as a standard formation for air fighting, and that whenever possible, Balbos — mass formations of six Squadrons — should be employed against enemy raids on this country. These proposals arose as a result of the remarkable results claimed in air combat by No. 12 Group, employing its Squadrons in Wings of four and five Squadrons on five occasions in September, operating from Duxford. Good results were reported against fighters as well as bombers.

62. As a result of the Air Ministry Conference, the Duxford Wing was invited to operate in No. 11 Group area on every possible occasion during the last half of October. In view of the results obtained in No. 11 Group when employing mass formations, the operations of the Duxford Wing have been watched with close interest. The [table of] patrols by the Duxford Wing shows that in ten sorties, it effected one interception and destroyed one enemy aircraft. On only few days was the weather considered fit for the Duxford Wing to operate. On several days that were unfit for these large Wing formations, the Squadrons in No. 11 Group were operating at high pressure, in Pairs.

63. The intensity of the air fighting over No. 11 Group territory during the second half of October can be gauged by the fact that its Squadrons account- ed for 83 enemy aircraft destroyed, plus 62 probably destroyed, plus 66 dam- aged; a total of 211 aircraft accounted for in the period covered. . . . Moreover, during this short period, the Squadrons in No. 11 Group by successful inter- ception, prevented scores of enemy from proceeding inland and bombing vital objectives. On numerous occasions the enemy turned about and retreat- ed at speed before our fighters could come within effective range.

64. From watching the operations of the Duxford Wings of four Squadrons during the second half of October, confirmation was obtained of the lessons

previously learned in No. 11 Group in the employment of smaller Wing formations. Other lessons appear to have been brought about as under:

1) Mass formations require the assistance of good Sector Controllers if they are to effect interception of enemy fighter formations;

2) Large Wings of four or five Squadrons suffer serious difficulties in R/T communications;

3) Increasing the number of Squadrons in a Wing does not appear to increase the chances of interceptions or the area of search effectively covered;

4) It is inadvisable to concentrate four or five Squadrons on one aerodrome in the Autumn, because all are likely to be weather-bound together;

5) The maximum size of a Wing should be three Squadrons, not four or five as previously practiced in the North.

(Signed) K.R. Park
Air Vice-Marshal, Commanding,
No. 11 Group, Royal Air Force.

# APPENDIX "C"

# *Dowding's Rebuttal of*
# *Balfour's Duxford Memorandum*

6th November, 1940

1.  With reference to your letter dated 3rd November, on the subject of the 12 Group Wing, I agree that this operation is causing so much friction and ill-feeling that I must withdraw the control of combined operations between Nos. 11 and 12 Groups from the Group Commanders themselves and issue the orders through my own Operations Room.

2.  At the same time, the story which Balfour has collected by his direct methods is wrong in its conclusions and in the facts on which those conclusions are based.

3.  The conclusions may be summarised as follows:

    (a) That No.12 Group is not allowed available RDF information.

    (b) That the Duxford Sector has been unnecessarily denied Observer Corps information from the Bromley area.

    (c) That the Duxford Wing is not called upon by No.11 Group until too late.

    (d) That in consequence valuable opportunities for destroying the enemy are being lost.

4.  As regards (a), 12 Group have all RDF information down to the latitude of Dungeness - Gris Nez. They get it simultaneously with 11 Group.

5.  As regards (b), the Duxford Sector has certainly been stopped from using an unauthorised system which has caused confusion and inefficiency in the work of the Observer Corps. They have been using the inter-centre teller line to pass distant tracks between Bromley and Duxford, whereas it is required to pass adjacent tracks between Bromley and Colchester. 11 Group had nothing to do with putting a stop to this practice. It was done at the request of the Southern Area Observer Corps Commandant.

6.  As regards (c), my criticism is that the recent conference and all the fuss that has been made has resulted in 11 Group calling for assistance not only too early, but without the slightest excuse. On 29th October, for instance, the first plot of the first attack of the day appeared at Gris Nez at 1025 hours and

the Duxford Wing was called on at 1030 hours. The raid turned out to be a small one, and 11 Group employed very few of its own squadrons.

7.    There are indications that No.11 Group, in order to get the Duxford Wing into action, is calling upon that Wing to patrol at a certain hour without even knowing whether there is going to be enemy activity at that hour or not. On the 5th November, AOC No.11 Group at 0930 hours, approximately, asked Controller No.12 Group to have the Wing on patrol over Maidstone at 1100 hours, a request which could hardly have been related to any situation that he could positively foresee at that time.

8.    As regards (d), no-one will deny the advantages of a 3, 4 or 5 Squadron Wing against a determined enemy attack, whether it be large or comparatively small, providing it can bring the enemy to action. A month ago the Duxford Wing, used against strong enemy attacks which took time in their building up over the Gris Nez area, and which came in with determination to reach their objective, would have been very effective. Now, however, against loosely formed high altitude fighter sweeps there is less time for the Wing to come into action and less for it to bite on when it gets there. The Wing absorbs the energies of 4 or 5 squadrons which have to be kept concentrated and at readiness if there is to be any hope of their operating successfully. Even so, it does seem that the time taken to form up is too slow for the present phase of tactics. No.11 Group allege that in the first attack on the 29th the request for the Wing was passed at 1030 hours, it left the ground at 1047 and did not leave the neighbourhood of Duxford until 1107. This may be inaccurate but tends to confirm that the Wing has just the limitations one would expect.

9.    There are, incidentally, other disadvantages to this Wing operation at the moment. It absorbs 4 or 5 squadrons of a very weak Group and thus diverts them from the tasks of No.12 Group, which are the defence of its own area, including some highly important industrial districts. On 29th October, the Duxford Wing was in operation between 1600 and 1700 hours. Only small fractions of the Wing were ready to operate again when the enemy attacked the East Anglian aerodromes at 1750 hours.

10.    I am inclined to the conclusion that for the moment in this present phase, the use of the Duxford Wing is a misemployment of a valuable element of our very limited strength. I think that Park was slow to take advantage of the possibilities of this Wing when they were first put forward by No.12 Group at a time when its operations might have been very valuable, but for the moment it is probably no longer an economical or effective use of 5 squadrons. There is always a possibility that, even now, the Wing might [added in ink:, with luck,] achieve a resounding success, but in this phase I think the odds are against that.

11. There remains the question of an Under-Secretary of State listening to the accusations of a junior officer against the Air Officer Commanding another Group, and putting them on paper with the pious hope that the officer will not get into trouble. Balfour has been in the Service and ought to know better. I think that, as a matter of fact, a good deal of the ill-feeling which has been engendered in the controversy has been directly due to young Bader, who, whatever his other merits, suffers from over-development of the critical faculty.

12. I must take counsel with my Group Commanders as to my precise action, but two things are quite clear to me:-

    (i)   that, as stated above, the Command must take control of these combined operations when they are necessary; and

    (ii)   that the continuous employment of this Wing of 5 squadrons cannot be justified in existing circumstances.

Leigh-Mallory has many commitments of his own, and should "keep his eye in the boat" more.

13. There is a growing tendency for the enemy to increase the frequency and weight of his attacks in the North and the West; and, although it is perfectly obvious that his object is to weaken the London defence, the intensity of his attacks on London has fallen off recently and I may soon be compelled to make some re-distribution of my force.

14. This might give an opportunity of moving young Bader to another station where he would be kept in better control. His amazing gallantry will protect him from disciplinary action if it can be possibly avoided.

# APPENDIX "D"

# *The Removal of Other*
# *Distinguished Officers*

The two stories related here are appended to this account of the appalling treatment of Air Chief Marshal Sir Hugh Dowding (as he was then) by the Air Ministry, in order to show that conduct of that kind, and which went unaccounted for, was far from rare.

## I. Group Captain A.G. 'Sailor' Malan

Group Captain Malan was the supreme fighter pilot of the RAF in the Battle of Britain and indeed in the European theatre of war. He was never shot down and he was scarcely ever shot at. There are few individual pilots whom Dowding has singled out for praise. Malan was one of them.

> I probably knew Sailor better than I knew most officers serving in squadrons during that time of stress which has become known as the Battle of Britain. I looked on him as one of the great assets of the Command — a fighter pilot who was not solely or mainly concerned with his own "score", but as one whose first thoughts were for the efficiency of his squadron, and the personal safety of his junior pilots who fought under his command. I know that he was regarded as a heroic figure by the small fry over whom he spread his influence, and I personally shared their opinion.

Apart from customary rests in staff jobs, he fought throughout the war. Towards the end, in 1945, he was Commander of 145 Fighter Wing of 2TAF (Second Tactical Air Force), which was engaged in operations in Europe in support of the Army offensive and the escort of bomber formations.

Malan had been Commander of this Wing since 1944. Suddenly he was removed from his command. The event has been described by his great friend, the New Zealand ace Alan Deere:

> It is right, I feel, that I should touch on Sailor's retirement from the Royal Air Force.[1] Although he wrote to me in a letter [from Plymouth, in February 1946, from the liner which was to take him home to South Africa]

"I don't think I could have faced a peacetime Service," I believe the decision was forced on him by his treatment as the war ended. He was then still commanding 145 Wing of 2nd TAF, which he had formed for the Invasion and led up to within weeks of final victory. But then he was relieved of his command — mysteriously, as all in the Command who knew him thought at the time — and replaced by a much older officer with no operational experience.

What could have been the reason for this? Authoritative opinion had it that his wealthy and socially acceptable successor knew the right people in the right places and wanted to be seen at the sharp end when the final whistle blew. Inexplicably and coincidentally, Sailor had been treated with much the same sort of medicine as had been prescribed for his earlier Commander-in-Chief of Fighter Command, 'Stuffy' Dowding, some five years before. Like Stuffy, he took his medicine without complaint. But what a loss a man of his calibre was to the peacetime Service!

This incident is not as insignificant as it appears. In the first place, it is apparently not impossible for a staff officer, who has no training or preparation, to take over another's command and who, puffed up with his own importance and powers on finding himself emancipated from the inhibiting mindset of the Air Ministry, could give orders which might put his pilots' lives at unnecessary risk and even jeopardize the operations.

Secondly, that such a deed is possible — the replacement of a master fighter pilot and operational commander by a desk jockey who happens to be in a position to pull the strings — is one more proof of the moral climate which, at the end as at the beginning of the war, seemed to prevail in high places in the Air Ministry.

## II. Wing Commander Sidney Cotton

Reliable Intelligence is one of the most decisive factors in the winning of wars. One of the chief contributing factors in the Luftwaffe's defeat in the Battle of Britain was its lack of reliable Intelligence. In the Second World War, the Allies' victory owed an inestimable debt to Intelligence. After Ultra, Britain's most prolific and fruitful source of accurate Intelligence was provided by photographic reconnaissance. The pioneer and the perfector of photographic intelligence was an Australian named Sidney Cotton.

Sidney Cotton began his flying career in the First World War; but he was one of the most extraordinary airmen of the Second World War — and indeed in the history of aviation. Not only was he the inventor of the Sidcot flying suit, the tear-drop window permitting the pilot to see below and rearwards, of which over 100,000 were fitted to RAF aircraft during the war, and aerial target illumination by 'Turbinlite ' for night fighter interception. He is renowned above all for his pioneering technical work in aerial photography and in the establishment of the first successful Photographic Reconnaissance Unit.

In the short space of time during which he operated his own aerial photographic unit from early September 1939 until March 3rd 1941, Cotton and his pilots and photo technicians performed prodigies of reconnaissance work, notably in France before the débâcle.

Cotton's interest pre-dated the Second World War. His activities between the wars had brought him into contact — a very fruitful contact — with many highly placed figures. Early in September he was consulted by Ian Fleming, who then worked with the Directorate of Naval Intelligence. Fleming wanted to know whether the Germans had any refuelling or maintenance facilities in neutral Southern Ireland. The Navy depended on the RAF's Photographic Section for aerial photography.

The RAF's aerial photography was worse than useless. Either its cameras froze at any altitude, or, at lower altitudes, its pictures did not turn out. Not only that: "On the outbreak of war, our total interpretation capacity consisted of two RAF officers at the Air Ministry, recruited from civilian ranks and with virtually no experience, two Army officers. . . , and a small nucleus at the Admiralty."

Cotton photographed the entire Irish Atlantic coast in the next few weeks. Word of such feats passes quickly. He got a phone call from an officer in Intelligence: the RAF wanted to see him. He was invited to a meeting. How could Cotton get such results when they couldn't? They were highly sceptical, and antagonistic. But they wanted to know how their Photographic Unit could get pictures of German naval units along the Dutch coast, which the Admiralty were demanding. The Air Ministry refused to let Cotton, a civilian, fly one of their aeroplanes. The meeting broke up, having decided only to hold another meeting the next day.

Cotton brooded; then decided. He went out and took the pictures. The following day the meeting dragged on and bogged down in trivialities, doubts and suspicion. Finally Cotton produced his pictures and said: "Is this the sort of thing you want?" There was general admiration and praise. But all present were convinced that they must have been taken before the war. Then Cotton announced calmly that they had been taken at three fifteen the previous day. It is unnecessary to describe the change of attitude and atmosphere, and the scene that followed. No doubt this demonstration by a civilian of superior professionalism to high ranking Air Ministry officers marked the beginning of their grudge against him.

A few days later he was called by none other than the Chief of the Air Staff, Air Chief Marshal Sir Cyril Newall, who invited him to lunch; and then, on his personal authority, authorized Cotton to form and to command the Photographic Development Unit, with the rank of Wing Commander, the unit to be under the aegis of Fighter Command.

It is impossible to recount the full story of Cotton's triumphs in aerial reconnaissance, and, precisely because of them, of his treacherous dismissal by the Air Ministry. But a few episodes must be told.

Cotton wanted Spitfires. (This in 1940!) He based his policy on the two factors of speed and ceiling. "If we used the fastest aeroplanes in the world, flying at the highest altitude, they could not be intercepted. Any fighter aircraft cleaned up, with guns eliminated, must be faster than the same plane as a fighter, and so long as such aircraft operated at their maximum altitude nothing could catch them."

All Cotton could get was a Blenheim IV. He cleaned it up, and got an extra 20 mph out of it. Dowding heard about it; and visited Cotton at Farnborough. The upshot was that Cotton managed, miraculously, to wangle two Spitfires out of Dowding. One writer has put it fittingly: "The turning point [in the formation of the RAF's Photographic Reconnaissance Unit] was reached when Cotton managed to charm two Spitfires out of Dowding, a remarkable event which reflects great credit on both men."

Cotton 'cleaned' and stripped them; and, with the installation of an extra fuel tank in the fuselage, increased their range to 1,250 miles at 30,000 feet with a cruising speed of close to 400 m.p.h.

During the Battle of France his unit performed prodigies of aerial photographic reconnaissance. The Air Ministry still considered the work of interpretation "a job that any intelligence officer ought to be able to do without special training." Their record in actual photography manifested the same dilettante, and casual unprofessional attitude.

Before Cotton "the RAF had photographed 2,500 square miles of enemy territory in three months for the loss of 40 aircraft, mostly Blenheims."

The French Air Force was more advanced than the RAF in this work, notably in interpretation. But their reconnaissance record was not. They "had photographed 6,000 square miles of enemy territory in three months for the loss of 60 aircraft."

Enter Cotton. His Heston detachment "photographed 5,000 square miles of enemy territory in three flights without loss."

Cotton, who was also working closely with the Admiralty, fought persistently to have his unit receive official recognition, status and backing from the Air Ministry, but was equally persistently frustrated. It was only the intervention of Winston Churchill that effected it. One of Cotton's Spitfire pilots had taken some excellent photographs of German capital ships, including the Tirpitz, to prove where they were located. Churchill was the First Lord. He saw the pictures and had a meeting with Cotton. Cotton had also been trying to get the Air Ministry to requisition his special photogrammetric equipment, without success. Churchill cut the Gordian knot by announcing that if the Air Ministry did not requisition it, the Admiralty would.

Cotton was convinced from his contact with members of the Air Staff that they were jealous of his unit's successes and reputation. He became aware "that there were men in the Air Ministry intriguing against (him)." He was not alone, however: others were in the same boat. So much so that he felt a certain consolation in knowing that he "wasn't the only one who was fighting on two fronts — the Germans and the Air Ministry."

But exasperation was another strong emotion: " The attitude of the Air Ministry appals me. God help the Allies unless our leaders wake up or we get new leaders." It was a further triumph of the skilled work of his unit that produced graphic evidence of massed German armour in the Ardennes on May 7th 1940. Cotton showed the photos to Air Marshal Sir Arthur Barratt, the AOC of the British Air Forces in France. Barratt was disturbed by the implications. It was "news of vital importance, because an attack from that quarter was totally unprepared for." Barratt informed the Air Ministry in London; they pooh-poohed the report.

Barratt sent one of his senior officers to London with the photos. On the 9th, he sent Cotton to put the evidence personally before the C-in-C of Bomber Command, who was then Air Marshal Sir Charles Portal. "Portal," wrote Cotton, " clearly regarded me as a nuisance, his orders for the targets he was to bomb were given him by the Air Staff after they had been approved by the War Cabinet". Cotton had assumed that the Air Staff, on receiving the photographs from Barratt's emissary, would have put them immediately before the Chiefs of Staff Committee or even directly before the War Cabinet. They had done no such thing. Apparently they had just sat on them.

The next day the Germans launched their *Blitzkrieg*. Cotton speculated:

> I have often wondered since what might have been achieved if a determined fire-raising attack had been mounted against the hidden German armour on the Luxembourg frontier on the night of 9th–10th May, by the 200 heavies that then comprised Bomber Command. It may well be argued that not much damage would have been done in such an attack with the weapons and aircraft then available. . . . However, whether such an attack would have achieved material damage or not, I believe it would almost certainly have postponed the assault that opened on the morning of the 10th, because it would have served notice on the Germans that their plans were known. It would quite possibly have resulted in a drastic revision of the Ardennes plan, a plan in which the German military leaders had little confidence, as we learned after the war. What might their fears and apprehensions have been if their armour on this front had been bombed that night, only two or three hours before it was due to roll forward? The whole course of the war might have been changed.

Cotton and his unit — pilots, ground crews, photographic experts, interpreters — continued to function and to produce evidence of military formations and movements, bridges blown and unblown, etc., during the perilous weeks of the Battle of France, until forced to evacuate.

On June 16th the first bombshell arrived, in the form of a letter from the Air Council.

> Sir,
>
> 1.  I am commanded by the Air Council to inform you that they have recently had under review the question of the future status and organization of the Photographic Development Unit and that, after careful consideration, they have reached the conclusion that this Unit which you have done so much to foster, should now be regarded as having passed beyond the stage of experiment and should take its place as part of the ordinary organization of the Royal Air Force.
>
> 2.  It has accordingly been decided that it should be constituted as a unit of the Royal Air Force under the orders of the Commander-in-Chief, Coastal

Command, and should be commanded by a regular serving officer. Wing Commander G.W. Tuttle, DFC, has been appointed.

3. I am to add that the Council wish to record how much they are indebted to you for the work you have done and for the great gifts of imagination and inventive thought which you have brought to bear on the development of the technique of photography in the Royal Air Force.

The reader may be able to form a very slight idea of the feeling experienced by Sidney Cotton on receipt of this summary and cowardly dismissal. Ever since forming his Photographic Development Unit he "had suffered experiences which had filled him with resentment, but (he) had never felt quite so sickened as now."

Cotton lists a number of things for which the Air Staff never forgave him. Most of them boil down to jealousy over his overwhelming technical superiority, his unorthodox methods which flew in the face of approved Air Staff ways, and "the continual war (he) had waged on apathy and delay." To these he added: "The fact that this had been my brief from the Chief of the Air Staff . . . probably angered them still more."

Cotton had his consolations. Among them were the satisfaction of knowing that he had placed the future of aerial photographic reconnaissance on solid foundations and see it, renamed the Photographic Reconnaissance Unit (PRU), play a signal role throughout the war in gathering intelligence; and the pleasure in seeing his unit taken over by his own highly capable administrative officer, Geoffrey Tuttle, whom he had trained.

The story is a long way from being over. After this dismissal Cotton imagined there would no lack of important work he could get involved in. Tuttle had actually warned him previously of what was in the wind but he did not believe it. Now, he was not to imagine "how vindictively" he was going to be pursued. Sad to relate, so powerful and long-reaching were the tentacles of the Air Staff, Cotton could get no employment during the Battle of Britain.

The beginning of the *Blitz* caused Cotton to turn his inventive mind to problems of defence against night bombers. He came up with the Aerial Target Illumination scheme (ATI). This involved a very powerful searchlight, a Turbinlite, fitted into the nose of a Boston DB7 twin-engined fighter. The Boston was equipped with AI radar, and the aircraft was accompanied by two Hurricanes. The Boston locked on to an enemy bomber, switched on its light, and the fighters moved in and 'killed' it.

Knowing that he was in bad odour with the Air Ministry, Cotton prepared a complete dossier and delivered it to Ernest Bevin in January, with the request that he pass it on to Churchill. Bevin passed it instead to Sinclair, the head of the Air Ministry — into the hands of the enemy. (Cotton did not learn of this until several months later.) From this moment, all his contacts with the highest RAF officers — Salmond, Sholto Douglas, Freeman, Joubert — turned sour.

On March 3rd he received the second bombshell from the Air Ministry:

Sir,

I am commanded by the Air Council to inform you that as it is no longer necessary for you to retain the acting unpaid rank of Wing Commander, or to wear Royal Air Force uniform, the authority granted in this Department's letter of the 3rd October 1940, numbered as above, is hereby withdrawn with effect from the date of this letter.

You will, therefore, remain on the Unemployment List of Officers of the Royal Air Force Volunteer Reserve in your substantive rank of Squadron Leader, but as it seems unlikely that your services will again be required on the active list of the Royal Air Force, the Council would be prepared to give favourable consideration to an application by you to resign your commission, in order that you may feel entirely free to follow civilian employment.

Cotton tried to join the Naval Air Arm, for whom he had done so much, and who had always offered him a position if he were free. Admiral Sir Dudley Pound arranged for him to be enlisted. When the Air Ministry heard of his imminent appointment, the Navy cancelled it. The explanation was that the Admiralty had "to kow-tow to the Air Staff" for their services. Said Rear Admiral A.L.St.G. Lyster: "The knees of my trousers are worn out crawling to the Air Staff to beg for equipment. . . ."

Things went from bad to worse. Cotton was arrested. He had been declared *persona non grata* at the Air Force establishments but had not been notified himself. His Boston was first hijacked and flown to Kinloss, and there it met with an accident resulting in a total write-off. The subsequent inquiry concluded that it had been sabotaged. The case was conveniently closed.

Cotton found himself under constant surveillance. A colleague who had worked with him on the ATI scheme, and who had also been eased out of it, suggested that the Americans would be interested. Suddenly he found himself summonsed to appear before Air Commodore D.L. Blackford, Director of Intelligence (Security), at the Air Ministry. He was made to understand that he could be interned under wartime regulations for the duration of the war, without right of appeal. His interrogation lasted for hours — that day and the next.

He was having difficulty in disproving the allegations against him, until friends came upon the scene, out of the blue, and provided him with the documentary evidence he needed. Among those friends were Ian Fleming, and Charles Morgan the writer, then in Naval Intelligence. The Air Ministry's vendetta collapsed.

Cotton then approached an MP he knew well, a W.J. Brown, with the idea of raising the matter in the House of Commons and instigating an official inquiry into the Air Ministry's persecution. There followed "weeks of wrangling . . . in which Sir Archibald Sinclair, the Air Minister, did his best to get the Air Ministry off the hook."

It was at this time that Major Sir Desmond Morton, one of Churchill's personal assistants, heard of the affair and when Morton had heard the full story he told Cotton he would take it up with Churchill. He said: "It's the most fantastic tale I've ever heard. The only story I can think of that compares with it is that of Captain Dreyfus."

Morton was true to his word. Churchill ordered an investigation, which cleared Cotton completely. When Churchill learnt also of Cotton's intended appeal to the House of Commons, he dissuaded him. Churchill's advice was this: "If I (i.e. Cotton) were to beat the machine, or the Establishment, as he called it, they would eventually get even with me somehow. . . ." Cotton finished by accepting Churchill's advice, as coming from someone who no doubt knew the Establishment better than anyone.

He felt well rid of the Air Ministry and its satanic machinations.

## NOTE TO APPENDIX "D":

1. Alan Deere (now, alas, the late Alan Deere) told the author that the officer who took over from Malan was a Group Captain Lowell Guinness, who was then at Fighter Command Headquarters, and that the posting was engineered for him by an Air Commodore Teddy Huddlestone of the Air Staff. Malan was sent to the RAF Staff College to serve out the war.

# APPENDIX "E"

# *Rivalry, Jealousy & Enmity*
# *in High Commands*

In this appendix our sole intent is to demonstrate that personal or inter-service rivalry and jealousy led to an enmity which was not at all uncommon in the past. This is true on both the allied and the enemy sides. It is a phenomenon older than war: it is as old as humanity. Whether there was, or is, any remedy to this kind of conflict depends on factors which themselves change with the circumstances and the personalities involved at the time. I intend to review some of the most notable instances of personal friction in past wars. (It is a pleasure to acknowledge here my indebtedness to my friend Murray Peden of Winnipeg, author of the acclaimed *A Thousand Shall Fall,* for an unpublished article on this topic which I have edited and modified with his permission.)

In the Canadian Army in the Second World War, the differences between General Simonds and General Crerar were of a personal nature. That they had scant regard for each other is undeniable, a fact which every student of the war has known for a great many years. The same criticism applies to the differences between Sir Arthur Harris and Sir Charles Portal. It is perfectly clear from the correspondence between them that their differences were conscientious professional differences, turning on what priority should be given to each of the many competing target systems they were charged with destroying. That the two commanders, in this case, had the highest regard for each other, is perfectly clear from the tenor of the correspondence. In the case of Crerar and Simonds there was personal antipathy, but such relationships are commonplace in war. Even so there is no evidence that the personal feelings of these two men had any prejudicial effect upon their performance or that of the men under their command. It would be difficult indeed to make such a case, for the antipathy between many other commanders was every bit as energetic. Field commanders seldom achieve their roles by being shrinking-violet wallflowers; a goodly percentage of the best have robust egos.

This is not a recent development; one can cite examples as far back as one wishes to go in military history.

In World War I, on the British side, the high-tension relationship between Lord Kitchener, then Secretary of War, Sir John French, General Haig and other senior commanders are, and were, matters of common knowledge. In his book *The Donkeys,* Alan Clark makes frequent comments on them. The views of General Horace Smith-Dorrien on Sir John French require little comment after the reported exchange:

> SIR JOHN FRENCH: "The British Army will give battle on the line of the Condé Canal."
>
> SIR HORACE SMITH-DORRIEN: "Do you mean take the offensive, or stand on the defensive?"
>
> SIR JOHN FRENCH: "Don't ask questions, do as you're told."

Clark makes frequent references to the strained relations between Kitchener and French, which "had been poor since the time of the South African War. Now they were worsened by Kitchener's reluctance to accept the restraints of a political, civilian appointment." Sir John French made a point of being difficult with General Sir William Robertson, the Chief of the Imperial General Staff. As Clark recounts: "He ignored Robertson socially, insulted him in public on a variety of oc-casions, refused to mess with him and continued to sit next to Henry Wilson at meals. . . ."

When Lord Haldane arrived for a discussion about the results of recent operations, in October 1915, Haig "submitted an impromptu report that was shamelessly critical of his superior." He had earlier confided to his diary, speaking of French: "It seems impossible to discuss military problems with an unreasoning brain of this kind . . . no good result is to be expected from so doing." Haig had the ear of the King, and did not scruple to air his sharp criticism of French at that level as well, telling the King: "French's handling of . . . the last battle, his obstinacy and conceit, showed his incapacity, and . . . I therefore thought strongly that, for the sake of the Empire, French ought to be removed." As Clark opines: ". . . one of Sir John French's few commendable traits, in the eyes of the politicians in England, lay in his implacable hostility to the Secretary of State for War (Kitchener). . . ." At any rate, Haig was instrumental in getting French sacked — and taking over supreme command himself.

Such squabbles and in-fighting were not confined to the British. When von Moltke was removed as Chief of Staff of the German army, following the failure of his modified version of the Schleiffen Plan and the Battle of the Marne, his successor, Lieutenant General Eric von Falkenhayn, quickly found himself warring strenuously with the two successful eastern commanders, General von Hindenburg and General Ludendorff, who differed strongly with his "western priority" strategy, pushing instead for an all-out offensive in the east. Both Chancellor Bethmann Hollweg and the Kaiser himself were soon drawn into the argument.

Robert B. Asprey, in his book *The German High Command*, recounts: "Temporarily brainwashed by euphoric briefings at Posen (from Hindenburg and Ludendorff), Bethmann decided that the eastern front must now have priority and that Falkenhayn must be replaced by Ludendorff." Bethmann's first overtures to the Kaiser in that behalf were rebuffed. But Ludendorff was not backward. "Ludendorff, in a remarkable display of insubordination that should have resulted in his immediate court-martial, had recently sent his intelligence officer, Major von Haeften, to the OHL in the guise of liaison officer. In reality Haeften was to lobby for an all-out eastern offensive. . . . Sharply rebuffed by Falkenhayn, (Haeften's) . . . appeal to Bethmann for a change of strategy and in consequence a change of command caused the Chancellor to approach the Kaiser over the heads of his military keepers. . . ." The Kaiser refused to consider dismissing Falkenhayn as acting Chief of Staff. Ludendorff would never be appointed to this post, because he "is a dubious character devoured by personal ambition." Wilhelm added an exclamation point a few days later by appointing Falkenhayn permanent Chief of General Staff. ". . . Bethmann was also beginning to suspect Ludendorff of unhealthy intrigues, and with good cause."

Perhaps one of the best examples of an extroverted field commander having a few unharmonious words with his superior, in the presence of witnesses, is found in the history of the American Civil War. It is, of course, trite knowledge that as commander of the Army of the Potomac, General McClellan scorned his Commander-in-Chief, President Lincoln, and showed his contempt publicly on several occasions. On the Confederate side, General Joseph Johnston made no secret of his view that "the real enemy" was his President and Commander-in-Chief, Jefferson Davies. But to see what real friction between generals can produce, perhaps we should consider the case of

General Nathan Bedford Forrest, rated by his contemporaries on both sides as one of the finest cavalry commanders ever to put a foot in the stirrups.

Special reference is appropriate here to Forrest's tender leave-taking of his commander, General Bragg. Having refused Bragg's proffered hand, Forrest gave him a tongue-lashing for five minutes, punctuating it by thrusting a forefinger in Bragg's face every few seconds, then concluded with his summation:

> "I have stood your meanness as long as I intended to. You have played the part of a damned scoundrel, and are a coward, and if you were any part of a man I would slap your jaws and force you to resent it. You may as well not issue any more orders to me, for I will not obey them, and I will hold you personally responsible for any further indignities you endeavor to inflict upon me. You have threatened to arrest me for not obeying orders promptly. I dare you do it, and I say to you that if you ever again try to interfere with me or cross my path it will be at the peril of your life."

With that, General Forrest turned his back on his commander and stalked out. General Bragg knew better than to take Forrest up on his dare and report him to Jefferson Davis; saying not a word to anyone, just as Forrest had predicted to the witness who had accompanied him.

It is tempting to put a disproportionate emphasis on the strained relationships between commanders, especially in cases where we have inadequate documentary information about their dealings with and their opinions of each other.

We have said that the emphasis placed by some historians on the Park/Leigh-Mallory dispute would lead us to believe that rivalry or tension between commanders was something highly exceptional. It was often exacerbated by the allocation of scarce supplies between different units, assignment of objectives, timing of attacks and a hundred other frequently unavoidable causes. Such differences between commanders, men under heavy and continuous strain, is far from rare, and is in fact almost routine. Let us look at some other well-known instances.

A reading of Daniel Dancocks's book, *The D-Day Dodgers,* gives a truer picture of top level camaraderie. Sir Oliver Leese, Eighth Army Commander, had no use at all for Canadian General E.L.M. Burns, who was Corps Commander for another General, Chris Vokes. Relations between Chris Vokes and Burns were very bad, to say the least. When a new Canadian Corps commander was appointed (Charles Foulkes), Chris Vokes's ire, before he left the theatre, was notable, for he had known Foulkes for some years and formed ineradicable impressions of him. As he said, he "had always disliked the man. I thought he was nothing but a military nincompoop, a complete horse's ass, a military politician."

Strenuous and bitter differences of opinion occasionally arose at the very highest level. The differences between President Roosevelt and Prime Minister Churchill are well known. We will cite the worst occurrence. Churchill became so angry about American insistence on implementing the invasion of southern France, and draining off large elements of the forces in Italy to do so, that, as Dancocks notes, he actually drafted a telegram to Roosevelt in which he threatened "to separate the British command from the American in the Mediterranean. Cooler heads prevailed, and the . . . telegram was not sent. . . ."

Lest anyone represent that during WWII such bristly relationships existed only on the Allied side, they should be reminded that General Rommel was forced to take his own life after it was discovered that he was involved in the plot to assassinate his Commander-in-Chief, Hitler. General von Kluge, too, was convinced of the necessity of killing Hitler, and also committed suicide (on August 19th, 1944) rather than face his wrath. Hitler also suspected him of attempting to surrender the armies in Normandy to the Allies.

Montgomery and Patton heartily detested one another, and took no pains to conceal the fact. Of course, General Montgomery had a generous amount of contempt for most other generals, particularly if they differed from his views. He had an extremely low opinion of the military skills of his own Commander-in-Chief in the field, General Eisenhower, and argued with him strenuously and in the most insubordinate terms — to the point where his outspoken criticism of Eisenhower's proposed broad-front strategy brought him to the very brink of dismissal, as General de Guingand has recorded. Montgomery did not endear himself to Omar Bradley either; he thoughtlessly humiliated him, and other American commanders, after the temporary change in the command structure necessitated by German successes in the opening stages of the Battle of the Ardennes. Bradley's own feelings for Montgomery were clearly revealed in his book, *A Soldier's Story,* and they were not those of a bosom companion.

As for Patton and Eisenhower, Patton bitterly resented what he saw as Eisenhower's policy of always siding with Montgomery against him. He seethed with frustration at Eisenhower's rulings on the allocation of supplies, and behind his back called Eisenhower a Limey. Underlying his bitterness was the feeling that Eisenhower had embarrassed him more than was necessary in punishing him for the slapping incident in a Sicily hospital.

The vocabulary, and the feelings, are all too familiar: personal and professional differences, antipathy, robust egos, strained relations, critical of his superior, implacable hostility, a remarkable display of insubordination, devoured by personal ambition, unhealthy intrigues, unharmonious words, "the real enemy", bungling, intrigue and stupidity inflamed by personal dislike.

Despite the almost continuous friction between all these king-sized egos, this group of commanders directed the Allied armies with such success as to drive 60 German divisions, which had had four years to prepare for the onslaught, all the way from Normandy to the Elbe and the Oder. Incidentally, beside the burning contempt that existed between General Eisenhower and his former boss, General Douglas MacArthur, the mutual distaste and suspicion between Simonds and Crerar paled to where they could have passed as Damon and Pythias by comparison. And the strained relations that existed between Park and Leigh-Mallory seem like child's play when seen in the perspective of some others discussed here.

# ACKNOWLEDGMENTS

Before I began the inquiries into the explanation of the removal of Air Chief Marshal Sir Hugh Dowding from his command at Fighter Command, which were to culminate in this book, I had been in touch with Wing Commander P.B. 'Laddie' Lucas, and had indeed contributed two pieces to books he had published about aspects of war in the air. It was due to Wing Commander Lucas's good graces that I met, first, in 1988, Air Commodore Henry Probert, then the head of the Air Historical Branch, Ministry of Defence, and his able colleague, Sebastian Cox; and the following year, also thanks to Laddie, the esteemed air historian, Denis Richards, and Air Marshal Sir Denis Crowley-Milling.

Air Commodore Probert was good enough, at the outset of my study, to spare the tirne to give me a summary of the facts and myths, and the main events and unsettled issues, of the Battle of Britain. He then passed me on to Mr. Cox, who made me aware of various informative files. Among them, in particular, was one from the archives of the Royal Air Force Museum, Hendon, containing private letters which passed between Lord Trenchard and Sir John Salmond.

Subsequently I met with Air Commodore Probert and Mr. Cox on a number of occasions; and after the former's retirement, I received from Mr. Cox invaluable help in locating files held at the Public Records Office. This service was especially appreciated in view of my remote distance from the United Kingdom, and enabled me to save much tirne which would otherwise have been spent in unearthing the sources I needed.

I had one meeting with Sir Denis Crowley-Milling in London, and we exchanged a few letters; but there was no possible meeting of minds: for his part, he could see no flaws in the leadership of Bader, his squadron commander in the Battle of Britain, his mentor and friend; and I, for my part, was not persuaded by his eloquence, nor able to convince him that there were flaws in Bader's views and methods.

Similarly I met once with Denis Richards; and there also seemed to be no likelihood of agreement on some of the major ideas I was then developing, and little enthusiasm on my part for his ideas, particularly with regard to the roles of Portal, Sholto Douglas and Leigh-Mallory in Dowding's removal from Fighter Command, and his eventual retirement, as well as the later performance of those three officers during the Second World War.

Subsequently, in a series of letters in which I put various vexed questions to him, Mr Richards was not only the soul of courtesy, but a mine of useful and unstinting information. I owe to him a great deal, even if, regrettably, I have had to question his conclusions on various issues. After the Air Historical Branch, I became acquainted with the holdings of the Royal Air Force Museum Library and Archives, and the Public Record Office. In the former I was able to study the private correspondence between Trenchard and Salmond, and the papers of Dowding, inadequate as they are.

It is, of course, no secret or surprise to any scholar or writer inquiring into historical issues, how vital and indispensable is the treasure-house of files, documents and other official papers, to the successfiil outcome of his search-es and quest. I am more than happy to express my gratitude to the staffs of the Museum and the Public Record Office for their unfailing help, courtesy, and professional expertise. It gives me a particular pleasure to offer my sincere thanks to the people named above, and to a number of people in the follow-ing public-spirited organisations, without whose help and cooperation I would have found my inquiries infinitely more arduous:

Dr Ruth Paley, Director, Reader Services Department, Mr Ian Malcolm and the Staff of the Public Record Office.

Mr.Peter Elliott, Royal Air Force Museum, Hendon.

I insist also on offering my ever-grateful thanks to Wing Commander P.B. 'Laddie' Lucas, CBE, DSO, DFC, RAF (Ret'd.) —now, alas, the late Laddie Lucas — who piloted my course to the Air Historical Branch, and whose understanding, if not forgiveness, I would like to have had for my uncompro-mising assaulting of the ideas of his hero and brother-in-law, Douglas Bader.

I cannot begin to express my gratitude to Air Chief Marshal Sir Chris-topher Foxley-Norris — whom I first came to know in 1950 when he was my Commanding Officer in the Oxford University Air Squadron — for three acts of kindness: for his constant encouragement in this enterprise; for his temerarious offer, made "out of the blue", to contribute a Foreword, without knowing much about what I was going to write; and for passing me on to Wing Commander John Young, Historian of the Battle of Britain Fighters Association. Wing Commander Young has spared no pains to discover and to send on copies of hitherto little known and unpublished papers, especially papers relating to the ideas and personality of the late Lord Dowding. And before these gallant gentlemen, I met and learnt much from both Group Captain Tom Gleave and Wing Commander Geoffrey Page, now both, alas, airborne at 'Angels Infinity.'

I am beholden to Mr Ernest G. Hardy, of Church Crookham, Hampshire, and Mr. Bill Duffin, of Harrow Weald, Historical Researchers both, who unearthed and photocopied for me many essential documents at the PRO when I could not go to the UK.

Closer to home, I take a very special pleasure in extending my cordial thanks to a number of friends, all members of the Aircrew Association, Vancouver Island Branch, who have read and commented on my manuscript, or expressed considerable interest and encouragement, in both writing and discussion, with a resultant inevitable improvement of it. They are: Charlie Plewman, Michael O'Hagan, Norman Emmott, Roger Napier, and, on the technical side, Derek Baker. Finally, I am greatly indebted to Erik Pedersen for his considerable skills in formatting the text of this book.

Of course it is a platitude to go on and say, after all these acknowledgments, that the author takes full responsibility for the views expressed in these pages, other than those quoted with attribution; and that had my many helpers and supporters known what I was going to write, they might have withheld their assistance.

Finally, and most importantly, I thank my eternally dear wife, Rika, who has never ceased to give me every support and encouragement to pursue this undertaking for fourteen years, and to accept with good grace my frequent absences, whether overseas or at home.

J.E.G. DIXON
Victoria, British Columbia
November 2002

# BIBLIOGRAPHY

## Unpublished Sources

Documents held in the Public Record Office, Kew, London; in the Library and Archives of the Royal Air Force Museum, Hendon; and in the Air Historical Branch, Ministry of Defence, London, which have been quoted in this book, are identified in the Notes attached to the end of the chapters.

*The Air Defence of Great Britain, vol.II, The Battle of Britain*
(Air Historical Branch Narrative, Ministry of Defence) AIR 41/15, 1-end.

*The Air Defence of Great Britain, vol.III, Night Air Defence*
(Air Histiorical Branch Narrative, Ministry of Defence) AIR 41/17 I.E.

*The Origins and Pre-War Growth of Fighter Command,* by T.C.G. James
(Air Historical Branch Narrative, Ministry of Defence)

*The All-Canadian Squadron* [compiled by Wg. Cmdr. F.H. Hitchins], in the Rare Book Room of the University of Western Ontario Library, London, Canada, held in The Beatrice Hitchins Memorial Collection of Aviation History.

## Published Sources

### HISTORY

Dowding, Air Chief Marshal Lord. *Despatch on The Battle of Britain.* Supplement to the *London Gazette,* September 10th, 1946.

———. *Twelve Legions of Angels* (London: Jarrolds, n.d. [1946])

*The Battle of Britain,* August-October 1940 (London: Air Ministry, HMSO, 1941)

*The Battle of Britain* (London: Air Ministry Pamphlet 156)

*Bataille d'Angleterre, La,* 3 tomes, publiés par Jean Lasserre (Paris: Icare nos. 93, 95, 99, 1980-81-82)

Bekker, Cajus: *The Luftwaffe War Diaries* (New York: Ballantine Books, 1975)

Bickers, Richard T. et al. *The Battle of Britain* (London: Salamander Books, 1990)

Bishop, Edward. *Their Finest Hour* (New York: Ballantine Books, 1968)

Butler, J.R.M. *Grand Strategy, September 1939-June 1941* (London: HMSO, 1957)

Churchill, Winston S. *The Second World War, vol.II: Their Finest Hour* (London:Cassell, 1949)

———. *Into Battle* (London: Cassell, 1941)

Collier, Basil. *The Defence of the United Kingdom* (London: HMSO, 1957)

Cooksley, P.G. *1940: The Story of No. 11 Group, Fighter Command* (London: Robert Hale, 1983)

Costello, John. *Ten Days to Destiny* (New York: William Morrow & Co., 1992)

Dean, Sir Maurice. *The Royal Air Force in Two World Wars*

Deighton, Len. *Fighter* (New York: Knopf, 1977)

Douglas, Sir Sholto. "Air Operations by Fighter Command from 25th November 1940 to 31st December 1941" (Supplement to the *London Gazette*, September 14, 1948)

Douhet, Giulio. *The Command of the Air*, tr. by Dino Ferrari (London: Faber and Faber, 1943)

Franks, Norman. *The Greatest Air Battle: Dieppe 19th August 1942* (London: William Kimber, 1979)

Gelb, Norman. *Scramble* (London: Michael Joseph, 1986)

Gray,C.G. *A History of the Air Ministry* (London: George Allen & Unwin, 1940)

Halliday, Hugh. *No. 242 Squadron. The Canadian Years* (Belleville, Ontario, Canada's Wings, 1981)

Haslam, E.B. "How Lord Dowding came to leave Fighter Command", in *Journal of Strategic Studies* (June 1981, pp.175–186)

Hough, Richard & Richards, Denis. *The Battle of Britain* (London, Hodder & Stoughton, 1989)

Hyde, H. Montgomery. *British Air Policy Between the Wars* (London, Heinemann, 1976)

Johnson, J.E. 'Johnnie'. *The Story of Air Fighting* (London, Hutchinson, 1985)

——— and P.B. 'Laddie' Lucas, eds. *Glorious Summer* (London, Stanley Paul & Co., 1990)

Jones, Ira ("Taffy"). *Wing Commander: Tiger Squadron* (London: W.H. Allen, 1954)

Jones, R.V. *Most Secret War* (London: Coronet Books, 1979)

Joubert de la Ferté, ACM Sir Philip. *The Third Service* (London: Thames and Hudson, 1955)

Mason, Francis K. *Battle Over Britain* (London: McWhirter Twins, 1969)

Overy, R.J. *The Air War 1939-1945* (New York: Stein and Day, 1981)

Parkinson, Roger. *Summer, 1940. The Battle of Britain* (New York: David McKay Company, 1977)

Pile, Sir Frederick. *Ack-Ack* (London, Harrap, 1949)

Price, Alfred. *The Hardest Day* (New York: Charles Scribner's Sons, 1979)

Probert, Henry & Sebastian Cox, eds. *Battle Re-Thought, The Symposium sponsored by the Royal Air Force Historical Society and the Royal Air Force Staff College Bracknell* (Shrewsbury: Airlife, 1991)

Ramsey, Winston G., ed. *The Battle of Britain: Then and Now* (London: After the Battle Publications, 1980)

Richards, Denis. *Royal Air Force 1939-1945, vol.I The Fight at Odds* (London: HMSO, 1953)

Smith, Malcolm. "Sir Edgar Ludlow-Hewitt and the Expansion of Bomber Command 1939-40", in *R.U.S.I. Journal* (vol. CXXVI, March 1981, pp.52-56)

Terraine, John. *The Right of the Line* (London: Hodder & Stoughton, 1985)

Townsend, Peter. *Duel of Eagles* (London: Weidenfeld and Nicolson, 1970)

Turner, John Frayn. *The Bader Wing* (Shrewsbury: Airlife, 1990)

Webster, Sir Charles and Frankland, Noble. *The Strategic Air Offensive Against Germany 1939-1945, vol.I Preparation* (London: HMSO, 1961)

Wood, Derek and Dempster, Derek. *The Narrow Margin* (London: Hutchinson, 1961)

Wykeham, Peter. *Fighter Command* (London: Putnam, 1960)

Zamoyski, Adam. *The Forgotten Few: The Polish Air Force in the Second World War* (London: John Murray, 1995)

Zimmerman, David. *Britain's Shield: Radar and the Defeat of the Luftwaffe* (Gloucester: Stroud, 2001)

## THE NIGHT BATTLE

Chisholm, Roderick *Cover of Darkness* (London: Chatto & Windus, 1953)

Howard-Williams, Jeremy. *Night Intruder* (Newton Abbot: David & Charles, 1976)

Johnson, David. *The London Blitz* (New York: Stein and Day, 1982)

Price, Alfred. *Instruments of Darkness* (London: Macdonald and Jane's, 1977)

Rawnsley, C.F. and Wright, Robert. *Night Fighter* (London: Collins, 1957)

Sansom, William. *The Blitz. Westminster at War* (Oxford University Press, 1990)

Winston G. Ramsey, ed. *The Blitz Then and Now, vol.2.* (London: After the Battle Publications, 1988)

Townsend, Peter. *The Odds Against Us* (New York, William Morrow and Co., 1987)

*See also* the relevant sections in Bekker, Churchill, Collier, Douglas, Johnson, Overy, Richards, Terraine and Wykeham, above; and, below, in Churchill, Douglas, Embry, Lindemann, Tizard and Watson-Watt.

## BIOGRAPHY

BADER     Michael G. Burns. *Bader and His Men*
(London: Arms and Armour, 1990)

————.     Lucas, Laddie. *Flying Colours* (London)

BALFOUR     Balfour, Harold. *Wings Over Westminster*
(London: Hutchinson, 1973)

BEAVERBROOK     Taylor, A.J.P. *Beaverbrook* (London: Hamish Hamilton, 1972)

COMMANDERS     Probert, Henry. *High Commanders of the Royal Air Force*
(London: HMSO, 1992)

CROSS     Cross, Air Chief Marshal Sir Kenneth. *Straight and Level*
(Grub Street, 1993)

CHURCHILL     Gilbert, Martin. *Winston S. Churchill, vol.VI:*
*Finest Hour, 1939-1941* (London: Heinemann, 1983)

COTTON     Barker, Ralph. *Aviator Extraordinary*
(London: Chatto & Windus, 1969)

DEERE     A.C. Deere. *Nine Lives* (London: Hodder & Stoughton, 1959)

DOUGLAS     Douglas, William Sholto with Robert Wright.
*Years of Command* (London: Collins, 1966)

DOWDING     Collier, Basil. *Leader of the Few* (Norwich, Jarrolds, 1957)

————.     Wright, Robert. *Dowding and The Battle of Britain*
(London: Macdonald, 1969)

EMBRY     Embry, Air Chief Marshal Sir Basil. *Mission Completed*
(London: Methuen & Co., 1957)

GRINNELL-MILNE     Grinnell-Milne, Duncan. *Wind in the Wires*
(London: Jarrolds, 1971)

HARRIS     Harris, Air Chief Marshal Sir Arthur. *Bomber Offensive*

KENT     Kent, J.A. *One of the Few* (London: William Kimber, 1971)

LEIGH-MALLORY     Dunn, Bill Newton *Big Wing* (Shrewsbury: Airlife, 1992)

LINDEMANN     Birkenhead, The Earl of. *The Prof in Two Worlds*
(London: Collins, 1961)

MALAN          Franks, Norman L.R. *Sky Tiger. The Story of Group Captain Sailor Malan,* DSO, DFC (London: William Kimber, 1980)

———.          Walker, Oliver. *Sailor Malan* (London: Cassell & Co., 1953)

PARK          Orange, Vincent. *Sir Keith Park* (London: Methuen, 1984)

PORTAL          Richards, Denis. *Portal of Hungerford* (London: Heinemann, 1978)

QUILL          Quill, Jeffery. *Spitfire. A Test Pilot's Story* (London: John Murray, 1983)

SALMOND          Laffin, John. *Swifter than Eagles* (Edinborough & London: William Blackwood & Sons, 1964)

TEDDER          Tedder, Marshal of the Royal Air Force Lord. *With Prejudice* (London, Cassell, 1966)

TIZARD          Clark, Ronald. *Tizard* (Cambridge: MIT Press, 1965)

TRENCHARD          Boyle, Andrew. *Trenchard* (London: Collins, 1962)

TUCK          Forrester, Larry. *Fly For Your Life* (New York: Nelson Doubleday, 1973)

TURING          Hodges, Andrew. *Alan Turing: The Enigma* (London: Burnett Books, 1983)

WAR LORDS, THE          Carver, Field Marshal Sir Michael, ed., *Military Commanders of the Twentieth Century* (London: Weidenfeld and Nicolson, 1976)

WATSON-WATT          Watson-Watt, Sir Robert. *Three Steps to Victory* (London: Odhams Press, 1957)

# GENERAL INDEX

## A

Abyssinia (Ethiopia) 28, 224, 227
Admiralty 203, 256, 258, 261
Air Sea Rescue Service 25
Alamein, El 186
Arabs 94, 167, 227
Ardennes 231, 258-259, 267
Armada, Spanish
    200, 204-205, 236, 240
Army, British 27, 44, 264;
    Canadian 263, 266; French 44, 83
Arnold, Gen. 'Hap' 188-190
Arras 17, 87
ASV (Anti-Surface Vessel) 224
Atcherley, S/L David 144
Atlantic Ocean 222
Auchinleck, Gen. Sir Claude 194
Australia 199

## B

Bader, S/L Douglas
    22, 54-71, **72**, 72-74, 95-96, 102-112,
    122, 133-134, 157, 202, 242, 253,
    269-270, 274-275
Baldwin, Stanley 10, 28, 215
Balfour, Hon. Harold
    6, 13, 102, 105-112, 115-116, 119, 150, 177,
    **196**, 208, 216, 218, 251, 253, 275
Barratt, AM Sir Arthur 258-259
Battle of the Atlantic 165, 195, 222-223
Baumbach, Werner 222
Bawdsey Manor 145, 147-148
Beamish, G/C Victor 184-185
Beauvais 14

Beaverbrook, Lord (Max)
    36-38, 89-95, 113-114, 122, 128,
    135, 138-139, 178, **196**, 275
Belgium 92, 215-216, 243
Bentley Priory
    32, 109, 158, 174, 209, 238
Berlin 196
Bevin, Ernest 261
Biscay, Bay of 225
Bishop, Billie 209, 272
Blackford, AC D.L. 261
*Blitzkrieg* 44, 101, 128, 142-149,
    153, 162, 170, 191, 215, 259-260, 274
Bodleian Library 97
Bomb Disposal Squads 165
Bonham Carter AC C. 81
Bournemouth 245
Bowen, Dr. Edward 81, 145, 148
Bowhill, ACM Sir Frederick
    38-39, 211, 224
Boyd, W/C O.T. 184
Boyle, AC 79, 88, 276
Bracken, Brendan 84-85, 205
Bradley, Gen. Omar 211, 267
Bragg, Gen. 238, 266
Brand, AV-M Sir Quentin
    **50**, 103, 122, 135
British Army 27, 44, 264
British Isles
    7, 44, 71, 199-200, 239
Broadhurst, S/L Harry 68
Broadstairs, Kent 240
Brooke, FM Sir Alan 194
Brown, W.J., MP 238, 262

# INDEX TO ILLUSTRATIONS